A Rose Blooms In Texas

Coming of Age in the Civil War Era

C A R L O S   R .   H A M I L T O N ,   J R .

2015

Revised Edition

2023

WESTBOW
P R E S S®
A DIVISION OF THOMAS NELSON
& ZONDERVAN

WestBow Press books may be ordered through booksellers or by contacting:

WestBow Press
A Division of Thomas Nelson & Zondervan
1663 Liberty Drive
Bloomington, IN 47403
www.westbowpress.com
844-714-3454

ISBN: 978-1-6642-9282-6 (sc)
ISBN: 978-1-6642-9281-9 (e)

Print information available on the last page.

WestBow Press rev. date: 04/05/2023

CONTENTS

PREFACE

In 1974, after the completion of my military service, our family returned home to Houston to establish our young children in a new school and to begin my medical practice. The following year my grandmother, Frances Wootters Denman, reached the end of her long life at the age of 94 years. Shortly thereafter, I discovered that she had left me a piano in her will, and arranged to have it moved to our new home. It was with surprise that I recognized the instrument from my childhood, an upright piano that had resided in a parlor in her home.

During World War II, when my father was serving as the medical officer for an artillery battalion in Europe, my mother and I moved to an apartment behind my grandparents' home in Houston. Although I was very young at the time, my memories of those years are distinct; I clearly recall the piano, a towering, antique giant of nine and a half feet that, due to its age, could not be appropriately tuned. The floor beneath the keyboard was ideal for a fort from which a five-year-old would defend his troops against the Nazis! I must have commented to my grandmother that I was fond of the piano, even though it had no other apparent use, and she must have remembered my comment well enough to count on me to provide a home for the instrument, at least for another generation.

The difficulty in moving and accommodating its over-size, even in the 20th century, was evident. It also made me wonder how – and why – a family would move it from North Carolina to a rural east Texas plantation in 1857 so that a ten-year-old child could continue her musical studies. That child, my great-grandmother as it turned out, eventually became the mother of seven children, including my grandmother. And although Berta Smith Wootters had died many decades before I was born, her children continued to express great affection and admiration for her.

My great-grandmother became a single parent when her husband, John Wootters, died at the age of 52, likely from complications of a wound received during the Civil War. Even so, Berta Smith Wootters persevered, managing her affairs, nurturing her children, and guiding all of them to university educations and productive lives as adults.

Some years after the silent musical instrument had been situated in our home, it occurred to me that I had little information about the original owners and the circumstances of their lives. When I expressed an interest in learning about them to a cousin, Dr. John H. Wootters, a grandson of Berta Smith Wootters, I was invited to visit him in Crockett to learn what I could about that family. Dr. Wootters and his wife had moved to Crockett, Texas after his retirement from a distinguished practice of general surgery in Houston. He informed us that, although he wasn't certain of the plantation's exact location on the Trinity River, he knew someone who could help. As luck would have it, a man named Mr. Edgar Pouncey knew the way to the property and the site of the graves of Major John Smith and Anna Jane Pouncey Smith.

Mr. Pouncey not only directed us to the plantation site and the graves, but he shared new information about the Smiths which was unknown by their descendants. Edgar Pouncey was a descendant of a family of slaves that had come to Texas with the Smith family and whose own ancestors had served earlier generations of Smiths and Pounceys. As he related stories of the Smith family, he spoke with great respect and warmth for them.

All of us recognized the institution of slavery as a sad mark on American history, a tragic blight with no redeeming qualities, and whose effects will take generations to heal. Even so, according to Mr. Pouncey, the Smiths had assured at least some of their slave families, including his forebears that they and a child that was apparently mentally impaired would always have a secure home with their family. A site for a church had been dedicated for the use of the slaves and, at the time of emancipation, ownership of homesites was transferred to the freedmen. Educational opportunities had been encouraged and a Cedar Branch School was eventually created near the church. Edgar Pouncey had served as a Trustee of the Grapeland Independent School District with which the school is affiliated. He was rightly proud of the opportunities that had been offered for many children through the school.

This information, unexpected and thought-provoking as it was, motivated me to learn what I could about the Smith family as well as the turbulent and tragic times in which they lived. One can often understand more about a person's character and personality from reading what they have written or said and two items may illuminate these aspects of John Wootters and Berta Smith. These are the comments of John on receiving the company flag for the Crockett Southrons at the onset of the war and the essay of Berta which she read at her graduation ceremony from Fairfield Female College in 1865.

Special appreciation must be given to my assistant, Jasmin Dimayuga Cambel for her help in the preparation of the manuscript; to my reviewer, Eileen Flynn DeLaO for her patient and thoughtful suggestions; to Dr. John Boles, professor of history at Rice University and the Susanne M. Glasscock School of Continuing Studies; and to the Texas State Historical Association and other sources of information mentioned in the bibliography. A special thanks to Cristina Adams, my very helpful editor and to Lucy Herring Chambers, Publisher, Bright Sky Press. This work could have never been completed without the support of my wife, Carolyn Burton Hamilton, who recognized that the story of these families, borne out during the most difficult era in American history, needed to be told and encouraged me to try to tell it in the best way I could.

Carlos R. Hamilton Jr. — 2012

ADDENDUM TO PREFACE FOR ABRIDGED VERSION — 2023

The re-publication of A Rose Blooms in Texas was prompted by the desire to make it available for those preferring an audio presentation or an on-line access to the text. It was also an opportunity to correct typographical errors and to re-edit some of the narrative descriptions. As the story is based on factual occurrences, considerable documentation and supportive material was presented in the Appendix of the first edition to validate these conclusions. Although useful in documenting the historical validity of the story, this was likely not of interest to many casual readers. These extensive Appendix entries have been omitted but the footnotes remain as many of the references are available on-line for the interested reader. Reading habits and new methods of presenting literature are not the only changes that have occurred in our society in the decade since the book was first published!

This interval has seen changes in the reactions of many to any consideration of the reality of the historical issue of slavery in the American past. Extreme conclusions about this tragic institution have solidified in the minds of some individuals and publications. There are those that hold opinions for which I can find no evidence or rationale. Some persist in the belief that slavery was not the principle cause of the Civil War and their counterparts hold that slavery was not only the cause of the war but was the critical issue throughout all American history. They then conclude that present day citizens of non-African ancestry should accept feelings of guilt for the actions of their forebears. This so-called critical race theory has divisive effects on the American public rather than the much needed bringing together of all citizens in appreciation for the freedoms and opportunities that our United States provides. The encouragement of class conflict is an example of pitting sectors of our society against each other for purposes of gaining political advantage and power.

This book should not be interpreted in any way as an apology or excuse for the presence of human bondage that existed for over two hundred years on our shores. Slavery was a great blight that was only resolved by the catastrophic War Between the States which resulted in more casualties than all other military efforts combined from the earliest colonial times to the present. A study of ante-bellum America makes it clear that the willingness of the colonists to accept slavery was related to the critical shortage of laborers in the pre-mechanical agricultural economy. In the early colonial period of our nation's history, indentured workers who had few options in England accepted the risks of working in the colonies. As the availability of indenture workers decreased in colonies able to sustain large scale commercial agriculture and produce profitable exports, slavery became ingrained as an institution in the colony's culture and was sustained by their legal system. There were many colonists from all backgrounds and in all colonies that believed that slavery was a fundamental moral wrong but the desire for economic success was clearly a higher trump card. Even colonies with little need for slave labor benefitted greatly from the economic effects of the agricultural wealth without which the entire colonial venture would not have had the level of ongoing support of the European homelands so critical for success in the seventeenth century.

From the distance of several centuries and an awareness of the civil war disaster that was the ultimate solution to the slavery issue, one can speculate about what might have been done about this terrible situation. Such speculation at this time seems of little value other than realizing that without compromise the Constitution and union of the states would not have occurred. The issue of what the American culture should or could do about these past wrongs is incompletely resolved and deserves consideration.

Some suggestions may be appropriate based on the awareness that the quest for economic success was the cause of the acceptance of slavery. Any attempt to eliminate slavery would have required a level of compromise that could not be achieved. Wealth in the early days of the colonies and continuing to the past century was significantly associated with the ownership of land. The provision of land to the newly freed slaves at the end of the civil war was briefly considered but was never accepted. The availability of productive public land has greatly changed in recent centuries and is not the unique key to wealth that it had been in earlier years. This source of personal advancement has been replaced by education which is now the most reasonable pathway to economic success and social mobility.

It is my opinion that the consideration of education as an effective pathway to improved economic conditions for a large part of our population requires several changes in political thinking. Just as the availability of land for the initial colonists was a start, the individual had to put a great deal of their own effort and talent into the venture for it to succeed. Just as with all land, all types of "higher education" are not equally economically productive. Our society has taken the bait that a college degree is essential for economic success when many college programs, even if they can lead to degrees, are not likely to raise one to a desired economic level alone. It is a reality that not all persons are suited for advanced academic endeavors. Training in skills and crafts in addition to basic academic skills and knowledge may be more likely to lead to productive careers in many cases.

Recent publicity concerning high levels of college debt incurred by students who have no ability to repay should be considered. The commercial loans used to pay tuition charges for student programs which may not be within the students capacity or not leading to productive careers but which yield significant debt are counterproductive. Much more effort should be spent on middle and high school counseling and guiding students into career fields for which they have the appropriate talents and interest. Debt to a public agency could be forgiven or reduced after a period of active employment following completion of their training. It is clear that this would take more than one generation to spread new wealth widely, but meaningful social and economic progress in families can rarely be measured in shorter intervals. Similar opportunities should be available to the children of recent immigrants and established residents of all races and backgrounds. Such a program could be considered a part of public school systems and levels of administration could reflect the commitment of the states and local communities to this and other educational opportunities. The families of both races described in this story reflect the benefit of mutual respect and opportunity for everyone.

DEDICATION

This work is dedicated to the present generation of ladies in my family that carry on the spirit, values and devotion reflected by the subjects of the story:

My wife, Carolyn Burton Hamilton; our daughters Patricia Hamilton Blalock and Marci Curry Hamilton; and our granddaughters Madeleine Janes Hamilton, Grace Elizabeth Hamilton, Frances Carolyn Hamilton and Carolyn Hamilton Bivins.

This work could not have been completed without information gained from the Handbook of Texas Online, a service of the Texas State Historical Association. Their extraordinary information resource is greatly appreciated.

I

May 1863 – Fairfield, Texas

Berta was startled awake with an intense sensation that she could hardly describe. It wasn't a feeling of fear or dread, but one of acute expectation. Sleep came easily for the fifteen-year-old, so she wondered what could have roused her on this night. Did she have a nightmare? Maybe, but she could not remember. Brushing a few wayward strands of hair from her eyes, she sat upright on her bed, the fading light of a gibbous moon in the western sky illuminating the room and her pale face. No dream came to mind, but as she gradually awoke, she sensed that this day would be unlike any she had ever experienced. This was the day she would return home to the Smith Landing Plantation. Her first session at the Fairfield Female College was ending, and the seniors would have their farewell ceremony that afternoon.

Berta could hear birds singing in the oak tree outside her bedroom window. She quickly put on her robe and slippers, and stepped through the French doors that opened onto the veranda, which extended around the entire second story of the college. It was the largest building she could remember, although the Tremont Hotel in Galveston, where she and her family had stayed on their arrival from North Carolina six years earlier, may have been of similar size. The Fairfield College[1] building and its views of the surrounding fields and forest had been her home since January. Berta walked around the veranda and saw the morning mist rising from the

---

[1]   Appendix II, Item 1. Fairfield Female College.

pasture and the small creek that ran across the back of the property where a small group of deer were quietly browsing near the water.

As she reached the south side of the building, she noticed three raccoons heading away from the building, likely lumbering back to their dens after feasting on scraps left for them by the kitchen workers. Stone pillars formed the foundation of the building, and the first floor was above the ground such that small creatures could easily hide underneath. Towards the rear of the building, the cave-like cellar connected to the pantry on the first floor, providing a cool storage room for preserved foods. Given the early morning hour, Berta knew she would soon hear the first bell ringing to awaken the students and signal the beginning of the day's activities.

As her stroll carried her to the east side of the building, she marveled at the beauty of the impending sunrise, at the rose-colored reflections from strands of clouds considered by the ancients as the fingers of Eos, goddess of the dawn. On this morning, she and her classmates would be meeting with their instructors for a final review of their efforts during the session. Berta continued to feel an unexpected sense of excitement and anxiety about the day. Perhaps it was the idea that school was ending and she would soon return to her beloved family, or perhaps it was the anticipation of meeting one last time with her music instructor, who would be leaving Fairfield College at the end of this session.

The helpers at the college had cleaned and pressed her clothes for this special day, and Berta took greater care than usual to arrange her lustrous red hair atop her head in a neat bun. She had a vague sense of guilt about the pride she took in her hair, as its unique hues were a trait she shared with her mother. She had also inherited her mother's pale skin, which would glow pink when she became overheated. Berta's complexion made it impossible for her to hide her emotions, as she would blush at the slightest provocation. Her father often teased her about this. Guile, he said, was not a trait that she should cultivate because her face would always reveal her true feelings.

The final detail of her preparation was to see that her hands and nails were presentable, as every pianist should. Although she didn't expect to perform on this occasion, she refused to neglect this detail of her routine. Her hands were smaller than she would have liked, which limited her ability to play some of the more intricate chords in her pieces, and her pinky finger extended outward noticeably. As she studied her hands, she thought, with a twinge of sadness, of her dear departed brother Lucius, who, because of the shape of her hands, had often teased her about having four thumbs.

Shaking off the sad thought of her brother, Berta turned to anticipating the final meetings with her instructors. The senior girls had already finished their meetings; the only activities left were to prepare for the trip home and the closing ceremonies that afternoon.

Not all the girls were enthusiastic about the immediate future. Berta's friend, Molly Rather, whose family had sent her to Texas to avoid the anticipated warfare in their home state of Mississippi, was one of those girls. She was graduating now, but the future was looking uncertain, as the Rathers had fled their home following the Union army's push into Mississippi after the Battle of Shiloh in Tennessee the previous year. Molly's family had relocated to an area on the Brazos River in Texas, where her mother's relatives had settled some years earlier when the state was still part of Mexico.

Berta's first meeting of the morning was with her piano instructor, Count Rudolph von Godski. The Polish aristocrat sported a slight limp from the battle at Shiloh and an exuberant mustache, held in place with beeswax, which threatened to catch fire every time he leaned over the candelabra on the forte-piano. The Count eased her anxiety that morning by pronouncing her talent exceptional and her performance technique excellent. But he then went on to suggest she would need to work harder to reach her full potential; she was very good, he noted, but she could be even better.

After thanking him for his encouragement and instruction, Berta thought about what activities she could give up to follow his advice. She already spent several hours every day practicing different pieces, such as etudes, mazurkas, waltzes and barcarolles. Her other pursuits, which included reading for pleasure and visiting with friends, played an important role in her life, and she wouldn't want to give them up. Music was wonderful, even necessary, Berta decided, and she would continue to develop her musical skills. But her playing would be for pleasure, not as a full time effort.

Between meetings with faculty members that morning, she encountered Betty Graves, the older daughter of the college president, Dr. Henry L. Graves. Betty taught younger students at the academy and had become her friend. Dr. Graves and his family which included his wife Rebecca and their children lived in the college building. Betty was the oldest and Ophelia-who preferred to be called Mollie-was in her class. A younger son, Henry, attended the academy which was a school for local children attached to the college which also provided teaching experience for the college students. In addition to teaching the younger students, Betty had assumed the responsibility of protecting and cultivating a rose garden that flourished in the Freestone County environment. She would permit older students to walk among the bushes and occasionally pick a bloom. When Betty had learned that Berta had lost her brother, Lucius, in the war, she went out of her way to show her kindness and compassion, even teaching her some of the gardening techniques she used.

That day, Betty was beautifully groomed, as usual, with her abundant dark hair neatly arranged atop her head and her long dress adorned with a colorful ribbon that matched the one in her hair. Berta was surprised when her friend offered up a rose plant to take as a reminder of her happy year at Fairfield Female College and a token of Betty's affection and respect.

"I know you have experienced a great loss with the death of your brother," Betty said. "I have marveled at the resilience of your spirit and thoughtfulness toward others. Give this small plant similar attention, and it may grow and bloom as I know you will."

Touched by her friend's words, Berta promised to nurture and treasure the plant, even as she wondered aloud why her friend seemed a little unsettled. As Betty looked around to see if anyone was within earshot, it was clear that she wanted to talk to her about something other than the weather and the garden.

"I do have something I want to discuss with you, and I must ask you not to reveal to anyone what I'm about to tell you," Betty said.

Berta flushed, slightly indignant at the notion that she couldn't keep a secret, but Betty shook her head and continued.

"Do you recall the flag ceremony earlier this spring? And if so, do you recall the man at the end of the procession who was somewhat taller than the others?"

Berta nodded, not certain that she remembered all the details and every soldier, but eager to hear the rest of the story. Betty obliged by telling her that the tall soldier, William, who had been away for training since the flag ceremony, was returning to Fairfield that evening. He would remain there for two days with his company before heading east to fight in the war. While this was somewhat interesting to Berta, she couldn't understand what about this solider and his company was making her friend anxious. And then Betty revealed her splendid secret.

"This evening, after the graduation ceremony, William and I will be married," she said. "Except for the two of us and the minister at the church in town, you are the only person who knows of it."

Berta's surprise left her breathless. "Oh! I cannot get my breath from such a shock," she gasped. "I don't know what to say!"

"Dear Berta, you don't need to say anything," Betty replied. "It would perhaps be best if you didn't respond immediately to what you have been told. My purpose in telling you this is that I trust you to keep the secret and to comply with my next request."

Betty then gave Berta a sealed letter to deliver to her parents the following morning, when they were likely to be alone. If pressed to answer questions, Berta was to say that their daughter and her fiancé were very much in love and that, given the war and the resulting uncertainties that accompanied daily life, they didn't want to be apart for even one more day. With William going away to war, there was simply no time for the formalities of a traditional wedding. Happily, the minister at her family's church had agreed to marry them, despite the possibility of upsetting her parents.

"Whatever the future may hold, we will always know that our love has been declared and blessed and that no human act can ever disrupt that bond," Betty said.

The two young women walked over to a garden bench and sat down together. The morning sun brushed the treetops of the surrounding forest, chasing away any lingering clouds. Berta gently grasped her friend's arm.

"With William going away to war, where will you live?"

"William has property of his own with a house that will be adequate for my immediate needs if my family does not want me to stay," Betty smiled. "I am confident that I can support myself in some fashion by teaching young children somewhere. With that and my faith, I do not fear the future."

Berta, however, had enough fear for both of them. She would not hear of her friend living alone and insisted that Betty return with her to Houston County, as her own family had rooms available and was always welcoming to both visitors and family. Smith Landing Plantation wasn't too far from Fairfield, and if Betty wanted to open a school, there were plenty of children who could benefit from experienced instruction. It was a heartfelt offer, one that Betty graciously refused.

"You are as thoughtful as you are gentle, however, having faith means that I look forward even though I have no idea what the future holds," Betty said, as she stood up.

She pressed the letter into Berta's hands, asking her again to keep it safe until the following morning, and promised to return in two days. The young women then bade each other a tearful goodbye as they walked toward the college building.

Until she could calm her racing heart and flushed face, Berta knew she was in no condition to have a review session with Dr. Graves. As she waited in the foyer, she distracted herself by recalling his lectures on the botanical sciences and the beauties of natural philosophy as portrayed by the Swedish scientist Carl Linnaeus. As she held the rose Betty had given her, she tried to remember how it would be classified but gave up after several minutes, concluding that its greatest significance was as a token of affection from a dear friend.

When she was called into Dr. Graves' office, Berta did not know what to expect from the meeting but the conversation that ensued caused her to blush with surprise. He congratulated her on being admitted as a member of the local Baptist church one month earlier in April.[2] As happened with all those seeking new membership in the faith, she was required to meet with the minister and at least two of the deacons of the church who would question her about her faith, her understanding of the Scriptures and the significance of membership. She remembered the evening very well, as they had asked her some difficult questions, and she had replied with answers that were, on occasion, somewhat unexpected. Dr. Graves, who had recommended her to the church for membership, already knew about her responses and was curious to hear Berta's side of the story.

---

[2]   Berta Smith was baptized into church membership April 26, 1863.

It was a tale of faith and will, of a congregation that thought a fifteen-year-old too young to understand the importance of spirituality, and of a young woman whose unshakeable faith and cast-iron will proved them wrong. The questions were, in Berta's mind, at times pointless and puzzling. Did she think it was God's will that she publicly declare her faith? She did. Did she think it was God's will that she attend the College? She did. Was it also God's will that the Confederacy and the Union go to war? Her answer – that God would want people to treat each other with love and respect, and would never want the world to be at war – no doubt perplexed the interrogators.

"Tell me," Dr. Graves said. "How do you think we should react when bad things happen to us or our loved ones?"

Berta chewed her lower lip slowly as she composed a response.

"I don't think God wants bad things to happen to us," she shook her head. "But they will anyway, so His presence and comfort are available to help us deal with what does happen. Sometimes God can use those things to achieve good results, although we may not understand or believe it at the time." Using her own family as an example, Berta pointed out that her mother, despite ongoing illness and a lack of strength, refused to let the situation overcome her. The illness might weaken her body, but not her spirit.

"They even wanted to know if I thought slavery in the Southland was also God's will," Berta said. "And I am sure that my answer was not what they expected from a girl like me."

"It is an unusual question for such a situation," said Dr. Graves. "What did you tell them?"

"I told them about Hannah, a slave who especially helps mother and who has more faith in God than anyone I've ever known," she said. "I told them that when we march through the gates of Heaven someday, Hannah will be near the front of the procession."

Berta's opinion of slavery was unusual, if not downright unconventional. She suspected that slavery had begun long ago as a result of sin, between two groups of people, and that subsequent generations had been unwilling to remedy the situation. God may not have placed Hannah in a perfect world, but she was certainly a blessing to those who lived in this one. And while the deacons might not have approved of her opinions, they had accepted her into the congregation, and for that she was grateful.

"I presume that church deacons don't think women reflect on faith and public matters very often," Berta frowned. "So I believe that most any answer they agreed with would have been adequate."

"You have considerably greater insights than most people your age," Dr. Graves smiled, clearly showing his approval. "Now on to lighter matters, such as that lovely rose bush you came in with. I recall that Betty mentioned your interest in gardening."

"Yes, by happy coincidence, Betty gave me this plant just now," she said. "I'll plant it at our home in Houston County and call it the 'rose of love.' As Betty has taught me how to provide for the plant, she has also taught me about love, and I will do my best to keep these lessons in my mind and heart."

The implications of what she had said didn't hit Berta until it was too late. The words were out, and she couldn't take them back. Fortunately, Dr. Graves just seemed bemused by her thoughts on love.

Realizing that the conversation had gone on too long, Berta excused herself, noting that she need to place the rose bush in water until, once back home, she could properly plant it. Dr. Graves excused her, cautioning that he expected a report on the health of the plant, her mother and Hannah when she returned to school in the autumn. With the good-byes finished, Berta slipped out the door before she could say anything else.

A large gathering of family and friends, faculty and staff of the college, and town residents attended the Fairfield Female College graduation ceremony that afternoon. The building's front veranda served as a stage for the proceedings as well as the seating area for Dr. Graves, his wife, several members of the school committee and the minister of the Baptist church. Girls from the other classes sat in the audience, in neat rows just behind the new graduates, perhaps so that they would be impressed by the gravity of the moment and therefore eager to continue their own studies. Behind the rows of students were the families, friends and supporters who had come to enjoy the celebration. Several visitors in the audience were young men wearing their Confederate Army uniforms; Berta could not help but wonder which one might be Betty's co-conspirator in the secret wedding plan. Even though she realized that her ruminations on the rose plant must have seemed odd to Dr. Graves, she was grateful not to have inadvertently revealed anything. As she watched the different people on the stage, she understood for the first time how many would be affected by that evening's events, and could only admire the minister for being so sympathetic to the young couple.

It was anticipation and daydreams of young love that kept Berta's mind from becoming too restless during the lengthy ceremony. But not everyone had something else to think about. In a sign that the introductions, prayers and admonitions had gone on too long, some of the younger children and students were beginning to fidget. Just as she wondered whether the fidgeting would become a disruption, a final amen was spoken and the tearful graduates joined their families for a reception in the grand hall and chapel of the college.

Following the reception and a light supper, Berta went back to her room to arrange her belongings in preparation for the arrival of Hannah and her son, Edgar, the next morning. They would pack her things, load the carriage and then, together, they would all make their way home. At first, sleep was impossible, so she turned to writing. In the flickering candlelight, she composed a letter to Betty, who by this time was a married woman:

My dear Betty: It is late in the evening, and I know that you and William are now man and wife. I want to wish you the greatest happiness and joy on this day, which will be forever in my mind. You will both be in my prayers daily. Please tell William that his safe return to you from the war will be my greatest wish. Remember that you are always welcome at the Smith Plantation and in Houston County for a visit of any duration. Thank you for the rose bush. I will cherish and nurture it as a symbol of the love that you have shown me and will share with your beloved William. I will ask your parents to give this letter to you on your return, and I expect that they will feel the same happiness about you and William that I do.

Love from your friend and admirer, Berta.

She sealed the letter with drops of wax from the melting candle, and was soon overtaken by sleep.

*   *   *

A familiar voice awoke her the next morning; Hannah and Edgar had arrived, and it was time to go home. In an instant, Berta remembered her obligation, and the promise she'd made to Betty. She dressed quickly and, with Hannah's help, finished packing all of her belongings. Even as Hannah assured her that Edgar would carefully move her trunks to the waiting carriage, Berta fairly ran down the broad stairway to Dr. and Mrs. Graves' rooms. There was no time or inclination for breakfast; the tension and excitement she felt about delivering her news had banished her appetite. She found the couple on the veranda and noted, with some relief, that they were enjoying a quiet breakfast alone. That would make her job easier. With a combination of uncertainty and nerves, she approached their table to deliver the letter that Betty had given her.

"Won't you join us for breakfast?" Dr. Graves said, motioning to an empty chair at the table.

"Yes, please join us," Mrs. Graves said. "We haven't seen Betty this morning, have you?"

"Thank you so much for the invitation, but I really can't linger," Berta said. "I have a note to give you, but I don't want to delay our leaving for home as Hannah and her son are already loading the carriage."

Dr. Graves opened and read the letter before Berta could gracefully exit the scene. His usually stoic expression quickly changed, as his eyes filled with tears and a genuine smile crossed his face. Mrs. Graves took the letter from him and read. Her reaction was equally emotional, confirming that Betty and her new husband would find only love and acceptance in her family.

Dr. and Mrs. Graves were understandably full of questions. Did Betty share their plans? Did Berta know when they were returning? Berta answered simply what Betty had told her, that their daughter's love for William and the uncertain future had spurred them to the altar without delay. The bride's parents smiled; the marriage had their blessing. They understood the decision and approved, but they would have enjoyed taking part in the celebration.

Betty, they said, was twenty-three years old and capable of making her own choices, and William's family was highly respected in Freestone County. All in all, it was a wonderful step in their daughter's life, and they looked forward to seeing her soon. In two days, Berta told them, convinced now that Betty and William would receive an enthusiastic welcome. It had been a day of revelations, but none more puzzling than the discovery that love was a matter of both one's mind and one's heart. As she left, Dr. Graves called out to her, "Berta, be sure to tend to your rose of love and we will all look forward to your return in September."

The carriage ride to Houston County passed in the blink of an eye, and Berta soon spied her parents standing on the embankment as the ferry approached Smith Landing Plantation. The journey had given her an opportunity to think about the past few days and to wonder whether she would ever feel about someone the way Betty felt about William. Perhaps it would happen sooner than expected. The only person outside her family that she had ever had any such interactions with was her friend John Wootters, and her feelings about him had grown in the nearly two years since he had left to fight with the Crockett Southrons.

The last time she'd visited with him was at a church service in Crockett nearly two years ago. He had exuded a strength and confidence she couldn't easily forget. The words he had spoken the next day at the flag ceremony remained prominent in her memory and reinforced her daily prayers for his safe return. He even wrote to her with stories about life in the army camps and on the battlefield. Those rare letters had an effect that she knew would take time to resolve.

II

July 1861 ~ Crockett, Texas.

Tuesday morning dawned warm and humid as the Smith household rose early to prepare for a trip to Crockett that afternoon. The family anticipated the next day's celebration with a mix of pride, hopefulness and concern. The occasion, deemed patriotic by politicians and local citizens alike, featured the presentation of a special flag to the first unit of volunteers to leave Houston County for the war in Virginia. Sewn by a group of ladies from the Baptist, Methodist and Presbyterian churches, this flag would be carried by the company and serve as a rallying point for the troops.

John Smith had seen the banner and had told his family that it was a replica of the Texas flag with the name 'Crockett Southrons' embroidered in an arc across the top. It was to be presented by Miss Sarah Jane Monroe, an articulate young lady and a contemporary of many of the departing troops. Her family boasted a storied patriotic heritage: her father, A.T. Monroe, who had relocated to Houston County from Virginia in 1854, was the grand-nephew of former U.S. President James Monroe. It seemed ironic to John Smith that a descendant of one of the country's founding fathers would advocate so fervently for the dissolution of that country.

John Wootters, who had been elected by the troops as their First Sergeant, would accept the flag on behalf of the company. Well known to the Smith family, John was the nephew of Lodwick Downes, an owner of the Long and Downes mercantile business in Crockett. Downes was a friend of John Smith's and a fellow Mason. Wootters, who attended services at the same Baptist church frequented by Berta and her family, also worked at the mercantile store as a clerk. He graciously tended to the needs of Berta and her mother whenever they stopped by the store.

The nearly fourteen-year-old Berta had been surprised by both the courtesy and congeniality of this young man, seven years her senior, who had expressed interest in her musical talents. She had been both flattered and flustered by his attention and approval. She also noted and appreciated the courtesy he had shown to the slaves, Hannah and Oscar, who were so important to her family's household.

The Houston County company of soldiers to be honored had been organized by Dr. Edward Currie, who was also their captain. On Wednesday, the company would leave for New Orleans, where they would officially become part of the Army of the Confederate States of America. While their exact assignment and command wasn't yet clear, similar groups from other Texas counties had become part of the First Texas Voluntary Infantry Battalion. As Captain Currie believed they would become Company I of that group, they had selected the name "Crockett Southrons" to identify their unit. Once officially mustered into service in New Orleans, they would travel by railroad to Virginia to join the battalion being organized by Colonel Louis T. Wigfall.

This last bit of news worried Berta's father somewhat since Wigfall, a South Carolina native, was widely known as a fire-breathing secessionist whose enthusiasm for war with the Northern states predated the hostilities at Fort Sumter. His career as a lawyer and politician had been marred by a propensity for dueling, and his military experience was limited to brief participation in the in the Seminole wars that did not dampen his enthusiasm for combat. Indeed, perhaps no one welcomed the events the past six months more than Colonel Wigfall. He had been present in Charleston during the bombardment of Fort Sumter and had personally received the truce and surrender of the fort from U.S. Army Major Robert Anderson. As a member of the Texas Legislature, Wigfall had been a staunch opponent of Governor Sam Houston.

On the other hand, Smith believed that quick and decisive victories by the Confederate army would encourage the Federal leadership in Washington, D.C. to be more accepting of an independent Southern nation. To that end, Wigfall's intensity and zeal for action could help the

Confederacy succeed. However, Smith also knew that military victories were achieved, not by colonels, but by committed, well-trained army officers and troops. He could only hope that Wigfall would provide that type of leadership. Thanks to the military background of the Confederacy's provisional president, Jefferson Davis, Berta's father was confident in the fledgling nation's prospects.[3] He felt certain that Davis would appoint experienced senior military leaders capable of channeling secessionist enthusiasm in a more productive direction.

So it was with a sense of hope that the Smith family arrived in Crockett for a prayer meeting at the Baptist Church the evening before the big event on Wednesday. John, Anna Jane and Berta had been warmly received by the church's membership after their move from North Carolina. And although the distance from their plantation home to town precluded their regular attendance, they were held in high regard by the congregation. Some members of the church were aware of Hannah and Oscar's deep faith and spirituality, as the slave couple usually accompanied the Smiths to town and often attended church services with them. Like all slaves in attendance, they were expected to sit in a designated balcony area. At some meetings they would have their own church services either outdoors or in a nearby building. When not in Crockett with the Smith family, they would be leading services for slaves at the church building on the Smith Landing Plantation.

Hannah and Oscar had encountered Mr. Wootters at the mercantile store and been surprised by the courtesy he showed to them. Slaves, who were expected to act deferentially toward all white people, were accustomed to a level of indifference or rudeness from that segment of the population. What they weren't accustomed to was being treated with respect; Wootters' attitude was a surprise, albeit a pleasant one. It meant that Hannah and Oscar were looking forward to attending the church service and celebration, and recognizing his leadership.

The prospect of war left many slaves feeling uncertain and anxious. Even after two centuries and many generations of slavery, the hope for freedom burned brightly. While some of the Smith Plantation slaves understood their good fortune in having generous and temperate owners, kindness was no substitute for the freedom to determine one's own future.

---

[3]   Appendix II, Item 2

The impending war could actually harm their interests. Even if they did shake off the shackles of slavery, it would mean entering a world of hostility and danger, especially for the very young and the very old. Either way, one thing was certain: opposing their owners' immediate interests could only lead to trouble. The possibility of obtaining their freedom by peaceful means had vanished with the onset of the war; now, they could only depend on their faith in God to determine the future.

Berta felt particularly passionate about these events. The prospect of so many young men from her community leaving for the dangers and uncertainty of war – as her brother, Lucius, had done just one month earlier – filled her with fear. The terrors that had been rousing her from sleep since his departure would, no doubt, intensify once her friend John Wootters also decamped for the war. She had come to know him as a kind and sensitive person; he seemed to lack the rough edges so prevalent in many young men of their area, and that filled her with concern about his ability to withstand a life of danger and hardship. His designation as First Sergeant of the company, however, suggested that his fellow soldiers and officers had seen in him a depth of character and leadership that would serve them all well.

The long summer days meant that the church service would begin in full afternoon sun, before the cool of evening. The Smith family took their places in the church sanctuary, along with the rest of the community. As the service progressed, Berta's eyes scanned the congregation. An observant young woman with a keen eye and an excellent memory, she could recognize many of them by the backs of their heads. In front of her to the right, sat a farmer named Abner who, as far as she knew, had never missed a service. He was easily identified by the deep furrows on the back of his neck as well as the mop of carefully trimmed hair that was, at other times, constrained by a well-worn hat. Abner and his wife, who seemed as tired as her husband's hat, had nearly enough children to fill an entire row. Berta was always impressed by their well-behaved brood and how they never seemed to move a muscle during services.

Near the front of the sanctuary sat the town physician, his shiny bald pate surrounded by a circle of white hair. He was flanked by his wife and an older son, whose main duty was to keep the aging doctor from falling out of the pew when he inevitably nodded off. Berta smiled to herself, recalling a Bible story about Eutychus, who not only went to sleep but fell out of a third-floor window during one of the apostle Paul's sermons in the ancient town of Troas. According to that story, Eutychus was miraculously restored to health by Paul, so Berta concluded that the sleepy doctor would likely be forgiven if he slid to the floor. [4]

Sitting in the front rows of the sanctuary were the soldiers being honored. She saw John Wootters sitting at the end of one pew and could only imagine what thoughts might be occupying his mind. She had never seen him in uniform before, and was impressed by how well the suit fit him and how dashing he looked. Berta found herself becoming tearful as she asked God to afford him special protection. The prayer service went on and on with what seemed to be no end in sight. She hoped to personally give Wootters her best wishes; the next day would surely be too filled with activities and confusion to offer such an opportunity.

As the evening progressed, the atmosphere grew still and heavy, with only the ladies' hand-held fans stirring a warm breeze. The minister and countless deacons expounded at length on the biblical importance of warfare and called upon divine support for their cause.

On hearing this, Berta couldn't help but wonder whether congregations in Northern states were having similar prayer services and also calling on the same God for intervention on behalf of their troops. She didn't have a clear solution to this conundrum. But she was sure that all soldiers needed a full measure of divine assistance to carry out their mission with duty and honor, and she, as one who stayed behind, would only ask that their lives be preserved and that their hearts and minds supplied with the assurance of God's love for them. When they were finally blessed with the last "Amen" of the evening, the congregation was released from the confines of the church into the cool of the evening.

Berta exited the church and spied John Wootters standing aside near the doorway. She could not take her eyes off him, from the gray tunic adorned with the braid of his First Sergeant rank. As their eyes met, Berta was overcome by feelings she didn't understand. Despite attempts to maintain her composure, her eyes filled with tears and her cheeks flushed red. She struggled to smile.

---

[4]   The Holy Bible, New Testament, Acts 20:9-12.

"Now, now young lady, you should put on a joyful face," John said. "This is supposed to be a time of celebration and enthusiasm, not one of sadness. If for no other reason, you should rejoice that we can, at last, breathe some fresher air. I think the only person that didn't offer an oration or a prayer was your friend Hannah. Perhaps if she had, it would have had a positive effect."

Berta dabbed at her tears with a handkerchief, as she didn't want to seem silly to her elegant friend. Even so, as she approached him, she noted that his clean-shaven face made him look both innocent and years younger. Surprised, she stumbled slightly over her words.

"Mr. Wootters, I trust that is not a hint of sarcasm that I hear in your description of these services, but I do welcome the chance to breathe more freely," Berta said, pushing a wayward strand of hair from her face. "I recall from the Scriptures that our Lord preferred shorter, more private prayers, rather than such oratory. Nevertheless, I am sure that every utterance was made with heartfelt sincerity."

Wootters nodded as she noted that her prayers for his safe return – and that of all the Crockett Southrons – would accompany them on their journey.

"My gentle-hearted friend, I greatly appreciate your kind words," he said. "But I must say that I haven't sensed any fear in my comrades, and I am sure that we will meet our challenges without hesitation. Your prayers will be most welcome, and I can assure you that I will also pray for our safety as well as the will to carry out our duties."

Berta immediately regretted her words, thinking they were more childish than she would have liked. Following his gracious response, she was more confused: his face and smile suggested a softness to his nature, but his eyes revealed a steely determination that revealed very different trait. In the months that followed, she would try to remember her feelings at these moments but could only recall the sense of confusion that swirled in her head.

"Mr. Wootters, I know that I should act braver than I really am but I must admit to a great sense of fear about the departure of so many for a war whose cause is hard to understand," Berta said. "You seem so strong and determined, and I don't understand why I can't be braver than I am."

John smiled, acknowledging the sense of Berta's words. The difference between fear and uncertainty, he explained, lay in the fact that most people lived through uncertainty at some point in their lives; fear was born from a perceived lack of control. Moreover, people would always experience circumstances or situations that were beyond their ability to manage. It was during those times – those fearful, seemingly helpless times – that people should depend on their faith in God.

"He will be with us whatever the situation," John said. "We can only pray for our faith not to falter in these times of such challenge."

Buoyed by his words, Berta curtseyed her thank-you as John excused himself for the evening. The hour was late, and he was expected to speak at the ceremony the following day. "I will be thinking about you as I express our thanks for the flag."

*　　*　　*

On Wednesday morning, July 17, Berta awoke to a cloudless blue sky so typical of summertime in Texas. The bright sunlight reminded her that the day would be warm, and shady spots would be at a premium during the flag presentation ceremony scheduled for noontime. She met Hannah and her mother in the hotel lobby; her father had already gone to the town square to secure comfortable seats in the shade so that Anna Jane would be reasonably comfortable throughout the afternoon. The town was abuzz with activity as they made their way toward the square, where a podium had been erected in front of Mrs. Hall's Hotel. The structure was festooned with colorful red, white and blue bunting to represent the new Confederacy and its "Stars and Bars" flag.

As the band began playing, more people arrived. Berta and her party scanned the crowd for her father. On spotting him, Oscar and Hannah helped Anna Jane make her way to the seats he had reserved. Prone to fainting spells and exhaustion, she had never regained her full measure of stamina since Berta's birth. The severe hemorrhage that had complicated the delivery of her last child had nearly killed her. She never fully recovered. Although her mind and spirit were alert and energetic, her body could only endure a limited amount of physical activity.

Mercifully, the speeches were short. According to crowd gossip, Captain Currie was eager to begin the trek to Louisiana and did not want to linger any longer than necessary. The men – more than one hundred of them – would march on the Old San Antonio Road. Once they crossed the Sabine River and reached Natchitoches, they would head south toward Baton Rouge and New Orleans. Currie expected them to complete their journey within two weeks; importantly, it would be the first opportunity he and his officers would have to assess the fitness of the new volunteers. Enthusiasm notwithstanding, he felt certain they would meet his expectations.

This last public display of support was eagerly welcomed by the recruits. Currie understood that separation from friends and loved ones would be one of their greatest challenges in the coming months or years. This festive event was an opportunity to make the most of a final, if temporary, farewell. Once the dignitaries were introduced and prayers offered, the county judge welcomed Miss Sarah Jane Monroe to present the flag to the company.[5]

Sarah Jane was older than Berta, who watched with admiration as the young woman move to the center of the podium. Berta thought she was dressed perfectly for the occasion: a long dress of red and blue with white lace on the bodice and generous petticoats, which made a striking contrast to the severe black suits of the men sitting behind her. They all stood as she moved to pick up the neatly folded flag from the low table. At the end of the row, First Sergeant John Wootters stood at attention. Once again Berta was surprised by his aura of authority and strength. He stood erect, motionless, as Sarah Jane began her presentation in a clear, confident voice.

She referred to the new flag as a glorious symbol of Southern independence and admonished the soldiers to never permit it to be dishonored. As she continued her speech, there was hardly a dry eye in the audience, although there was much clapping. At the conclusion of her remarks, Sarah Jane held up the flag. The crowd remained silent as John Wootters advanced to the stage and took the flag in his arms. In a calm voice, he spoke of the honor he felt in receiving the flag on behalf of his company and expressed his appreciation for this gift.

"As long as a heart pulsates and an arm is nerved, the banner will be protected," John said. "As long as one of us survives, the flag will never be sullied or dishonored by any act unworthy of a soldier or gentleman."

---

[5]   Appendix I. Transcription of Crockett Argus newspaper report of The Flag Presentation, July 17, 1861.

With these words, Berta fully grasped for the first time that this man who seemed to her larger than life might never return – and she began to weep. Her sobs were obscured by the applause and shouts of the crowd around her. As John Wootters rejoined his troops to the side of the podium, the banner of the Crockett Southrons was unfurled and raised high on a standard. With the flag-bearer leading them, the men marched quickly around the town square and turned east on the Old San Antonio Road toward Louisiana and the unknown dangers that lay ahead.

A gentle hug from her father reminded Berta that their return trip home would begin soon, as evening was approaching. Oscar had the carriage and horses waiting as they left the town square, where many of the Crockett residents continued to mingle. Some spoke with excitement in their voices, while others appeared more somber, reflecting the realization that their beloved Southland was embarking on what could be a dangerous and costly war.

Smiling, John Smith held Anna Jane's hand as she began nodding off. The strenuous day had taken its toll on her fragile body. Hannah, having established that her mistress was comfortable and the other riders were situated, took her place atop the carriage next to Oscar, who had been waiting patiently. The occasional whinny of the horses and the sound of their hoofs scratching the ground was a sure sign they were ready to go. With a soft whistle, Oscar prompted them into action. They made their way through the thinning crowd and headed north toward Smith Landing Plantation.

The carriage made its way down the road and out of town, and was soon engulfed by the lengthening shadows of the pine forest. Berta noticed that her mother was now asleep and that her father encircled her shoulder with his other arm. While her parents seemed to be resting quietly, she kept going over what John Wootters had said to her the previous evening. Berta could not stop thinking, wondering whether it was God's will for her brother, Lucius, and her friend, John Wootters, to be leaving their homes for war. She was certain that the answers to her questions would be slow in coming and would remain a lingering problem in her mind. Anxious for a distraction, Berta remembered her promise to learn a new song on the piano, one that seemed so popular with the Houston County band and everyone at the celebration. Even though she had no written music, she thought she could remember enough to play the lively tune titled "I Wish I Was in Dixie's Land."

John Smith smiled contentedly, tightening his embrace of his wife, as the carriage proceeded the twenty miles to their home. Berta watched him, wondering what he was thinking as he periodically glanced at her and then at the passing forest. How could she know that he was recalling the day of her birth nearly fourteen years earlier, an event that had so profoundly affected his life?

III

September 1847 - Bladen County, North Carolina

F or three days, the rain fell in torrents. The wind howled and whipped its way across the countryside, snapping branches and shaking the shutters of Desserette, the Smith family plantation.[6] When the weather finally tapered off, Major John Smith mounted his horse and rode one mile to the main turnpike leading to Elizabethtown, hoping to at last greet Dr. Beauregard Harvey. Nearly one week earlier, the doctor had been summoned to care for John's wife, Anna Jane, during the delivery of their long hoped-for second child.

Her labor, which had lasted more than a day and a night, and delivery had been fraught with problems from the beginning. Despite the assistance of Hannah, the household slave who had attended Anna Jane since before her marriage thirteen years earlier, the infant refused to enter the world until Dr. Harvey used his considerable skills to move her into the proper position. Anna Jane had rejoiced with her husband at the birth of their only daughter, her joy made even greater as the baby came fully crowned with a shock of red hair, clearly marking her as her mother's child. Major Smith, as John was known around Bladen County, North Carolina, was delighted at the prospect of another beautiful girl in his family, one who would surely be as bright and lively as his adored wife.

---

6   Appendix II. Item 3. Desserette--The Smith Plantation in Bladen County, North Carolina.

Their joy, however, was short-lived. By the second day, Anna Jane, who had been weakened by the prolonged labor and delivery, began hemorrhaging. Hannah tried every remedy she had learned from her mother and aunts in South Carolina, but the bleeding continued, with Anna Jane becoming more frail and pallid. By the second day, it was clear that her condition was deteriorating; the situation was made worse by her refusal to take food or water.

Both Hannah and Major Smith knew the situation was desperate. They also knew that for Anna Jane to survive, they would have to fetch Dr. Harvey. The river was swollen from the pounding rains; high water and a swift current made it impossible to navigate the twenty miles upstream from Elizabethtown. The only way to reach Desserette was by the turnpike road, which was more of a trail through the pine forest. It followed high ground on the west side of the Cape Fear River, but in most places it was a river of mud. Hannah suggested that Oscar could get through to Elizabethtown to find Dr. Harvey. Frantic with concern for Anna Jane, Major Smith agreed and dispatched him on this uncertain mission.

As the afternoon wore on and streaks of sunlight began to peek through the clouds, Major Smith left Hannah in charge and rode the mile to the main road to await Oscar's return and to view the storm and flood damage. Riding to wait for Oscar, Major Smith had time to size up the situation and to reflect on the events that had led to this day.

Oscar, he knew, held a very special place at Desserette as he was both responsible and very intelligent. He was also devoted to Hannah, whom he called his 'special woman,' and to the Smith family. Major Smith had designated him as overseer of the slaves who worked in the cotton fields, an increasing source of the family's prosperity. Oscar was respected, or at least feared, by the slaves who worked the fields, picked the cotton, removed the seeds, created the bales and stored them until their shipment downriver to the Port of Wilmington. Maintaining control of this workforce was essential, and Major Smith had learned over the years that having a slave serve as overseer was more effective than the harsher discipline used by many of his peers in Bladen County.

The possibility of unrest among the slaves was always a concern, and it was for this reason that the militia was such a constant presence. A leader of the local militia, Major Smith had a long tradition of military service in his family,[7] and he was highly regarded by the white population as a man of experience, skill and integrity. His own militia activities also meant that he was intimately familiar with that area of the Carolinas between the Cape Fear and Pee Dee Rivers and the counties to the south. It was there, further south, that he met Anna Jane Pouncey.

Following a period of intense courtship, he married Anna Jane, and persuaded her to leave her beloved Cheraw area of South Carolina and reestablish her life in Bladen County, North Carolina. Once established in her new home, the young Mrs. Smith had quickly become a welcome and gracious addition to genteel society. She was widely regarded in the area surrounding Elizabethtown as a person of faith, wisdom and style.

In their thirteen years of marriage, Anna Jane had given birth three times before the arrival of this new baby girl. Two children had died in infancy, but a son, Lucius, had survived and was now an active, intelligent five year old. Since the birth of Lucius, Major Smith and Anna Jane had wondered why they had been unable to conceive again – and then came the joyful news that Anna Jane was pregnant. It seemed like an answer to their prayers. But now, her sudden physical decline following the birth cast a pall over the happy house. It seemed unlikely that Anna Jane could live without a miracle, which also brought the infant's survival into question.

As Major Smith rode toward the banks of the Cape Fear River, he was amazed at the sight of the usually placid waterway between the plantation and the city of Wilmington. For now, in the storm's aftermath, the water was rushing downstream faster than he could have imagined. The sheer power of the river, engorged by the rains of the previous days, was a stark reminder of how he and his family existed through the whims of nature. Everything they did on the plantation depended on the weather and the abundance of the soil. Had these rains arrived one month earlier, they would have wiped out a year's worth of cotton production. Fortunately, however, most of the crop had already been picked and placed in storage barns to dry. The work of ginning the cotton to remove the seeds and prepare bales would be done over the next several months. In years past, this particular stage in the process had severely restricted the amount of

---

[7]   Appendix II. Item 4. The American Revolution in North Carolina, the Battle of Elizabethtown and the family of Major Smith.

cotton they could produce, as it was slow and tedious. But the invention of the cotton gin by Eli Whitney had revolutionized cotton production.

Desserette and its counterparts throughout the south were able to meet the demands of cotton mills in Great Britain, which enriched planters in Carolina and throughout the southland. Their ability to continue meeting this demand was limited only by the productivity of the land. Cotton, like tobacco two generations before, was highly profitable; however, the crop also quickly depleted the soil of its ability to sustain abundant production. The only remedy was to allow large tracts of land to lie fallow for two or more years before resuming production. The availability of suitable land, however, was becoming a problem, so much so that some Bladen County neighbors had moved west in search of acreage to areas in Alabama, Mississippi and Texas.

Access to routes for delivering the cotton to a shipping point was also essential. The Cape Fear River was a key route for Desserette, and it was nearly always navigable by the barges that carried their crop to Wilmington. Major Smith and his fellow cotton growers often wondered how long it would be before steam-powered boats fully replaced the water current and mule-team assisted transport. Given that the *SS Savannah* had crossed the Atlantic more than thirty year earlier, there was little doubt that boats would soon appear that were capable of navigating the Cape Fear and other rivers to deliver cotton to the ports and the markets of the world.

One of Major Smith's great concerns was the growing need for more labor to work the expanding acreage devoted to cotton and prepare the crop for market. Cotton, while highly profitable, required even more labor than the naval stores industry. And while the plantation had enough slaves on site to do the work, he worried about the increasing cost and difficulty in managing the labor. The price of an able-bodied male slave was rising and, as the land became less productive, it was clear that the plantation's future profitability was in doubt. Already planters in more northerly states, such as Maryland, Delaware, even Virginia, were reducing their slave numbers and selling them to the expanding plantations in Mississippi and Louisiana. New slave imports into the United States were illegal which had been signed into law by President Thomas Jefferson forty years earlier.

As for Major Smith's own opinion and perception of slavery and individual slaves, these had changed since his marriage to Anna Jane. In 1834, after their wedding, her parents Major James and Ann Kolb Pouncey, presented Anna Jane with two families of slaves whose ancestors had been owned by their families for a century. The respect that Anna Jane showed these individuals and the diligence with which they served her family had helped to tweak Major Smith's perspective. In particular, Hannah and Oscar, who had assumed responsibilities of the highest level of importance at Desserette, proved to be more like family than slave labor.

Never had this been more true than at the present moment, when the survival of his adored wife depended on Hannah's care and on Oscar's success in finding – and returning with – Dr. Harvey. As the day wore on and the shadows lengthened, Major Smith realized that if Oscar didn't bring the doctor soon, it might be too late. He prayed for Anna Jane's life to be spared. Indeed, Major Smith had learned much about faith from Anna Jane, who brought an awareness of Christian spirituality to their marriage. As a child, he had attended church services, but it was only in recent years that he had begun to understand and share Anna Jane's appreciation of God's daily presence in their lives.

Not surprisingly, Major Smith's increased understanding of faith and spirituality also affected his evolving view of slavery. Anna Jane's family had arrived in the New World one hundred and fifty years earlier in search of religious freedom. Those moving to South Carolina from Pennsylvania had founded the Welsh Neck Baptist Church in an area known as the Old Cheraw District. While many generations had passed since anyone in their area was familiar with the language of Wales, the virtues of loyalty, moderation and sincerity that often defined the Welsh character remained strong. These traits were based on a deep religious conviction and the Baptist faith, which Major Smith gradually made his own.

Membership at the Smith's church was not taken lightly. Not only were members expected to have a significant understanding of their beliefs but they were also expected to demonstrate a level of spiritual maturity and behavior consistent with expectations in the New Testament gospels.[8] Moreover, all believers had equal standing in spiritual matters and were

---

[8]   Appendix II. Item 5. History of the Welsh Neck Baptist Church.

individually responsible for their own relationship with God and their salvation.

Major Smith had known few, if any, individuals who reflected the values of Christian love more than Hannah and Oscar. He admired their devotion to each other and to their children, especially their youngest who was clearly impaired and would likely never function independently. They were loyal and trustworthy, and it was with complete confidence that he left Anna Jane in Hannah's capable hands.

Major Smith was roused from his ruminations by the appearance of a buggy with Oscar at the reins. A glimmer of hope reawakened in him as he prayed that the help Anna Jane so desperately needed was inside the carriage.

"Greetings to you my friend," came the familiar voice of Dr. Beauregard Harvey. "Surely your man, Oscar, is the most skillful of drivers. We could have never made this trip were it not for his ability to find alternate trails."

A short, middle-aged man with graying hair briefly stepped out of the carriage. Dr. Harvey's usual proper dress – a black waist-coat and necktie – was rumpled after the arduous trip, but his warm smile set Major Smith at ease.

"Doctor Harvey, you can't imagine how grateful I am that you are here," Major Smith said, trembling. "My precious Anna Jane seems at the very brink at departing this life."

"John, please call me Beauregard, as my mother did," Dr. Harvey said, shaking the other man's hand. "Now, let's put aside pleasantries and get to the house without any further delay."

Bladen County was fortunate to count Dr. Harvey as a physician-in-residence. A native of Virginia, he had pursued his medical education in Philadelphia, but, as he would often comment, the cold winters and city life were not for him. So he eventually made Bladen County his home. A well-known and respected member of the Baptist Church, Dr. Harvey treated slaves as readily as he did their masters and was, as a result, regarded fondly by all.

During his rounds to the area's plantations, he had also become familiar with the remedies used by slave women, many of whom had extensive knowledge of herbs and potions that were carefully passed from one generation to the next.

On arriving at the main plantation house, the men were greeted by Hannah, who took the took the doctor's top coat and held the large front door open as he entered the dimly lit hallway.

"Thanks to the Lord you have come, Doctor," she said. "We have been praying for your safe arrival, and we hope you can help Miz Anna. She has had a really hard time of it."

"Well, I know she has had the best nurse in Bladen County helping her," Dr. Harvey smiled. "So tell me what has happened since I was here last."

Hannah described Anna Jane's initial recovery and subsequent lapse. First came two days of bleeding, more blood than Hannah thought could be in a human body. When the flow finally waned, Hannah went to wash her mistress and found something she hadn't expected.

"I couldn't tell what it was, and then I saw it was piece of flesh," Hannah explained. "The flesh came a-loose, and I saved it for you to see. The bleeding stopped after that and there has not been any for at least an hour."

After studying the tissue Hannah had saved, Dr. Harvey told her that she had likely saved Anna Jane's life. The flesh was a part of the afterbirth, which didn't completely pass after the baby came, causing Anna Jane to lose blood until it did pass or Hannah removed it. At this point, Dr. Harvey turned his attention to the patient, noting that she could be roused but was clearly too weak to respond coherently or to move about without help. Her pallor seemed greater against the intense red of her hair; even the occasional freckle paled to the point of disappearing. Nevertheless, Dr. Harvey concluded that Anna Jane was making progress.

"And how is the baby, Hannah?" he asked.

"Oh, Dr. Harvey, little Abigail is just fine. Since Miz Anna wasn't able to nurse her, I took it on myself," Hannah smiled. "That child does have an appetite. She's hungry all the time except when she's sleeping."

John, whose attention was focused on his wife, heard that the baby was called Abigail and that Hannah was nursing her, and realized with some alarm that he had not stopped to consider whether his infant daughter was receiving nourishment, much less had been given a name.

"I didn't know you were still in a nursing way, but you must still be nursing your little one," Dr. Harvey said.

"I am," she nodded. "I'm hoping little Ossie gets stronger, and some days he does seem more like he should be."

Hannah had borne many children, but from the moment of his birth she knew that her last baby was not like the others. He lacked the strength and alertness of her previous children, and his face and eyes looked slightly different. Knowing how distressed she was about her youngest, Dr. Harvey had been able to offer Hannah some words of comfort, but no diagnosis. In the three years since Ossie's birth, he had not discovered either an explanation of the illness or an effective treatment. Although he could sit up and crawl a bit, Ossie was not as active or vocal as other children his age. His sweet nature, however, compensated for any shortcomings. And while Hannah did worry about her son, she was convinced that things happen for a reason, that God had a plan. She liked to say that God wanted her to have Ossie, so she would have to do for him as best she could.

It occurred to Dr. Harvey to tell Hannah about a visit he was planning to Philadelphia in the spring. Once there, he said, he would consult with other doctors about Ossie's condition. The boy had such definite features that it was possible one of his medical colleagues may have examined other children like him and would know what could be done to help."[9]

By this time, Anna Jane began to stir, asking for some broth and tea, and the ever-watchful Hannah promptly left to fulfill the request. Major Smith, while elated by his wife's improvement, was confused about the care of the new baby; he knew that Hannah was nursing her, but he regretted not being more aware of her immediate needs. All of his attention and thought had been focused on Anna Jane for the past days. He took advantage of Hannah's brief absence to express to Dr. Harvey his trepidation about the slave nursing his daughter.

Dr. Harvey reassured him that, when it came to nourishment, there was no difference between African milk and Anglo-Saxon milk. "I can't imagine a better wet nurse for baby Abigail," he told the anxious father. "And from the sounds coming from the next room, the baby is strong enough to fully make use of her substantial lung power."

Even as the doctor spoke, the cries increased in volume and frequency. Right on cue, Hannah came in with the tray, but rather than serving

---

[9] Although there is no definite evidence it is possible from the descriptions that this child had Down's Syndrome.

Anna Jane first, she went straight to cradle. A pair of loving arms and a few gentle words worked wonders to still the infant's distress, and Hannah took advantage of the quiet to present her to the gathered admirers. Anna Jane held her baby and wept.

"Oh John, she really is a beautiful baby," she whispered. "I am so thankful to God for giving her to us."

While those few words left her breathless, she went on to tell her husband that she wanted to name her only daughter Philomena Berta Smith.

"Yes, Anna, I have heard you mention those names, but Hannah is already calling her Abigail," Major Smith said. "At some point in her life, this baby may decide to name herself something entirely different."

Anna Jane mustered a slight smile. "Where in creation did Hannah come up with such a name for this beautiful baby?" she said in a subdued voice. "It is an interesting name but not as classically elegant as befits such a tiny noble figure."

Hannah, having taken the baby in her arms, turned to offer her mistress some more broth. Anna Jane seized the moment to ask how she had thought of the name Abigail.

"Oh, Miz Anna, Abigail was one of the wisest and prettiest women in the Bible," Hannah answered. "The preacher at church told us about how Abigail tried to save her man from the devil's rum, which had got hold of him something hard. She saved him from being killed by King David's men, but the rum got him anyway. Because she was so smart and beautiful, she became King David's wife." [10]

At this moment, the baby began to wail again, and Hannah went off to feed her. Major Smith, who had heard Hannah's explanation marveled at how much she knew about the world without ever having left the Carolinas. Taking his wife's hand, he reiterated his concern for her health and reminded her that all would be well as long as she was well.

"Whatever the baby is called, she will always be a blessing to her family," he said. "Now you let Hannah care for the baby, and you eat and rest. We all need you to recover."

Anna Jane put on a brave face for Major Smith's sake. In the back of her mind, however, she knew that her recovery would be a long, slow journey.

---

[10] The Holy Bible, Old Testament, 1Samuel 25:14-42.

Already she was overwhelmed with a weakness that felt insurmountable. As sleep began to overtake her, she prayed to God to let her live to see her precious new baby grown and to face the future, whatever it might hold, with her dearest John. And so she slept, her faith a constant reassuring vigil through the night.

IV

Spring 1857 -- Bladen County, North Carolina

Berta ran into the cooking house and was greeted by a wave of heat and a medley of mouth-watering smells. But she was much too excited to be distracted by the aroma of baking bread.

"Come quickly, Hannah, and see what is happening to the old possum!" she cried, tugging on the slave's apron. "The one you feed and worry about so much is in the smokehouse, and something is going on."

The kitchen at Desserette was Hannah's fiefdom, and there was little doubt as to who was in charge. With a fire usually going in the long fireplace, she would move the glowing coals to the end, where she worked her magic over the skillet or cauldron. Baked sweets. Spicy concoctions. Savory stews. There was always something delicious brewing in the Desserette cooking house.

Today, Hannah frowned her disapproval at the girl's outburst, even as Ossie, her own son, squealed with delight. He stopped shelling peas long enough to acknowledge Berta, then quickly returned to the job at hand. Hannah smiled while trying to appear indignant at the sudden intrusion of a hollering white child into her domain.

"Miss Abigail, you be careful," she scolded. "You are so riled up, you may faint away." Hannah was especially fond of the nine-year old, whom she had taken care of since her birth. Anna Jane's ongoing debilitated state meant that Berta often sought Hannah's company and counsel so as not to disturb her mother.

Ossie was several years older than Berta, but had never developed normally; his speech and mind were like that of a three-year-old child, not one who was already thirteen. While his limitations were many, he was content to spend hours shelling peas at a small table in the cooking house under his mother's watchful eye. When not occupied with this task, he would use charcoal fragments to create designs on wooden shingles. These artworks received Ossie's intense devotion, and only he knew what they meant. One thing was certain: he prized them and fiercely protected his stable of art projects. Even with his limited speech skills, he had no difficulty expressing his intentions or desires, and was fully capable of showing affection for Hannah and his father, Oscar. He was also fond of Berta and always greeted her with genuine affection, although he would refer to her at various times as either his "mudder" or his "sisser."

Caring for Ossie was a high priority for Hannah, and she was thankful that her mistress, Anna Jane, and Major Smith had promised to provide for him and for her as long as the child needed care. The family physician, Dr. Harvey, had not been able to explain the child's lack of development; even a discussion with medical colleagues had failed to enlighten the situation. Other physicians had cared for similarly affected children, but no remedy or explanation had ever been found. What they did find was that affected children usually did not live to maturity; indeed, Ossie had already surpassed most expectations.

"Old possum seems to do just fine," Hannah said, wiping her hands. "Now if you will let go of my apron, I will come with you to see what is such a worry. You finish your work, Ossie, while I find out what the commotion is all about."

Age had slowed Hannah somewhat, but her curiosity and alertness remained sharp. She was about ten years older than her mistress, and had spent most of her life helping to care for Anna Jane and her family. Her own parents had been slaves in the South Carolina household of Anna Jane's parents. As she followed Berta out to the smokehouse, she wondered what could upset the child so.

"Look, Hannah! Look in the window and you can see the old possum," Berta pointed. "What in heaven's name is happening to her?"

"I don't see anything happening to her. She's likely scared enough to jump out of her hide, so she's pretending she's dead. She's just playing possum."

"She does look dead now, but a minute ago she was lying on her back and seemed to have little bugs crawling on her stomach," Berta said. "I don't see any little bugs now so maybe they killed her! What could be the trouble, Hannah?"

"Miss Abigail, those weren't bugs," Hannah chuckled. "Those were her babies being born and crawling into her pouch, where they will be warm and can nurse until they get big enough to look like little possums and come out in the daylight. I knew she was expecting babies as she was getting bigger. She probably climbed in the shed to have the babies cause she still thinks that old tree is hers, even though it has been cut into firewood."

"That old possum sure is brave to lie there with her babies instead of running away like she usually does," Berta noted.

"I don't doubt that she is a brave possum, but as soon as she thinks you're gone, she will be out of the shed or hiding somewhere in the wood pile as fast as you can blink your eyes," Hannah said. "We'll let her be now. She's had enough excitement for one day."

Berta climbed down from her perch by the smokehouse window, reluctant to leave the wondrous sight of the possum and her babies. As they neared the kitchen structure, she chewed her bottom lip thoughtfully. Hannah could tell that something was on the child's mind, but she waited patiently until Berta was ready to talk. It took only a few minutes for Berta to ask her a question.

"I know that Mother tells me to do what's right, but sometimes it's hard to do just as she says and then to have to tell her what I did anyway," she frowned. "How do I know what's the right thing to do, and how do I make myself not want something else?"

"Miss Abigail, when you're young you haven't had as many chances to know what happens when you make choices. That's why you need to do what your Momma tells you to do as long as you are a child," Hannah said. "Even though people know what's right they sometimes act like they don't, so God gave us commandments to help guide us. An animal like old possum does what their nature tells them to do: run away, stay and fight, or play possum. God has put the nature that best suits the animal inside them so they don't need to think about anything. People are different. They have to find out what's right and then be brave enough to do it."

"I knew you would know the answer!" Berta said as they walked to the cook house. "You know so much."

Pleased but preoccupied with thoughts of preparing dinner, Hannah gave the little girl a hug and shooed her back to the main house. Berta skipped through the entry parlor to the back sitting room where her mother preferred to rest during the day near a fireplace that was nearly always in operation. Cold weather or any chill in the air made Anna Jane uncomfortable. She had not been the same since her last pregnancy. Her monthly menstruation had stopped altogether, and she had never been able to nurse her new baby. Hannah had come to the rescue and nursed Berta, who had grown into a healthy, active child. Anna Jane and John regretted not being able to have more children, but they were thankful for the son and daughter they did have.

As was the situation for many children of plantation owners in Bladen County, itinerant tutors would come to their home for several days at a time and add to the education that was provided by the parents. Berta had become an avid reader with an insatiable curiosity. Her questions were constant, her energy boundless. Anna Jane was also pleased to note that Berta was musically inclined, indeed talented. She had learned to play familiar tunes on the harpsichord that had been brought from South Carolina years earlier. Then one year, her music tutor mentioned that a modern forte-piano was for sale in Charleston; Major Smith had had it shipped to Wilmington and eventually to Desserette. When the instrument was found to be in good working order, he bought it for the price of eighteen bales of cotton.[11]

The arrival of the piano at the plantation was an event that none in attendance would ever forget. It was an upright piano of grand proportions, at least nine feet tall and weighing nearly a thousand pounds. Oscar and five other able men struggled to move it from the dock to a wagon and then into the main house. The piano had apparently been created by a craftsman named George Traegser from Covington, Kentucky. A small

---

[11] Personal communication from Frances Wootters Denman, daughter of Berta Smith and granddaughter of Anna Jane and Major John Smith.

silver plaque on the piano stated that it was registered as Patent No. 28, but no other information about its history was available. It was not clear to either the Smith family or to local musicians why it was patented, but they assumed that a louvered front panel operated by foot pedals that modulated the piano's tones and the fact that it had only eighty-six keys were likely its unique characteristics.

The piano soon became a cherished part of their home and a great source of pleasure for the entire family. Berta, in particular, came to consider the piano a close friend as entertainment for a young child on the plantation was limited. She saw white children of her age only when they gathered in Elizabethtown for shopping or church services, or during occasional visits to neighboring plantations. She had read more than once all the books from their library that she could master, and her mother did not permit her to wander about the plantation out of sight of the main house or Hannah. She spent hours playing etudes of varying difficulty provided by her tutor. As he also brought the music for their church services in Elizabethtown, much of Berta's repertoire consisted of religious music.

"Berta, I am so glad you have come into the house as I was wondering what adventure you had been up to," Anna Jane greeted her daughter.

"You won't believe what I have just seen," Berta said. "If it hadn't been for Hannah, it would have been terribly frightening."

"Indeed, what could have caused such concern for so intrepid an explorer as my little girl?"

Berta spent several minutes regaling her mother with the story of the old possum, the babies and the insight Hannah had given her into human and animal nature. Anna Jane listened intently, smiling and marveling at the morning's events. Berta's joy made her own physical limitations seem less important.

"Truly, the Lord has given you an inquiring mind and a gentle heart, and I know that you will grow into a very brave person who is also thoughtful and kind," Anna Jane said. "I do not believe you can teach a person to be brave, but you can certainly learn how to control your fears."

At the moment, Anna Jane was controlling her concern about her husband and son, who were down in Texas, and praying for their safe return. Once a part of Mexico and then briefly an independent country,

Texas seemed very foreign and far away to this Southern-bred girl. Major Smith had taken both Oscar and Lucius with him on this adventure. Rumor had it that the vast state had fertile acreage as far as the eye could see and a pleasant climate, too. Anna Jane's greatest fear was that the increasing population and scarcity of arable land in the South would propel her husband to move the family to Texas, a world away from Bladen County and her family in the Cheraw District. She also worried whether she would survive the trip if they did move.

Berta had her own private concerns, namely whether or not they would be able to take the piano. Given how large and heavy it was, she had her doubts. But she pressed her mother, pointing out that she would never feel lonely as long as she had her parents and her beloved instrument nearby.

"I am certain that your father would find a way to keep you and the piano together," Anna Jane laughed. "He is very proud of you for learning to play it so well and continuing to improve your skills. Why don't you play some tunes while I take a rest?"

A letter had arrived from Major Smith several days earlier with news of his return from Texas and indicated that the ship should land at Wilmington by the end of that week. He wrote that he and Oscar would waste no time in returning to Desserette, as he had obtained horses for the last leg of the journey; their baggage would arrive later. In the meantime, Lucius would remain in Texas with their new overseer, Elijah Chadwick, to take care of some business that had not been concluded. Brimming with enthusiasm and optimism, Major Smith's letter confirmed the bright economic prospects in this new state.

While he didn't say it outright, it seemed to Anna Jane that a move to Texas was now inevitable – and soon. In earlier letters, Major Smith had mentioned how much their son had grown and matured into a competent youth, capable of managing affairs and making thoughtful decisions. Both parents were proud of how Lucius was turning out; as a young boy, he had been more interested in riding horses and exploring the hills and forests of Bladen County. His tutors had initially recommended that he continue his education at the new Roanoke College in Virginia. They believed that its ties to the Christian faith would benefit both his educational and spiritual growth; Lucius, however, had never been partial to either scholarship or religion.

Anna Jane was startled from her reverie by shouts from the garden. Much to her surprise, John burst into the room moments later; his most recent letter still lay in her lap. Overwhelmed by joy and relief, Anna Jane felt a surge of strength from the emotion of the moment, a strength that propelled her from her chair and into John's outstretched arms. As she collapsed against his chest, she knew that whatever the future held for them, she would be a part of it.

"Oh, John, I am so thankful that God has returned you to me safely," she said, hugging him. "We have all missed you terribly, but it looks like the trip to Texas has certainly agreed with you."

Anna Jane sat back down and invited Major Smith to share the details of his trip, of how Lucius was faring and what was keeping him from coming home. Any thoughts Berta had of practicing the piano fled at the sight of her father. Eager to hear about the place that might be their new home, she climbed up into his lap. The dust from his long ride would have to settle later. The ladies wanted news, and they would not wait.

A tall man with broad shoulders and an air of authority, Major Smith possessed a naturally gentle expression and an ever-present slight smile. His hair was thinning, but he sported a well-trimmed beard; his remarkable blue eyes, surrounded by fine lines, lent him a certain air of wisdom. Hannah appeared then with a pot of warm tea and some cakes, along with a glass of sweet milk for Berta.

"The only things more beautiful than the blessed land of Texas are sitting in this room with me," Major Smith said. "I am so grateful to be able to return home to be with you."

Insisting that Hannah also serve generous portions of cake and tea to Oscar, he told the three women that not only could he not have made the trip without him, but he could only have left for such an extended period knowing that Hannah was there to care for his wife and daughter. For her part, Hannah informed him that "Missy Abigail" had diligently practiced her piano and that Oscar was already recounting their adventures in Texas – and how much he liked it.

"Texas is really a special land," Major Smith said, turning his attention back to Berta and Anna Jane "I think what makes it so special is the attitude of the people who live there, although the climate and soil are so blessed that God has surely had a special hand in it."

The best route to this 'promised land,' he said, would be overland to Mobile, Alabama or to New Orleans, and then by ship to Galveston, at that time the largest city in Texas. Calling it very busy and progressive, Major Smith noted that Galveston was much newer than Charleston and also lacked the long-established residents that could sometimes be hostile to newcomers. Texas, on the other hand, was an open place, ripe with opportunity. It was a place where hard work and honesty were rewarded generously and where everyone was welcomed.

Galveston, in addition to being the state's largest metropolis, was a growing port on the Gulf of Mexico. It boasted an active cotton market and, Major Smith noted, bankers who appreciated the value of that product. The city was also prosperous enough to attract musical groups and artists, especially architects. At least three rivers fed into Galveston Bay, the largest of which was the Trinity River. During their visit, Major Smith, Oscar and Lucius took a packet steamer up the Trinity to explore the countryside. It was a ten-day journey that changed the course of their lives.

Not only did the landscape – gentle hills covered with stately pine trees – look very much like Bladen County, but they passed acre after acre that had never been touched by a plow. Major Smith anticipated that cotton would thrive in this environment; indeed, as they ventured further upriver, they saw that some planters were already producing a fine crop. And then there was the climate: warmer than the Carolinas, with mild winters and enough rainfall. The most promising area he'd seen was in Houston County on the Trinity River, whose main city, Crockett, was named for Davy Crockett, who fought and died at the Alamo.

Houston County was not to be confused with the city of Houston, Major Smith pointed out. That city was also named for a Texas hero, Sam Houston, the first president of the Republic of Texas. But instead of rolling hills and crisp pines, it featured a lush, flat, humid landscape situated on the banks of Buffalo Bayou.

Major Smith spoke with the passion of a religious zealot. He had learned much about this new state and all it had to offer, and he was clearly eager to go. Anna Jane knew the decision was all but made.

"I can see that you are in love with Texas," she told her husband. "The only matter not resolved in your mind is when we should move, not whether!"

"It does offer good prospects for our plantation and our family," Major Smith agreed. "If we ever want to expand our property in this part of the world, some move will be necessary."

Anna Jane nodded, not wanting to reveal how heavy her heart was at the thought of leaving family and friends and everything familiar. Rather, she hoped that Major Smith's enthusiasm was contagious, and that his joy would become hers. Having prayed for guidance, she hoped now that this move would bring blessing and happiness to all in her household.

"Well, my dear, if the climate really is as warm as you suggest, I may be able to survive without a fire in the hearth and a sweater around my shoulders," Anna Jane said with a twinkle in her eye. "I think I might enjoy that circumstance."

"Father, will we be able to take the piano with us to Texas?" asked Berta from the comfort of his lap. "It's so big that I can't imagine a wagon large enough to carry it."

Major Smith reassured her that the massive instrument would have a place in their new home. He had, in fact, already secured passage for it and all their furnishings on a ship that would sail from Wilmington to Galveston. As the sea voyage was long and subject to weather delays, he planned for his family and the slave families to take the household goods and travel overland through Atlanta to Montgomery, Alabama and finally to the port of Mobile. From there, they would sail to Galveston, with a stop in New Orleans, arrive in Texas on practically the same day as their furnishings.

During his Texas tour, Major Smith had purchased a new property in Houston County, including four sections of some of the finest farmland he'd ever seen. Lucius had stayed behind to help Mr. Chadwick with the supervision of the new property and to ensure that there were enough slaves to clear the ground and plant a crop of cotton before the spring rains cleared out. The Smith family would also have a new house; by year's end, they would be living in a home on a high bluff overlooking the Trinity River. As Major Smith elaborated on their route and plans, Anna Jane ticked off a mental list of people to visit on their way down to Mobile, including friends in Georgia and a close cousin in Marengo County, Alabama, people she'd thought never to see again. Surely this was a sign of happy times ahead.

"I know that you have always wanted Lucius and Berta to attend college in Virginia, but I have learned of a university with a reliable reputation that is promoted by the Baptist convention," Major Smith's voice interrupted her daydream. "And thinking of Berta's musical talent, I have also been told there are tutors who should be able to visit our new home to help her with her studies and musical training. I expect to provide every opportunity for Berta whether it is in Texas, the eastern states or the music centers of Europe."

Berta's ears perked up at the mention of her name. "I will be happy to go to Texas as long as I'm with you and Mother and Hannah and the piano," she said. "I will pray to God to make me brave enough to overcome any fears. If the old possum can overcome her fears, then I can, too."

A puzzled Major Smith ruffled his daughter's hair and requested that she entertain them with a lively tune on the piano. Noting that Hannah was waiting outside the parlor, no doubt listening to his description of their future home, he then mused aloud about more tea, and about wanting Hannah to hear about their new home.

Minutes later, as if by magic, Hannah entered, holding a steaming pot of tea.

"Would you be needing some more tea, Major Smith?"

"Yes, that would be most welcome," he said. "Please make sure Oscar tells you all about our trip, Hannah."

"Well, he told me he didn't see bears or wild Indians, but I'm still wondering about what's there," she said. "And I'm wondering who's going with you to Texas and who's staying here."

Major Smith knew this would come up, and he had a ready answer.

"I can't take everyone to Texas, but as I have told you before, you and Oscar your families will always be with us," he said. "No one knows what the future holds, but I am sure that it will be better for all of us in this new land. I will make good on the promises that I have made in the past."

He then turned to his daughter and said, "Indeed, Berta, we will take your piano to Texas. Now, can you play my favorite song 'Standing on Jordan's Stormy Banks?'"

"Oh, yes! I will be glad to play it for you," she clapped her hands and jumped down off his lap. "We could even change the words if you and Mother will sing it."

And so they sang:

> *On Cape Fear's stormy banks I stand, and cast a wishful eye,*
> *To Texas' fair and happy lands where my possessions lie.*
> *I am bound for the promised land, I am bound for Texas*
> *land.*
> *Who will come and go with me, I am bound for the promised*
> *land.*

Together, they joined in this new version of the song. The clearest voice of all was Hannah's, which floated out the windows and up in the bright afternoon sky.

V

Christmastime 1857 –
Houston County, Texas

In December, darkness comes early to East Texas, and the dense forests further mute the effects of the fading sunlight. On this night, the moon was nearly full and reflecting off the pale roadway as the Smith family's carriage rumbled toward a new home in Texas. This was the final leg of their journey, one that had begun in Bladen County, North Carolina and taken more than two months to complete.

The first weeks were very tiring for Anna Jane as they traveled through Georgia and Alabama. Stops in Atlanta and Montgomery had allowed her some respite, and a visit to her cousin's plantation in Marengo County, Alabama had boosted her mood and energy level.

The remainder of the trip had been by water; down the Tombigbee River to Mobile and then by ship to New Orleans. A fair breeze had filled the sails from New Orleans to Galveston, where they remained for a week while Anna Jane and Major Smith made needed arrangements for their arrival in Houston County. When the day of departure finally arrived, the entire party was eager to see and be settled at the new plantation. The autumn rains had been gentle, and the current of the Trinity River did not unduly prolong their trip to Crockett.

No one was more excited to land in Houston County than Anna Jane, whose desire to see her son after nearly a year gave her an energy and strength she hadn't had for years. Lucius had been awaiting their arrival for several days and would meet them near Crockett at the Trinity River landing known as Hall's Bluff. He would have a carriage for the family, wagons for their luggage and several of the slaves who had been with them since leaving North Carolina. They would go by roadway through Crockett to their new home; the boat would continue upriver with their furnishings, including Berta's piano, to the landing at their new plantation, which was as far as the river was navigable. That landing would serve as a future loading point for the cotton produced on their land and at surrounding plantations for shipment back to Galveston.

In the time that he had been away from home, Lucius, now sixteen years old, had grown into a tall, handsome young man with a full head of dark-brown hair. He had also developed physically, thanks to his work on the land and the new home. On spotting him in the gathered crowd, Anna Jane recognized a younger, taller, perhaps even more attractive, version of his father, and her eyes welled up with tears of joy.

As the riverboat docked, Lucius immediately took charge, directing the unloading of the cargo and passengers. Both Major Smith and Anna Jane would later comment on how mature and confident their son seemed as he took control of their disembarkation.

With the luggage secured and the passengers in place, the Smiths proceeded on their journey from the landing to the town of Crockett, where they would spend the rest of that day and the night becoming familiar with their new hometown. Anna Jane and Berta visited the Baptist church and the mercantile store, while Major Smith called at the Masonic Lodge with Lucius where he renewed his acquaintance with friends made on his earlier visit. By late afternoon the following day, it was time to leave and head north, as it would take several hours to get to the new house.

The evening shadows had already begun to lengthen as Lucius took the reins to guide the carriage. Elijah Chadwick, the overseer, had preceded them with the wagons, luggage and household slaves. Major Smith joined his son atop the carriage, eager to hear what progress had been made on the building and the land in his absence.

"I think you will be pleased," Lucius told him. "There are only a few minor details to be finished in the house over the next few weeks, and Elijah's crew has cleared land for planting cotton, although next year's crop will be smaller than in the future."

He went on to confirm his father's suspicions that the soil was, indeed, very fertile, and announced that a small garden planted just a few months earlier had already provided a good crop of late corn.

Inside the carriage, Berta fidgeted with anticipation, chattering as the carriage rumbled through the night. She was delighted at the prospect of a new home, new surroundings, new friends – and particularly pleased that her piano, which she'd glimpsed as it was unloaded in Galveston, had survived the long trip seemingly unscathed. During their brief stay in Crockett, she had also met Mr. Rogerson, a piano teacher from Galveston, who played music she'd never heard before – compositions by Beethoven and Chopin that seemed much more complicated than the church hymns she'd grown up playing. He had high expectations, she confided to her mother, so she would need to practice quite a bit to prepare for her lessons.

"He thinks that you are blessed with talent, and he wants to help you use it well," Anna Jane smiled at her daughter's excitement. "Your piano and it's companions from Bladen County will be in their new home very soon, as will you."

"And I am sure that I will love it there, Mother!"

Watching her daughter speak with animation and conviction, Anna Jane realized that she had a very independent head on her shoulders and would soon become a young woman. Although Anna Jane had often prayed for greater physical strength, this had never been fully granted, and she was reminded daily of her limited stamina and dependence on her family for so many things. She was thankful that her spirit and mind were unaffected and thankful to have survived long enough to witness Berta develop a keen mind of her own, an insatiable curiosity, spiritual awareness and a significant, though untested, musical talent.

Indeed, listening to Berta's animated discourse during their two-month journey made her worry somewhat about the child's future prospects in this new land. She and Major Smith had already discussed educational opportunities, and they would continue her schooling at home as they had in Bladen County. While in Galveston, they had secured the services of two tutors: one whose skill was in mathematics and science, and another who could instruct Berta in Latin, history and literary matters. They would visit for several days every month for instruction and to help the Smiths acquire new volumes for their library. As for Berta's musical education,

Anna Jane had no doubt that it would be well maintained and challenged by her third tutor, Mr. Rogerson.

Anna Jane had always assumed that Berta would be able to continue her studies in Virginia, at such a place as the newly created Hollins College. But that now seemed very far away, perhaps too far. Nevertheless, Major Smith had assured her that when the time came, he would send an appropriate member of Hannah and Oscar's family to accompany and look after their daughter.

Like other members of Anna Jane's family, Berta's most striking feature was her red hair and fair complexion, which was highlighted by constantly pink cheeks and an occasional freckle. These features had been passed down to Anna Jane from her grandmother, Sara James Kolb, and her mother, Ann Kolb Pouncey. If she could have changed anything, it would have been to give Berta some curl to her red locks, which, although lustrous and thick, knew only to hang in a straight line. Consequently, the child had worn her hair in braids or pigtails for most of her life.

Berta was also unusually kind and patient, especially for someone her age. Perhaps she had learned this by witnessing her own mother's limitations, or by having spent so much time with Ossie, Hannah's son, whose limited mental and physical abilities meant that he needed constant care and supervision. Whatever the reason, Anna Jane was, once again, grateful for her daughters good nature. Her brief reverie was interrupted by Berta's continuing commentary.

"The trip has been a long one, but it was very exciting, especially the sailing from Mobile to Galveston. I had never seen so large a schooner and had never expected to really sail on one," Berta said as the carriage bounced along the rutted roadway. " Although after this trip, I am not sure I will ever be able to leave our new home in Texas. It seems that we have gone halfway around the world, and we still have a few more miles to travel."

In the interest of distracting her, Anna Jane steered Berta to the subject of Lucius and how much he had changed in such a short time.

"Lucius seems to be a grown man," Berta agreed. "I don't remember him being so handsome, either."

"Indeed he is," her mother smiled at Hannah, who nodded. "And only last year, he was still a boy."

And so the conversation went from topic to topic – from the paddle-wheeler trip up the Trinity River to the perils of sandbars as described by the riverboat captain. Berta worried aloud that their new home might be too isolated, but her mother quickly dispelled the notion, pointing out that Crockett was not only close enough, but that it also boasted a comfortable hotel, a welcoming church and a well-stocked mercantile store, which was owned by Col. John Long and Mr. Lodwick Downes. In a happy coincidence, Mr. Downes' wife, Harriet, was also from North Carolina, so she and Anna Jane had much to talk about in their first meeting.

As it happened, Mr. Downes' nephew, James Wootters, helped his uncle in the mercantile store. A native of Maryland, James had finished a college course in Maryland after both of his parents died. He hoped that his younger siblings, including a brother named John, would eventually leave the eastern shore of Maryland and join him in Texas, where he said, there were greater fortunes to be made.

* * *

By the time the Smiths reached their new home, night had fallen. The short days of winter made the trip seem longer than it really was, and as they approached the house, the candlelight from the windows was a welcome sight for the weary travelers. Even though Houston County was warm at Christmastime, at least by Carolina standards, a blazing fire in the entry parlor fireplace made for a cheerful reception.

Even more cheerful than the warm fireplace was the broad smile on Oscar's face. He had been waiting for them at the entrance that led from the roadway to the plantation. The main house, which was close to the Trinity River landing site, was still several miles from the turn-in off the main road. The carriage path to the plantation house, while newer, was an improvement over the muddy, rut-filled thoroughfare. The principal north-south roadway through Houston County continued northward, from Crockett to the town of Palestine. In Crockett, it crossed the long-established El Camino Real roadway, known as the Old San Antonio Road, which had been built by the first European settlers in Texas in the 1690s.[12] While the older road was in good condition despite its age, the

---

[12]   "Old San Antonio Road", Handbook of Texas Online.

north-south route remained a tedious and unpredictable route, despite increasing numbers of travelers.[13]

The new homes for the Smith family and the slaves that accompanied them from North Carolina, while incomplete, were enough to ensure their comfort and safety until Oscar and his crew could finish building them. The spring planting would demand their efforts soon enough.

Anna Jane and Berta were delighted to see some of their familiar furnishings already in their new home, including the oversized piano which had a special room of its own off the entry parlor. Oscar had arrived at the plantation with their household goods and a complement of able-bodied men to move the furnishings from the dock to the home. but the task had been accomplished and added to the sense of familiarity and welcome felt by Berta, her mother and Hannah.

"I know the piano will need to be tuned," Anna Jane said to her daughter with a hint of fatigue in her voice. "But I believe you have some of the written music that we brought from North Carolina. This has been a fatiguing day, and I would like nothing better than to sit with your father in the new parlor and listen to you try out your instrument. Songs of the Christmas season, perhaps?"

Berta hurried off to find her music among the various crates in the entry hall, glad to have a job to do. Her parents' relief was palpable as they savored the silence, the warm fire and the end of the journey they had undertaken.

"I am so thankful that we are at last home again," Anna Jane said, embracing her husband. "I hope we will never be apart for such a long time again."

"Darling Anna, your presence and love warms my life better than any fireplace ever could," Major Smith said. "No one could be as happy as I am that we are finally here."

He would not have any reason to be away, he said, except for occasional trips to Galveston to look after their financial affairs. There was a great deal of work yet to do to make the plantation productive and prosperous, and he planned to be there every step of the way. Those words were music to Anna Jane's ears. Nothing mattered to her more than family, which led her to broach a subject she had been turning over in her mind since leaving Bladen County.

---

[13]   Bishop, E. Houston County, Handbook of Texas Online.

It was about Hannah, Oscar and their families. While Anna Jane's greatest regret was her lack of strength and stamina, she found herself tonight sitting in front of a fire with her husband in Texas. The journey, previously unthinkable, had been made possible because of Hannah's efforts and devotion. Since the day Berta was born, Anna Jane had depended on Hannah, as a helper and a trusted friend. After all, Hannah, Oscar and Ossie were God's children, just as she, Berta, Lucius and Major Smith were; God, she reminded her husband, was color-blind and did not distinguish between black and white, slave or master. Anna Jane's thoughts on slavery struck a slight note of discord in an otherwise very happy marriage. It was a pity, Major Smith pointed out, that the country had not been able to resolve the problem of slavery, all the more so because he could not envision a peaceful solution to this contentious issue that had divided families, communities and states.

Eager to avoid an unpleasant discussion, Anna Jane applauded loudly when Berta finished her first piece.

"Just listen to her play, John!" she said. "I am so fortunate that you are here to share this blessing with me. Now tell me all about what you, Lucius and Oscar have done to provide us with such a welcoming new home."

As it turned out, there was much tell. His first trip to Texas and subsequent meetings in Galveston had led to the property opportunities in Houston County. Through his affiliation with the Masons, he met Samuel May Williams,[14] whose introductions led to Houston County. After he traveled the Trinity River with Lucius, Oscar and Elijah Chadwick for a first-hand look at the area, it was clear that the delivery of cotton to the port would be both swift and efficient. Moreover, much of the land had never been cultivated, which was good for planting but also meant that clearing it would be a challenge. The pine forests provided enough timber for any construction needs, with enough left over to sell to help meet the growing demand for new buildings in Galveston and the expanding town of Houston.

Crockett proved to be a progressive town. Col. Long, an owner of both the hotel and the mercantile store, had played an important role in persuading the Texas and Red River Telegraph Company to bring its service to Crockett several years earlier. Barring any storms, which could

---

[14]   Appendix II, Item 6. Samuel May Williams.

interrupt the lines, the telegraph allowed them to communicate with cotton brokers and financial contacts in a matter of hours, rather than days. It also connected Crockett to Galveston and cities to the east, such as Shreveport, New Orleans and Natchez, thereby enhancing its own importance.

By the time he returned to North Carolina to arrange for the family's passage to Galveston, the building process was underway, and Elijah Chadwick and Lucius had the job well in hand. Major Smith was especially impressed with his son's efforts and didn't hesitate to say so.

"I am certain that Lucius will be able to contribute to the direction that our property will need in the future," he said. "He has matured in the past year and is showing qualities of which we can both be proud."

"Indeed, he seems very confident in his abilities," Anna Jane said.

"There is still much for you to see," Major Smith said. "Now I want you to rest and recover strength. I will show you the property tomorrow in the daylight."

Berta, having finished playing the carols, entered the parlor to inquire about dinner first, and then whether she could play Christmas melodies all year long. Her parents laughed.

"Sweet Berta, you can play them every day if you wish," Anna Jane said.

"It's just that they remind me why Hannah told me on the ship that we don't need to be afraid," the child said, frowning with concentration. "It's because God is with us."

"As you grow older, you will understand even more how God's presence in your life will help you overcome your fears," her mother nodded. "I am thankful that Hannah has told you those things and she is very correct in doing so. But now we should see what Lucius and Mr. Chadwick have provided for our first meal in our new home!"

On entering the new dining room, a generous banquet awaited them. Berta hopped from one foot to another in anticipation of the meal. There was venison, sweet corn and an abundance of freshly baked bread and tarts. The corn, Lucius pointed out proudly, was from the first harvest of their very own garden.

"We aren't the best of cooks, but Elijah and I hope the meal is an adequate welcome," Lucius said. "We have had more practice with the cook-fire since being away from Hannah! We have many reasons to welcome your arrival."

"Well, you must be getting enough to eat as you seem to have grown a foot since I last saw you," his mother said. "I am just so thankful to see you looking so well that I can scarcely keep a dry eye. And this delicious meal is an extra gift."

Over dinner, Lucius brought them up to date on how he had been spending his time in Houston County. Constructing the house and other buildings had been his principle task, one that could not have been done without the help of their new neighbors, the Wallings. Their son, Hosea, had become a real friend. On the few days that Lucius didn't work on the property, Hosea had taken him to nearby fishing and hunting areas. Hosea's older brother, Robert, was a skilled craftsman who had also helped with the construction. The Wallings lived nearby on the road to Crockett in a small community called Daly's.

"I am delighted that we have such pleasant neighbors, and I look forward to meeting Mrs. Walling," Anna Jane said. "Your father and I are very proud of what you have accomplished, Lucius."

Berta, in the meantime, was looking at her brother in a new light. During the day that she and Lucius had been together for the first time in nearly a year, she had been astonished at his growth and newly acquired manliness. She realized that the brother that seemed near her age had now moved to the adult world.

"Well, I must say that I am certainly glad to see our property so productive," Anna Jane said, shaking out her napkin before putting it in her lap. "But I want you to remind all of you to use your knife and fork when eating the corn-on-the-cob, as we don't want our children to eat with their hands like savages!"

A proper Southern lady, Anna Jane always insisted on good manners and high standards, no matter the levity of the occasion.

"Indeed, my dear Anna Jane, we will expect only the highest degree of decorum at the Smith Landing Plantation," Major Smith smiled broadly. "Especially when enjoying an outstanding meal of corn and venison."

And with that, the reunited Smith family joined hands to express their thanks to God for bringing them all safely to their new home.

VI

Autumn 1860 – Houston County, Texas

In the three years since moving his family to Texas, Major Smith had frequently traveled to Galveston, as that city was the center of banking, commerce and trade on which his expanding plantation depended. He used those visits, as during this particularly warm week in late autumn, to attend to his cotton shipments and other business matters. In his opinion, the move to Texas had been the right one to make: this season's cotton harvest had been the most abundant in his memory. Enough rainfall and the labor of more than ninety slaves had yielded a bumper crop, more than anyone had expected.

Lucius, who was assuming more of the daily management of the plantation, had accompanied his father on this trip, and Major Smith was pleased to have the company. He appreciated the extended time available to visit with his son, knowing that opportunities for such conversations were becoming less and less frequent.

Perhaps more important than the cotton was the change in Anna Jane. Over the past three years, she had grown much stronger, an improvement she attributed to the warmer climate. Berta, too, had grown remarkably and exhibited a significant talent for playing the oversized piano that was such a prominent presence in their home. Although still maturing, Berta bore an uncanny resemblance to her mother, not only physically, but also in her intelligence and sensitive spirit. Moreover, she was blossoming into a beautiful and talented young woman.

During his Galveston visits, Major Smith would also come with a list of requests from Anna Jane and Berta for items of clothing, decorations for their home and books for their expanding library. On this trip, he was especially interested in acquiring the final installments of the serial publication of Charles Dickens' novel, A Tale of Two Cities. Over the past year, these chapters had gradually made their way to the book dealer in Galveston, and the return trip up the Trinity River to Smith Landing would give him an opportunity to read this fascinating book.

The description of that particular era as "the best and worst of times" and by its characterization of "wisdom or foolishness, and belief or incredulity" struck a chord with Major Smith. He could not but feel that these contrasts reflected what he was witnessing in Texas. The United States had recently come through the most intense and divisive presidential nomination effort in its history. People were angry, even more than Major Smith had imagined,[15] and there was an undercurrent of uncertainty rippling through the population. Despite the rosy outlook for his plantation and his family, he was not at all positive that things would turn out so well for the country.

Having finished breakfast on the first morning of their return trip, Major Smith and Lucius were enjoying a view of the marshlands from their deck chairs. The packet steamers that made the trip from Galveston to the towns and plantations along the Trinity River were shallow draft boats; they were able to cross Galveston Bay to the deeper waters of the river and avoid the changing locations of sandbars. During the first day on the river, they passed through swamps before reaching the piney woods further upstream. Once in the piney woodlands, they would see more settlements, towns and plantations, where the trees had been cut and the land planted in cotton and other crops.

Despite his optimism about their own situation, Major Smith was anxious about the political climate he had just observed in Galveston. It was obvious that the voters of Texas had already made up their minds about the upcoming presidential election on November 6, and he sensed that the possible results of the election would bring about, in Dickens'

---

[15] Appendix II. Item 5. The Presidential Nomination and Election of 1860.

words, a "winter of despair." On the one hand, there were those determined to impose their will on a nation regardless of the outcome of the election; on the other side were those calling for dissolution of the union if their interests were not preserved. The two groups appeared to be on a collision course as surely as if they were steam engines barreling toward each other on the same track. Lucius, noting his father's somber expression, decided to lighten the mood.

"It would appear that every bird in the land has migrated to this swampy marshland in Texas," he laughed. "When the birds arise together, it's like a cloud dark enough to blot out sunlight. Their sounds drown out our voices!"

Major Smith looked at his son, who was often described as a younger version of himself, and smiled. He could see the physical similarities – Lucius shared his father's dark hair and tall stature. But his mind and thoughts were more akin to those of his mother, whose gentle, contemplative nature he had also inherited.

"Indeed, Lucius, the wonders of nature are greater than our minds can comprehend. More creatures of every sort all sharing a small part of the Earth and living at peace with each other!" his father replied. "I only wish we humans could live with each other in such harmony, despite our differences. I have to say that I am very glad you have made this trip with me, and I want to hear your thoughts about what we've seen."

Lucius seized on that comment to bring up something that had been bothering him since their departure from Galveston.

"Actually, I have more questions than thoughts," he said. "I was very surprised to overhear so many conversations critical of Governor Sam Houston. I have always heard of him referred to as the "Father of Texas" and thought he was held in high regard. I don't understand what has caused some to dislike him so intensely."

Major Smith paused in his reply, knowing that Lucius and members of his generation would be among the most affected by the turmoil brewing in their midst.

"Here's the thing: the problem that has led to such anger is one that has plagued our nation since before its independence," his father said, choosing his words carefully. "That problem is the institution of slavery."

"I don't understand why we, as a nation, haven't been able to deal with this in a peaceful and civilized manner."

"The answers to these questions are beyond our complete understanding," Major Smith said. "I do know that early generations of slave owners assumed that Africans were intellectually and spiritually inferior, simply because they looked, acted or thought differently. Of course, now we know that is utter nonsense, and yet slavery continues to be the law of the land."

"Truly, I know Oscar to be a man of great capacity and spiritual strength," Lucius declared. "We have spent time together building our homes and hunting in the forests, and he is clearly a person of excellent character and ability."

His father nodded his agreement. He and Anna Jane had gone back and forth discussing the best possible solutions for their slaves but had yet to come up with a satisfactory answer. They had repeatedly assured Oscar and Hannah that they would always have a home with the Smiths and that they would never have to worry about providing for Ossie. Freeing them was the logical choice, but it did not always work. Major Smith had heard that Hosea Walling sought to grant freedom to a family of his slaves, but Texas laws prohibited him from doing so. In fact, many political leaders throughout the southern states were insisting that the only possible solution was secession from the United States. Governor Houston vigorously opposed that idea, which made him unpopular in some quarters.

"I have heard many in Daly's and in Crockett talk with enthusiasm about the Southland leaving the union," Lucius said. "What do you think would happen then?"

Major Smith shrugged. Predicting how the federal government would respond to such a movement was no easy feat. The election in November would determine everything. The Democratic Party, which had until then supported the Southern agrarian interests, had been unable to agree on a candidate. At its convention in Charleston, it split into two smaller groups, which would seem to have no chance of success in the national election. The northern Democrats nominated Stephen Douglas, who favored giving residents of the new western territories the ability to vote on the issue of slavery. The southern delegates loudly opposed this and refused to support any restrictions on slavery. Many of them, including the delegates from Texas, quit the Democratic convention and later nominated John Breckenridge of Kentucky as their candidate. Apparently, secession from the union was preferable to any compromise on slavery.

"Father, I often heard in Galveston that most of the men dislike the Republican candidate, Lincoln, even more than they do the other candidates," Lucius said.

"That's true. It is unlikely that Lincoln will receive a single vote in Texas or the rest of the Southland," his father nodded. "With the voices of moderation so badly divided among the other candidates, it is possible that he will be the next President. He has vowed to oppose secession at any cost. That could result in war. And only a mad man or one who had never experienced warfare would want that to be the outcome"

Major Smith had also heard whispers of secession in restaurants and business establishments across Galveston. He was afraid that the call for careful deliberation would be drowned out amid the shouts calling for war. Lucius, sensing that a shadow had once again moved in, got up.

"I know you would like to read your new book, so I'll stroll around the deck and take in the view."

As Lucius walked away, Major Smith's gaze fixed on the river bank, unable to focus his thoughts. The riverside terrain abruptly changed from the coastal marshland; the raucous cry of a raven roused him from his reverie. Suddenly, Major Smith was afraid. He could not explain it, but in the pit of his stomach was the fear that his only son would likely be one of those who would respond to a call to arms. After a brief moment, he realized that he was gripping the Dickens manuscript as if his life depended on it.

*   *   *

After an uneventful trip upriver, the packet steamer was at last nearing its destination at the landing in Houston County. This location, twelve miles west of Crockett, was the principle stopping point for steamboats near the main town. The vessel blew its whistle to alert the dock hands of its arrival. Crockett was the last major stop for the boat, although it often continued to Smith Landing when cargo needed to be loaded. On this occasion, Major Smith could see two red-haired companions on the dock, but was surprised by their glum expressions. He was equally surprised by the absence of Hannah, who had accompanied them on every previous trip to Crockett. Lucius was in the stern of the boat supervising the proper unloading of their goods as John descended the gang plank to his waiting ladies.

"What is it that makes my sweet girls so gloomy on this otherwise fine day?" he asked.

"Oh, Father," said a tearful Berta throwing herself into Major Smith's arms. "Little Ossie has died!"

"Dear Lord in Heaven, whatever happened to the child? When did he pass away?" her stunned father exclaimed.

"We don't know," Berta sobbed. "He didn't seem ill the day before and the next morning Hannah found him without any sign of life."

"My darling child, I am so very sorry," Major Smith said, comforting her. "You have never experienced the loss of someone you knew and loved so well. It is perfectly natural to cry. Anna Jane, please tell me what happened."

Distressed herself, Anna Jane told him that Ossie had seemed quite himself until three days ago, when he began struggling somewhat for breath. But he did not seem ill otherwise. Then the day before yesterday Hannah had gone to wake him and found that the life had gone out of him during the night. There was nothing to be done as he had died quietly during his sleep.

"Hannah and Oscar both are as stoic as ever," Anna Jane said. "But I know that she feels her soul deeply grieved by this loss."

"My dear Berta," Major Smith said, gently embracing his daughter, "I know you and Hannah are very sad that Little Ossie is gone, but you know that he is now with the Lord. From his earliest days we had been told that he would not live for very long. He has now completed his earthly life and God has taken him home to a much better one."

Berta nodded, not fully believing that Ossie would think it was better to be separated from his parents but trusting her father's words. She told herself that she would miss seeing Ossie in his usual place, shelling peas or working on his art, but she would not be afraid for him. Hannah and Oscar, Anna Jane told them, were having a service today. They had chosen a burial site near where the slaves' church building would be built. Ossie would be the church graveyard's first occupant.

"Now, my precious girls, let's see if Lucius has gotten our luggage in the carriage and we can return home unless you have other things we need to do in Crockett," Major Smith said. "If you need to stop by the Long and Downes store, Lucius needs a strap for his saddle, and I would like to have a brief conversation with Lodwick."

"Wonderful idea," Anna Jane said. "Berta needs some new ribbons for her hair, and I'm sure Mr. Downes has a good supply."

*   *   *

The previous year had seen the unexpected death of Col. John Long, and his widow had recently married Mr. James Wootters.[16] As the new couple was on a trip to Galveston, the Smith family would need to wait for another opportunity to congratulate them on their marriage. Earlier in the summer, James Wootters' brother and sister had moved to Crockett from Queen Anne's County, Maryland. They were presently living with the Downes family, and the younger brother, John Wootters, was working at the mercantile store.

The Long and Downes Mercantile Store contained a vast collection of supplies, but the emphasis was on equipment parts, hardware and saddlery that was sold both to the plantation owners and farmers with smaller acreage who lived throughout Houston County. There were entire rooms filled with grain and other commodities as well as medicines – at times questionable – for almost any ailment. Ladies clothing was not their specialty; the styles on offer were mainly of interest to those who worked outdoors. The more fashionable attire was often bought from traveling vendors, whose visits to the larger towns were widely advertised and eagerly anticipated. Families would also plan periodic visits to more urban locations, such as Galveston. On this occasion, however, Berta and her mother were more interested in diverting their thoughts from the recent tragedy and in giving John Smith a chance to visit with his friend.

They were examining the selection of ribbons when John Wootters, Lodwick Downes' nephew and one of the store's principal workers, appeared and offered his assistance. Berta though it amusing that this

---

16   Miller, A.S. Wootters, James C., Handbook of Texas Online.

young man would have a useful opinion concerning ribbon colors, but she politely welcomed his suggestions. He introduced himself even though they had already met at church.

"Of course I know your name," she said. "I recall that you and your family prefer that it be spelled with two 't's. Indeed, Mr. Wootters, I would certainly value your opinion of these ribbons and which one would best keep my hair from blowing in the wind and match my new dresses. I didn't realize you were an expert on fashion matters."

"I am no expert on such matters, Miss Smith, but almost anyone would know that any type of ornament would be made more attractive by your own beauty," the young Wootters said. "I'm no musical expert either, but I certainly admired your piano playing last Sunday. I had no idea you could play so well or that you had such an extensive repertoire."

"Mr. Wootters, two such agreeable compliments would be welcome under any circumstances, but on this day, they are especially pleasant," Berta said. "The Smith family is bereaved by the unexpected death of our household servant's youngest child."

"I am very sorry to hear of your loss" he said.

"My father thought a bit of shopping would ease the pain a bit," Berta said, showing a bit of a smile. "At least, it keeps our minds occupied while he visits with Mr. Downes."

"I heard that you learn from Mr. Rogerson of Galveston, who comes by our store occasionally when he visits your home for your tutorials," he said. "He also has commented that you seem to have more talent than he usually finds in other students."

John Wootters had heard Mr. Rogerson perform in Galveston several months earlier during a trip to take delivery of some merchandise. The music was very pleasant, he noted. A new music style – something called German Romantic – that was currently very popular in Europe. Berta was surprised – and pleased – to hear that this young man had such musical interests as well as such an agreeable manner.

After half an hour of examining various ribbon sizes and colors, Berta chose four ribbons. "One spool of each should keep my mother's and my own wind-blown hair nicely controlled."

While Anna Jane and Berta were poring over merchandise, Major Smith was visiting with his friend Lodwick Downes to share his impression of his trip to Galveston. Downes expressed no surprise over the secessionist rumblings in the state's largest city; he was aware of similar feelings in even the smallest villages of Houston County. He agreed with Major Smith that the outcome of the presidential election was inevitable in Texas, and assumed that the results would be the same throughout the South.

Sam Houston had never held much enthusiasm for slavery, he reminded Major Smith, and although he was an owner, he never depended on slaves for his major business activities. Houston's principal efforts had always been to bring Texas into the Union, and the threat of dissolution was too great for him to consider. It was Lodwick Downes' opinion that Texas would overwhelmingly vote for secession and that Houston County might be unanimous in its assent.

What neither man could predict with certainty was the extent or the outcome of secession. States that had abandoned the Democratic Party at the Charleston convention would surely join in leaving the Union. But they couldn't predict how the remaining states or the federal government would react. They also wondered if towns and cities in the Northern states would concern themselves with the departure of distant Southern states from the Union. Following a brief discussion, Major Smith and Lodwick Downes concluded that the federal government would be the most likely to object and that, without widespread popular support, secession could possibly proceed without great opposition. But this outcome wasn't certain. An alternative course – the abrupt emancipation of the slave population – was even more distasteful and unacceptable to many across the Southland.

As the Smith family returned home, the warm sunshine on an autumn day made the trip a pleasant one. However, concern continued to gnaw at Major Smith's core. Despite his prayer for guidance, he continued to wonder if whatever the future held was destined to be the 'worst of times.'

As he felt agitation over the state of Texas and the nation, he was somewhat surprised at how much happier Berta seemed. He could not imagine how something as insignificant as hair ribbons could have such an effect on what had earlier seemed to be a very somber mood. Anna also smiled, although more inwardly, as she could not help having overheard the conversation between Berta and John Wootters. And she had to agree with her daughter that Mr. Wootters was a very charming young man.

VII

Late March 1861 – Crockett, Texas

Springtime had been delayed by the lingering cold of winter, but when it arrived, the once dormant flowering trees of the Texas piney woods seemed more exuberant in their blooms than in previous years. The dogwoods and redbud trees seemed to light up the forest, and the magnolia trees with their dark, waxy green leaves showed the promise of flowers yet to come. Everywhere the light green glow of emerging leaves indicated that spring was on the way.

These signs of nature's rebirth were especially meaningful to the Smith family as they were traveling to Crockett for Easter services. Berta planned to help with the piano music for the church services, and the family would be staying at Mrs. Hall's Hotel. Having once served as a boarding house, it was now the best inn in the town. Sadly, the Long Hotel had been destroyed in a fire the previous winter.

Oscar was guiding the team of horses and would return to the plantation that afternoon as Major Smith and Anna Jane had agreed that his presence would be needed at the Sunday church service for the slaves on the plantation. New clothing had been ordered from Galveston for Berta and her mother, who would use the day to make the necessary alterations in time for the Easter celebration.

In the meantime, Major Smith and Lucius would make arrangements for Oscar to pick up supplies from the mercantile store. If time permitted, Major Smith would also take his son to the Masonic Lodge and make introductions all around. H was pleased that Lucius had expressed interest in continuing their family tradition of associating with this organization. As the carriage followed the road through the quiet forest, each of them understood that the future of the Southland would likely be anything but quiet. The secession of Texas and the threat of war was the topic of every conversation.

Anna Jane was in a particularly somber mood. She spent the ride gazing at the passing forest, while Berta tried to read a book despite the frequent bouncing of the carriage. Major Smith was sitting in his usual place, next to his wife and facing his son, who was wearing his Sunday-best jacket and pressed shirt. Lucius studied his father who was riding quietly, apparently lost in thought.

"I am very pleased with the progress we have made with the new mare you brought to our stable last month," he said finally. "She is very spirited, but she seems willing and able to learn."

"I am glad to hear you say so, Lucius," Major Smith said. "I thought she was a good horse and worth the bale of cotton I paid for her. I am, however, a little concerned about her stamina when the weather gets warmer. Nevertheless, she may provide us with colts that could be very useful on the plantation."

"Do you think she would be suitable for a mounted military group?" Lucius said. "Hosea told me just the other day that he heard one was to be formed soon, and if that is the case, he and I will be interested in joining."

That declaration woke Anna Jane from her reverie. She sat forward with a sharp gasp.

"Surely you aren't considering joining an army unit!" she said, her voice wavering. "I know you are now a man and can make your own decisions, but I am still your mother and have a right to an opinion about your plans."

"Mother, please don't become tearful as I have not made any plans and would only do so if such joining became a duty and a necessity."

Anna Jane blanched, her skin more pale than usual. She could not prevent the tears the began coursing a delicate path down her powdered cheeks.

"John, please tell Lucius that we need him at home and not in some army that likely will not have any need to form," she said.

"Anna Jane, none of us knows what the future holds," he answered. "But all of the information we've heard cannot be reassuring for a peaceful future."

A grave stillness fell over the carriage. Scarcely a month had passed since Texas had voted overwhelmingly to join the other cotton states in seceding from the Union; federal troops in Texas didn't hesitate to peacefully leave their fortifications and supplies to the state government. Whatever happened next depended on the actions of the new president, Abraham Lincoln, as he had the power to order military force to prevent secession from proceeding. And the latest news to reach Houston County involved South Carolina men firing on a federal government ship trying to deliver supplies to a Union-held fort in Charleston Bay.

"Is there no way for reasonable people to resolve their problems without the threat of war?" Anna Jane asked.

"Unfortunately, the voices of reason are too easily obscured by the strident cries for secession on one hand and the abrupt abolition of slavery on the other," Major Smith shook his head. "The Peace Convention failed; Texas and other cotton states did not even send delegates. I believe the enthusiasm for secession is too great for the small, quiet voice of reason to be heard."

"Surely, the new president will not send troops into battle against his own citizens!" Anna Jane said, trembling.

"That is why there is much talk about forming companies of troops across the south," Lucius chimed in. "We must be ready to respond and defend our constitutionally protected rights. Perhaps the northern states will be less likely to engage in a war that doesn't greatly benefit their way of life if they understand that we will stand strongly for our rights."

"At this point, we can only pray that such will not be the result of human stubbornness," said his father, whose expression showed no evidence of optimism.

It was unlikely, Major Smith thought to himself, that the new self-proclaimed Confederate States of America, with Jefferson Davis as its president, would succeed unless North Carolina, Virginia and Tennessee joined the secessionist states in breaking away from the Union. President Lincoln had stated in his inaugural speech that he had no plan to change the status of any slave; he had also flatly rejected the idea of secession. Tensions were running high in the North and South, as the political stand-off mushroomed into something more consequential and far-reaching.

Berta, who had been listening to the conversations, was aware that there was much that she did not understand about the circumstances. She wondered if her family could, indeed, be affected by this war. She looked at her brother, whom she adored and looked up to, unable to imagine him marching off to the dangers of war.

"Lucius, I do not want you to join the army," she said, her voice unsteady. "Please tell me that such is not going to happen."

He smiled at her fondly and took her hands in his.

"These are times, Berta, when men must be prepared to face danger to defend their homes and their freedom," he said. "If war comes to this country, I would feel obligated to defend our homeland."

Berta couldn't respond. Up to this moment, she had not realized – or accepted – that her brother really had become a man, one who was clearly aware of his adult responsibilities. Her impression of him as a big brother and an older child in their family would have to change. The remaining distance to Crockett passed with Berta quietly dwelling on this new reality and wondering how her role in their family might evolve. Was she prepared to leave behind the amusements provided by her piano and her books? The prospect of accepting more responsibility for herself and how that might occur occupied her mind until their arrival at the hotel.

As their luggage was unloaded from the carriage, Anna Jane and Berta were informed that packages had arrived for them from Galveston. This news seemed to cheer up both Smith women, as new clothes were a far cry from the image of a battlefield.

"Will the seamstress really be able to fit the new clothes in such a short time?" Berta asked. "I don't know how anyone can do such a thing!"

It was a matter of skill, her mother informed her, a skill that the seamstress practiced daily, just as Berta practiced her piano. Sewing was an art that could be acquired and developed with practice. On their return home, Anna Jane promised to teach her daughter how to better use a needle and thread, perhaps even how to knit, as a lady could only benefit from such practical skills.

As Major Smith, Lucius and Oscar left for the mercantile store, the ladies excused themselves to attend to their fittings. Once that was done, they would proceed to the church building, where Berta would practice the music she was to play at Easter services.

*   *   *

On arriving at the store, the Smiths and Oscar were informed that their supplies were there and ready for loading. Major Smith thanked Lodwick Downes for ensuring the prompt delivery of their shipment, as his plans for clearing additional acreage for planting depended on those supplies arriving before the springtime rains.

A portly man of with a jolly demeanor Lodwick Downes always wore a smile and was on a first-name basis with nearly everyone in Houston County.

"It is a privilege to be of service, John," he said. "I am thankful that there is such great demand for your cotton product and that you and your peers can meet that demand. I only wish that I could be as content in my mind about our future, considering the turmoil pervading our land."

For the past two years, business had been brisk and profits abundant, Downes noted. Any disruption would be unwelcome, if not catastrophic. He could not imagine having to import equipment from a foreign country, especially if that foreign country was New England. With talk of war and secession trickling into the conversation yet again, Downes invited Major Smith to join him for a spot of better-than-average bourbon whiskey.

"Lucius has certainly grown up," the proprietor said, pouring two glasses and setting them down on the counter.

"He certainly has, right before my eyes," Major Smith agreed, taking a long pull of bourbon. "But I can't help, being anxious about his zeal for defending the new Confederate nation. I'm sure he will waste no time in volunteering."

"You seem to know about what is happening in ways that I have not heard or read" Downes said. "Please tell me what you have learned."

So Major Smith brought him up to date on what Lincoln had said in his inaugural speech. With the Republicans controlling the Presidency and both houses of Congress, he added, there was no chance that the Peace Commission and its recommendations could have reversed the secession process. Moreover, Lincoln would not hesitate to prevent the success of the Confederacy with whatever means necessary.

Downes' normally jovial expression fell. "I suppose this means war is a certainty."

Major Smith put an arm around his friend's now-slumped shoulders and nodded in defeat. While much would depend on the Northern states' willingness to support a fight, it did seem that war was inevitable. Without saying it, both men feared the outcome: that the United States of America would cease to exist.

"It is difficult to swallow, as my own father and his father served and suffered in the revolution that gave birth to the United States," Major Smith said. "But the rule of law and personal liberty require all of us to stand firm in our beliefs and to support our states, our communities and our freedom to the fullest extent."

Downes, noting that John Wootters had come into the room, turned toward his nephew and attempted to take a lighter tone.

"Has the shipment for the Smith Landing Plantation been accounted for and made ready for delivery?" he asked.

"Yes sir, and Lucius has seen that it is stowed on the carriage for transport," John Wootters replied. He paused for a moment and then continued. "Major Smith, I couldn't help but overhear what you were saying, and I value your thoughts on these matters. It concerns me that many think this war will be fought to protect the institution of slavery. Slavery may have been the spark that started the fire, but many of us have other reasons for going to war."

"Young man, I appreciate what you are saying," Major Smith said, taking Wootters' offered hand. "I also pray that you and your comrades will stand firm for the homes and freedoms we hold dear and that God will protect you all."

John Wootters thanked Major Smith for his kind words and relayed the news that Lucius had spoken to him about joining up. A Mr. Redding Pridgen was organizing a company with a mounted unit and had recruited Lucius to serve. Somewhat surprised that Wootters knew his son's plans before he did, Major Smith confessed that Lucius had only confirmed his intentions that very morning. Sensing a potentially uncomfortable moment, the younger man changed topics altogether.

"Lucius also told me that Miss Smith will be providing piano music for the church services on Sunday," Wootters said.

"Berta's music is an important part of her activity," Major Smith said. "I believe she is practicing her music there now, that is if she and her mother have finished with their wardrobe fittings. They have ordered new Easter dresses from Galveston."

"Since your ladies bear such a resemblance to each other, do they have matching outfits?" Wootters smiled.

Major Smith chuckled. "I confess I do not know, but blue and green seem to be their usual preferences."

With the carriage packed up, the Smiths and Oscar made ready to leave. The slave would return to the plantation, while Major Smith and Lucius proceeded to the Masonic Lodge for the planned visit.

"We hope to see you on Sunday and trust that Berta will be playing in the proper key!" Major Smith said to Wootters as he left the store.

"I am certain she will perform perfectly," Wootters said. "I will look forward to hearing her play."

As soon as the Smiths had left, Wootters asked his uncle if he could leave early. He had a mind, he said, to stop by the church and welcome Miss Smith to Crockett. Downes waved the young man out the door.

"I see no reason for you to stay any longer on this fine afternoon, John," he said with a sly grin. "I am pleased that you are developing such an interest in religious matters."

*　　*　　*

As the afternoon shadows lengthened and the heat of the day gave way to cooler evening temperatures, John Wootters quietly took a seat in the back row of the church. Berta Smith was playing passionately, seated to face the choir and unaware of her new audience. As she completed one of the pieces, Wootters surprised her with applause from the back of the room. She gave a brief squeal of alarm as she turned to see him standing and clapping.

"Bravo!" Wootters said, smiling broadly. "A beautiful presentation of one of my favorite songs, Miss Smith."

"Indeed, Mr. Wootters, are you in the habit of surprising people so?" Berta asked "If you have been listening for very long you know that I missed some notes in my previous attempts. Hopefully I won't miss too many on Sunday."

"I would say that your playing is good enough for a concert in Vienna." Carrying a burlap bag, he walked to the front of the church to join the smiling Berta.

"I doubt that I will be going to Vienna or anywhere else, especially if the packet boat stops running and we really do have a war," Berta frowned.

"I wish you wouldn't let these prospects weigh so heavily on your mind, Miss Smith," Wootters teased. "Your father told me that you and your mother have new dresses for Easter service this Sunday. I don't know the exact colors, but we had a supply of blue and green ribbons in the store so I thought I would bring you some choices."

"You have brought a smile to my face, Mr. Wootters," Berta said, pushing stray strands of hair out of her eyes. "I am very pleased to have such choices. A ribbon will surely help me keep my hair under control!"

"I am sure that any of these choices will help with that," Wootters said. He was taller than Berta remembered. And more handsome.

"I suspect that these are an attempt to make me more cheerful than I was on our ride from the plantation this morning," she continued. "My father probably told you that we were rather taken aback by the news that Lucius is considering joining an army unit. It is still a shock to me."

Wootters nodded. "Your father did tell me, but I hope you won't let it detract from your joyful Easter celebration," he said. "Indeed, Berta, a smile on your face will be a welcome accompaniment to your pleasant music. I hope I am not being rude by addressing you by your given name, am I? Although I would almost prefer calling you Abigail as it has a somewhat more lyrical quality."

"How do you know that I am called by that quaint name?" said Berta. "The only person who ever calls me that is Hannah, although my mother uses it when she is more exasperated than usual."

"I wouldn't know that special name of yours, except that Hannah told me about it when she was in the store recently," Wootters confessed. "I hope my attempts at cheering you up don't seem too clumsy, but I really do not want you grieving over something you cannot control."

Berta said nothing for a moment, and then nodded at him. "You may call me Berta or Abigail, whichever you prefer."

"Your father mentioned that your mother's grandfather had lost his life during the American Revolution," Wootters said. "I am very sorry for that loss. I know that the memory of those stories can remain with us for generations."

Berta, now sitting in a pew, was tying ribbons with her fingers but her thoughts were clearly elsewhere. She didn't know all the facts, but she did know that Anna Jane's grandfather, Colonel Abel Kolb, had been a leader of the patriotic Whig forces in the upper Peedee River area of South Carolina.[17] One day, she recalled the story, he was confronted by Tory troops while on a visit to his home. In defending his home and his family, including Berta's grandmother who was a child at the time, he gave himself up, only to be murdered in the sight of his wife and children. Had it not been for the loyalty of the small group of slaves, who stayed behind when they could have fled, the family would have been in desperate straits.

"Oscar, who helped load our carriage today, and Hannah, the household slave who cares for my mother, are descendants of those slaves," Berta told him.

"They must be very special people, and they must deserve special respect," he said. " Now, Miss Smith, we have had enough of these burdensome thoughts for one day. Please share the ribbons with your mother, if they aren't all tied into small knots!"

Berta thanked him for the ribbons and for his kindness. But the day had grown dark, and it was time to find her family. Wootters offered to escort her to the hotel. His words of encouragement lifted her mood.

"I know that your music will be perfect for the Easter service," he said. "I will be listening carefully if my attention isn't too distracted by your presence."

---

[17] Appendix II. Item 8. Colonel Abel Kolb and the American Revolution in South Carolina.

VIII

Late June 1861--Smith Landing Plantation, Houston County

As Independence Day approached, the residents of Houston County had no plans to celebrate the founding of the United States of America. With their patriotism shifted to the new Confederate States of America, most young men across the southland and their families were preparing for a war that had already begun. No one could predict how long it would last, but virtually all U.S. federal military stations and supplies in the South had been taken over by the new Confederate government.

The call for men to serve had gone out to the people of Texas, and the response was impassioned. Already, there were units forming in communities throughout the state. Men who were highly regarded in their counties many of whom were also military veterans recruited for units that they themselves would command; young men often joined units with friends or family members.

Redding S. Pridgen, a planter well known to the Smiths, lived in northern Houston County and was recruiting mounted riflemen. Born in Alabama in 1822, he came to Texas with his parents in 1840 . During the Mexican War in 1846-1847, Pridgen served with First Mounted Texas Riflemen in McCowan's Company.[18] Redding and his wife, Elizabeth, now owned a plantation in the Elkhart area. During the first weeks of

---

[18]   Redding Scott Pridgen, www.findagrave.com

summer 1861, rumors of recruitment for Sibley's brigade were widespread in Texas; those rumors were confirmed as Pridgen began recruiting mounted rifleman in June. Robert Walling, overseer on the Pridgen plantation, enlisted and was appointed third sergeant.[19] Elijah Chadwick, overseer at the Smith Landing Plantation, also joined, followed by Hosea Walling and Lucius Smith, who enlisted as privates.

Lucius had already told his father of his intention to join this unit, and they both agreed to wait before telling Anna Jane. Major Smith thought it would be better for her physical and emotional health if Anna Jane were to receive the information gradually, rather than as a sudden revelation. Although she was distraught as any mother would be, Anna Jane was comforted by the knowledge that Lucius have friends nearby.

On this warm afternoon at the end of June, Anna Jane and Major Smith were sitting on the front veranda gazing at the languid Trinity River as it flowed past their high riverbank. The field sloping toward the river was awash in a blanket of yellow flowers and punctuated by the constant hum of honey bees from Hannah's own hives. The pastoral scene belied the momentous occasion: Lucius, who was indoors packing, would be leaving to join his army unit in just a few hours. Hannah, now slightly stooped and her hair streaked with gray, emerged to offer tea while they waited for their son.

"Indeed, Hannah, some tea would be appreciated, and it may help to calm my grieving heart," Anna Jane said. She had done her best over the past few days to maintain a cheerful and optimistic demeanor, but on this day she dropped all pretense. As Hannah withdrew, Anna Jane turned to Major Smith, her eyes brimming with tears.

"If I didn't know that Lucius was going to be in the company of capable friends, I believe my mind would dissolve with grief."

"It is truly a blessing that he will have someone close to share his army life, but I have the greatest of confidence in his own strength of character and ability," Major Smith said. "He has truly become a man of determination and integrity. All we can do now is to support his decision and assure him of our approval and love."

Anna Jane nodded, not trusting herself to speak. She understood the truth of what her husband was saying, but she found it nearly impossible

---

[19]   Appendix II. Item 9. The Wallings of Houston County, Texas.

to say such things when she had no idea where her son was going or when – or if – he might return. Lucius had told them that Captain Pridgen planned to move the company to San Antonio, where they would join other groups under the direction of Colonel Tom Green, a Travis County lawyer and clerk to the Texas Supreme Court. Having commanded a company in the First Texas Regiment of Mounted Riflemen in the Battle of Monterrey during the Mexican War, Green was generally thought to be one of the state's most experienced military leaders.[20] It was not clear, however, where the company would go once it left San Antonio, and that uncertainty worried Anna Jane more than anything. A few minutes later, Oscar approached his owners and quietly cleared his throat to announce his presence.

"Oscar, have you made sure that Lucius has the equipment and mounts I asked you to provide for him?" Major Smith said, turning to his trusted slave.

"Yes sir, I've made sure he has the guns and both of the horses. He didn't want to take your Magnus, but I told him that you wouldn't have it any other way," Oscar said. He said he wanted to leave his usual horse for you and Miss Berta to ride and he would take one of the other horses to carry his bags. Believe me, Lucius will have the best horse in the army and guns as good as anyone."

"Thank you for helping Lucius with his packing," Major Smith said. "I will count on you and Hannah keeping him in your prayers."

"I am praying for him already," the slave nodded. "There he comes now. Don't he look like a fine soldier?"

And there he was, already looking like more of a man than he had even that morning. Major Smith beamed with pride, despite a nagging anxiety, as his son led the prize stallion, down the pathway to the front of the veranda.

"I can't believe you would insist on having me take Magnus as my mount!" Lucius exclaimed. "He is the finest horse in Houston County."

"Giving you the best mount and weapons I have is the least I can do to support your decision to join Pridgen's company," his father said. "As much as your mother and I want you here with us, we understand your

20   Alwyn Barr, "Green, Thomas," Handbook of Texas Online.

commitment to the cause of the Confederacy. Please know that with you go our love and admiration, and our prayers for your safe return."

With those words, even Lucius was perilously close to giving in to the emotion of the moment. His mother, understanding as only a mother could, stepped up to say her own good-bye.

"I want you to remain well and safe wherever you may travel, Lucius," Anna Jane said, her voice faltering. "Please give me a hug and one more for Berta. She will be very sorry not have to have arrived from Crockett in time to see you off."

"It's likely that we may pass Berta on the way to Crockett," Lucius said, mounting his horse. "If we do, I will give her a proper farewell. If I miss seeing her, ask her to say a special prayer for me and my friends."

As he rode away from the plantation home, Lucius felt a nervous anticipation. Any inkling of hardship or danger was obscured by the excitement of joining his friends in what would be the greatest adventure of their lives. As he disappeared from view, a fog of gloom settled over the Smith Landing Plantation. Anna Jane, having put on a brave face for her son's sake, gave in to tears and despair.

"Surely giving our son to the Confederate cause is enough torment for our family," she said, once her tears had subsided. "I trust that you will not be leaving me during this time."

"Anna Jane, I have thought about my responsibilities and what would be the best path to follow during these very difficult days," Major Smith said. "Even though I have some experience in the Carolina militia, my best service will be here."

He confirmed that the Smith Landing Plantation would continue planting and producing cotton, with the understanding that any profits would go to support the Confederate cause. Without Lucius to manage and supervise operations, Oscar's help as an overseer of other slaves would be more critical than ever.

Worrying about her son was at the top of Anna Jane's list, but other concerns abounded as well. Her many relatives and friends back in Bladen County were much closer to the battlefields than anybody in Texas. Since Virginia and North Carolina had seceded – and been the last states to do so – the Confederacy's seat of government had moved from Montgomery,

Alabama to Richmond, Virginia – bringing Jefferson Davis' government much nearer to the front lines.

"There is no way to predict what is in men's minds and hearts, but the best outcome for the Confederacy will be quick and decisive victories," Major Smith said, as if reading his wife's mind. "The longer and more extensive the conflict, the less likely that the South will be able to prevail, as the size of the northern population and their manufacturing resources are much larger than ours."

Although he did not say it aloud, he also wondered how the people of the Northern states felt about this war, whether they were willing to support a long, costly and perhaps bloody conflict. In the years since America's independence from Great Britain, many other Europeans had emigrated to the northern part of the country. Whether or not they were willing to take up arms for their adopted homeland was still in question. And it was a big question, particular since it seemed that much of the fighting was likely to occur in the Eastern seaboard states. Texas and other states would rally to their cause and enhance the chances of success.

"Did you know that Dr. Edward Currie is organizing a company in Crockett?" Major Smith said. "I understand his company will join the First Texas Infantry, which has been formed in Virginia."

"I know Dr. Currie is highly regarded as a physician," Anna Jane said, a note of skepticism in her voice. "I was not aware that he had any military experience."

As it turned out, the doctor, originally from Mississippi, had served under Jefferson Davis during the Mexican War. Once that conflict had ended, he settled in Texas to practice medicine.[21] According to Major Smith, a number of young men from Crockett were signing on with Dr. Currie, among them John Wootters, whose uncle, Lodwick Downes, owned the mercantile store. At an official presentation in Crockett, Wootters would receive the flag on behalf of his fellow infantrymen.

"You remember Wootters, Anna Jane?" her husband asked. "I believe you and Berta have met him during one of your shopping trips to Crockett."

At last, Anna Jane had something to smile about on this somber day.

"My darling John, how can you be so insightful concerning issues of our country and state and so effective in managing the affairs of our

---

21   History of Houston County, Texas. p. 312.

property, and yet be so blind to what is happening under your nose?" she laughed. "I believe that our Berta has more than a cordial interest in Mr. Wootters; in fact, Hannah has confirmed it. I also think Berta would attend the flag ceremony even if it meant she had to walk to town in her bare feet!"

Major Smith was speechless. Berta was just a little girl, a child really, and Wootters was a man. An older man. Surely his wife was mistaken. Their daughter would never have noticed him if it weren't for the fact that he attended their church and waited on them at his uncle's store. Anna Jane laughed and shook her head as her husband gave voice to his thoughts.

"Let me remind you that the age difference between this young man and our young Berta is no greater than the advantage you had over me when I lived a protected life on Pouncey Plantation," she said. "And yet I noticed you and did not discourage your interest. Unless your vision has dimmed, you might have noticed our daughter has become a beautiful young lady!"

When she and Berta were at the mercantile store, she told him, John Wootters never overlooked an opportunity to inquire about her needs or to comment on her musical talents. But she asked Major Smith to keep this information to himself, as Berta hadn't yet expressed her feelings about John Wootters to her parents. Anna Jane did not want to cause her any embarrassment, particularly since affection at a young age often did not stay its course. In light of the news that Wootters was going to war only reinforced the idea that they should not interfere, especially since they knew how upset she would be at having missed Lucius' departure.

It wasn't long before the carriage arrived from Crockett. Hannah and Berta came into the entrance hall with a more somber air than usual.

"Oh, Mother, I am so glad to be back home, but I am very sorry to have not been here when Lucius left, " Berta said on entering the parlor and finding Anna Jane. "I didn't know this would be his last day at home before joining the company. Thankfully, Hannah and I passed their troop just outside Crockett, and I had a chance to visit with him briefly. I noticed that he was riding Magnus, and when I asked him why, he told me that he and I would both have new horses. I don't know what he meant by that, but he seemed very excited, and said that he would write us a letter when they reached San Antonio."

At that moment, Major Smith came in. "I heard the sound of your voice, Berta, from upstairs," he said, enfolding his daughter in a tight hug. "We are glad you are home. I hope your visit in Crockett was a good one, but I know you and Lucius will regret not having a chance to say good-bye."

"Had I known he would be leaving today, I would have found some other time to visit the church pianist," Berta said. "But I did see him and his troop on the roadway and was able to give him a farewell kiss. He seemed too excited for any longer conversation."

Anna Jane, whose pallor seemed greater than usual, sighed. "It has been an exhausting day, but I am relieved by your presence, Berta," she patted the seat next to hers. "Please come sit by me and tell me about all your visit in Crockett and with Lucius. Also, you must ask your father what Lucius was referring to about the horses."

John, who had assumed his usual place in the over-stuffed great chair that faced Anna Jane's favorite divan, informed Berta that Lucius had joined a mounted company and would be facing many, possibly arduous, treks. He told her about insisting that her brother take Magnus, as he was one of the strongest, most fearless mounts Major Smith had ever owned. In the stallion's absence, Lucius wanted us to ride Betsy, his own good-natured, dependable mare.

"She is a wonderful horse and gentle enough for me to ride comfortably," Berta said. "I am also glad she will be here with us as she is very fond of Lucius. I will think of him every time I ride her. I will miss him greatly."

"Did you and Hannah go to the store or have any other visits in town?" Anna Jane asked her daughter.

"We did, that is Hannah did," Berta nodded with great animation. "Hannah went to the mercantile store for some sugar and flour, and she must have mentioned that I was practicing piano at the church because Mr. John Wootters walked over to visit as I was finishing my session. He commented on how much he enjoyed the Beethoven sonata I was playing."

The picture suddenly became very clear to Major Smith. What his wife had told him was absolutely true. John Wootters had caught his daughter's fancy; he could see it in her eyes and the way she spoke his name.

"Your mother and I were just discussing plans to be in Crockett in the next several weeks for the flag presentation to the Currie Company, which will soon be leaving for New Orleans," he said. "I expect that you and Hannah will attend with us if you would like to. It should be a memorable ceremony and a suitable substitute for a patriotic display that in past years would have occurred on the Fourth of July.

"Oh yes, I want very much to attend!" Berta said. "Hannah has already told me that she wishes to be there. She holds Mr. Wootters in very high regard, and he has been chosen to receive the flag and offer a response on behalf of the company."

"I am sure that all participants in the ceremony will be pleased to have a large and enthusiastic crowd in attendance," Major Smith said, the corners of his mouth twitching. "But how has Hannah come to have such a good opinion of him?"

Berta was a bit surprised by the question, but she pointed out that Wootters often helped them during their visits to the mercantile store. He was, she noted, very polite and accommodating. Hannah had even told him about how she called Berta by a special name, Abigail, and the significance of that name.

"She even told him that she thought 'Abigail' was more in keeping with my nature than my proper name," Berta said. "I don't know why she would think that, but I told Mr. Wootters that he could use whichever name he preferred."

"Well, Berta, since you are on a first-name basis with the young man, it's only appropriate that he and I share the same name," her father smiled. "I have always been proud to share the name 'John' with both the prophet and apostle of the Bible."

"Father, I believe you are teasing me," Berta smiled back. "I only refer to him as Mr. Wootters. He is very kind and interested in our welfare, but I know him best from our church meetings. We should all go to Crockett for the presentation to show our support and appreciation to all the young men who will be leaving their homes to defend our freedoms."

As always, Berta's maturity and insights surprised and impressed her parents. They would definitely be going, Major Smith thought to himself. For the company from Houston County and especially for the young man named John Wootters.

IX

November 1861 ~ Crockett, Texas

It was a brisk autumn morning that saw Major Smith and Berta traveling from the plantation to the town of Crockett. The air was cooler than usual and the sky clear, as a north wind the previous evening had brought rain and clouds to the area. Anna Jane remained at home, where she found comfort by the warm fireplace in her sitting room. The sorrow that encompassed her since her son's departure hung over her like a shawl draped around her shoulders; even Hannah's cheerful demeanor could do nothing to rouse her from her melancholy. The colder weather seemed to only aggravate her frail health.

Despite obtaining the best medical advice in Houston County, the Smiths had received no satisfactory explanation – nor any possible remedy – for Anna Jane's physical decline. They had traveled to Galveston to consult with the most experienced physicians in Texas. Major Smith had even suggested that she go to New Orleans in search of answers. As a much larger city, it would naturally be home to a broader range of doctors with experience treating a variety of illnesses and conditions. But Anna Jane knew that her lack of strength would make such a trip too difficult. Instead, she followed the suggestions of various advisors – an easily digestible diet with additional salt, rest and a warm environment – and stayed put at Smith Landing plantation.

On her better days and despite her physical limitations, Anna Jane continued to take an active interest in her family and their lives. However, with Lucius gone to serve in the Confederate army, her usually cheerful mood had turned darker. Frequently overcome by a sense of hopelessness and the belief that her death was imminent, she prayed daily that she would survive to see Lucius and his friends, the Walling brothers, return safely. She also prayed that John Wootters would return from Virginia and that she would also be fortunate enough to see Berta with an established future.

As the carriage made its way toward Crockett, Berta noticed that with the recent frost and winds, most of the hardwood trees across the low-lying terrain had shed their foliage. The gray limbs reached skyward in stark contrast to the green pines silhouetted against a bright blue sky. She felt a sense of loneliness descend as she reflected on the passing countryside.

"Father, I must admit that it is hard for me not to feel sad these past few months," Berta said, after a period of silence. "I miss Lucius and the joy he brings to our household. The winter woodlands are so barren, they only add to my feelings of emptiness."

"I share your feelings of sadness," her father said. "I find myself thinking of your brother often and with some regret that I did not try to dissuade him from enlisting so soon."

Despite his misgivings, Major Smith found some measure of comfort knowing that Lucius was, at least, with his trusted, capable friends, Hosea and Robert Walling, and under the command of the experienced Redding Pridgen. He knew that they would face many hardships; that was the price of war. But he was also certain they would look out for each other. Just recently, he and Anna Jane had gotten word that Lucius' unit was leaving San Antonio and heading to New Mexico to secure that area for the Confederacy. The soldiers would trek across the western part of the state toward the town of El Paso del Norte, which had a substantial Army base and plentiful supplies, and cross into New Mexico from there. It was a long winter journey – much of it across an area scarce with water. Once again, Major Smith offered up a silent prayer for his son's safety.

"I also pray that John Wootters is well and safe," Berta said. "I have heard they are having a very cold winter in the East."

In fact, everything had changed with the change of season. Both Lucius and John Wootters were gone to war, along with so many other young men from the area, and those events had taken their toll on her mother's emotional and physical state. Moreover, since late July, the Union Navy had very effectively blockaded the Port of Galveston. With the threat of Union soldiers coming ashore, her piano tutor was unable to make the trip from that city. In fact, none of her tutors, musical or academic, had been able to make the trip to Smith Landing in several months. And given the tenuous situation, there was no telling when the packet boats would again be able to make regular trips up the Trinity River. Indeed, life as it had been just one year earlier would be unlikely to resume as long as the war continued.

On this particular trip to Crockett, Berta would be going directly to the Baptist church to meet with the woman who played piano there. Since Berta's tutor could not come, she had kindly offered to step in and help with her musical education. Major Smith, on the other hand, was intent on finding out the fate of a cotton shipment that had been delivered to Galveston. This year's crop had been among the largest in memory, but the Union Navy's blockade meant that the packet boats that usually delivered the cotton were only able to escape the port occasionally.

There was some hope among the planters that a few boats had managed to slip out and reach Mexico or Havana, where the cotton could be loaded onto other boats sailing under foreign flags. If not, then the warehouses in Galveston would soon be over-filled with cotton, and river traffic to Crockett would come to a complete standstill. Perhaps more importantly, the Confederacy was dependent on revenue from cotton sales to the mills in Europe. That money bought weapons and equipment that the Confederate Army desperately needed, and without it, they would be at a serious disadvantage.

"I know you have been very busy with the harvest and delivery of the cotton to the gin," Berta said, as if reading her father's thoughts. "What will happen if the ships cannot sail?"

"Our plantation and others across the southland have pledged the revenues from these crops to the cause of our new country," Major Smith said. "The problem is that our states have, in past years, been so occupied with agriculture that little effort has been directed toward manufacturing. We will need to import war material if we are to defend our homeland."

As their carriage continued through the forest, Berta was reminded that the roadways had been much improved since their first journey from Crockett four years earlier. She wondered aloud if other roads had been improved and whether it would be possible to deliver the cotton to Galveston over land, by wagon. Major Smith smiled, impressed by his daughter's keen intelligence and foresight.

"You are quite right; the roads have benefited from the efforts of the plantation owners who are required to maintain them," he said, also noting that the trip to Crockett was substantially shorter now with the improved roadway. "It's possible that some of the crop could be sent to Mexico by land. I will be meeting with Andrew Gossett about that during our visit. On these matters, he is the most knowledgeable person in Crockett."

Andrew Gossett's father, Elijah, was originally from Tennessee and had been a boyhood friend of the celebrated Davy Crockett.[22] The younger Gossett and his brother moved to the area with their father before the War for Texas Independence. When Crockett and his men came to Texas to fight the Mexican army, they stopped for a night or two at Elijah Gossett's homestead on the way to San Antonio and, eventually, the Alamo. The town was named Crockett in honor of that fallen hero. Andrew Gossett, who donated the land that was now the town square, had since served as sheriff and judge for the county and was one of its most respected citizens.

With Berta practicing piano at the church, Major Smith meeting with business and government leaders and Oscar loading supplies at the mercantile store, it would be a busy visit to Crockett. Major Smith agreed that, after his meeting with Andrew Gossett, he would first stop by the Masonic Lodge and then head to the church to collect Berta. Together, they would meet Oscar at the mercantile store.

"If I finish earlier I will meet you at the store, as it's very near the church, and I can amuse myself by looking at what they consider the latest fashions," Berta said with an impish grin. "I'm sure I can find some new music at the church, but I don't expect Mr. Downes to have any new, stylish clothes."

The grand piano, which played such an important role in their household, continued to be a source of pleasure for Berta and her parents. She practiced often and diligently, and her skills had improved tremendously as a result. Indeed, Anna Jane had expressed concern about the future of her child's musical talent. While the effects of the war throughout the South were still uncertain, she realized that their plan to send Berta back to Virginia or another Eastern location for school would not be possible for quite some time.

---

[22] Long, C. "Elijah Gossett", Handbook of Texas Online.

On arriving at the town square, Major Smith disembarked from the carriage and entered the building that housed Andrew Gossett's office. Oscar would drop Berta at the church before returning to the store. As John approached the door to Gossett's office, he was welcomed by a thunderous voice.

"Major Smith, I could see through the window that you were heading in this direction," Judge Andrew Gossett boomed. "Come in here, warm your hands and sit for a spell."

With the post office and telegraph station next door, Gossett was able to monitor the affairs of the state and the Confederacy in a more timely manner; the weekly newspaper, the Crockett Argus, could only provide limited current information. Rumor was that, if the Galveston port blockade went on for much longer, the paper might cease publication as all of its newsprint and printing paper arrived through that port. Major Smith entered the spacious, sparsely furnished office, and the two men settled into broad wooden chairs in front of the hearth.

"Judge Gossett, this fire is much appreciated as the carriage could hardly keep out the cold north wind," he said. "My only comfort on that chilly ride has been a warm conversation with my daughter Berta, who is growing up too quickly. While I would like for you to meet her some time, my primary purpose in being here is to talk business. In your opinion, what is the outlook for commercial activity in Galveston and in Texas? And what do you see as alternatives for inland planters and our crop?"

Gossett shook his head, knowing that the news was bad and the outlook bleak. Galveston was in a state of panic. The port was virtually shut down, and military leaders did not think the city could be defended in the event of an invasion, which seemed increasingly probably. At least half of the population has already fled inland seeking refuge with family and friends. In the past four months, the town of Houston, unprepared for an overwhelming influx of new residents, had almost doubled in population. Planters in Houston County had also seen the arrival of friends and relatives eager to find a safe haven until the situation changed.

"I am in a quandary about the prospects for our cotton crop," Major Smith told his friend. "It is abundant, as you know, but I'm concerned about being able to sell it and provide that value to the Confederacy."

"You're right to be concerned," Gossett said. "If the crops from our cotton states can be exchanged for armaments and supplies, our southland may be able to withstand prolonged hostilities. I have been told that no rifle has ever been manufactured in Texas, and that lack of industry across the region has us at a disadvantage."

Nodding his agreement, Major Smith asked the judge about the possibility of getting the cotton crop out from another port. The Texas coastline was vast, and it seemed unlikely that any Union naval force could secure every mile of it. He also mentioned the idea of transporting the cotton overland to Mexico and then transferring to ships flying under European flags.

"Although there are a number of ports along the Texas coast, the problems of delivering the cotton and securing its safe passage at sea are daunting," Gossett said. "Just outside this window is a part of the Old San Antonio Road, which could be a way to deliver the cotton to the Mexican border. It is a long and hazardous journey, but one that has been undertaken by travelers for many years."

While the road was well established all the way from Crockett to San Antonio, the journey grew more uncertain as one traveled further south. A trek to the towns of Laredo or Villa de Dolores on the Rio Grande River would traverse remote and barren terrain, much of it home to hostile Indian tribes. With the U.S. Army no longer in place to deter their raids, it was a brave, well-armed soul who traveled through that area.

"I am familiar with the local unit of our militia and I believe that, with appropriate assistance, they could manage such a venture," Major Smith said. "Adequate wagons and mules should be something that we Texans can produce, even if our foundry capabilities are limited. Wagons loaded with cotton bales would provide protection for armed troops as a bale could hardly be penetrated by any light firearm."

"I expect that by this time next year, our militia unit could be deployed in such a capacity," Gossett replied. "But, absent the troops, I know there would be concern about possible slave unrest."

Discontent, even rebellion, among the slaves was always a concern; Major Smith knew that. But his plantation was blessed with a population that was very loyal to his family and to each other. While newly acquired slaves could be unpredictable in responding to their circumstances, he was not at all worried about his own. That prompted his friend to issue a well-meant warning.

"I have overheard complaints from some of our local residents that your good treatment of your slaves may affect their attitude toward other white people, that it may not be respectful enough," Gossett said. "It has never been a problem for me, but you should be aware that some folks resent the situation."

Caught off guard, Major Smith expressed his surprise and concern. He knew that hard feelings could lead to unpleasant confrontations; he would mention the problem to Oscar and ask him to relay the message to the other slaves that they could all be in danger from some of the white population's rougher elements. They should take extra care to mind their manners when in town.

"I have found that those who do not own slaves often resent black people who show abilities and skills that they themselves do not have," Gossett said. "One never knows how this hostility may manifest; avoiding such problems is always the best solution."

The judge made his way to the fireplace, stoked the now dying embers and threw a new log on the fire. As the room grew warmer, the two men caught up on news of their respective families. Gossett noted that there was much talk about town and admiration for Berta's skill on the piano. He also asked after Lucius and offered a prayer for his success and safety.

"I appreciate those words, my friend," Major Smith stood up to go. "As the day is getting by, I must retrieve Berta and get back home before supper. Many thanks for your advice, prayers and friendship."

Following a brief visit to the Masonic Lodge, Smith passed by the church and learned that Berta had finished her session and would meet him at the mercantile store. He set off in that direction, his eyes searching the town square for her trademark red hair. Not immediately seeing her, he glanced toward their carriage and saw Oscar waving to him to come aboard. As he approached, he saw Berta already seated inside.

"I didn't expect you to be finished with your meeting so soon," her father said, reaching to open the carriage door. "I hope all went well for you and the church pianist."

It was then he noticed Berta trembling, huddled in the corner of the front seat.

"Whatever is the matter, child?" he exclaimed. "You are shaking like a leaf."

"Oh Father, I have had a terrible experience, and I just want to go home as quickly as we can," Berta moaned as the carriage lurched to a start.

"Tell me. what has you so upset?" asked her father, his fists clenched in a surge of protective instinct.

As her eyes filled with tears, the words seemed to lodge in her throat. But, amid the whispered mumbles, her father heard her say, "that old man Jencks really frightened me, and he must be the meanest person on this earth." Major Smith could not recall ever seeing his daughter in such a state of distress.

"What has that derelict Jencks done to cause you such unhappiness?"

"He said some really threatening things to me, and I was just walking down the street in front of the mercantile store," she sobbed. "He appeared out of nowhere and started accusing me of trying to teach Oscar to read and telling me that I was only going to make trouble for all of us if I kept doing that."

"What did you say to him? Where was Oscar when all of this was happening?"

"Oscar was in the store getting ready to load the carriage, and he came out when he heard Jencks yelling at me," Berta said, now looking more angry than tearful. "I'm sure Oscar did nothing to anger the old devil; I certainly didn't say anything to him. I was so surprised by his presence that I don't think I uttered a single word in his direction. When Oscar came through the door, Jencks turned around and walked away."

Major Smith wished for a moment that Anna Jane or even Hannah was present as one of them would likely know how to react more appropriately to an angry young woman who was probably not of a mind to be placated. He was angry himself, indeed furious that such a man as Jencks would speak to Berta in that fashion. Jencks was said to love his whisky, and people around town said that the sheriff often locked him up after a drinking binge, just to keep the peace.

"Now, Berta, please try to calm yourself," he finally said. "Tell me what you think caused him to act as he did."

"I don't know what he meant," she answered. "I have only once or twice answered a question Oscar asked about a particular word and it's spelling, and I have helped Hannah read Bible verses. Anyway, I don't see anything wrong with them knowing what a written sign might mean or being able to read."

"My dear, you have not been around people like Jencks," her father said. "Our life on the plantation, in our church and with your tutors has only exposed you to the more genteel segments of our society. I'm afraid that you need to learn about such individuals and how you should respond to what they might say. You must also be aware that you are becoming a young woman, and the way you behave around men, especially those of dubious character, must change as you do."

While he had every confidence that Berta's instincts would eventually guide her in these situations, he was grateful to have Anna Jane waiting at home. She would surely know what and how to teach their daughter in matters of proper behavior. Berta's outgoing nature could easily be misinterpreted by some men, particularly those who weren't gentlemen, as being something other than sociable and charitable. That and her beauty could, in the wrong situation, be a dangerous combination.

"I know you to be a brave young lady, but bravery should never be a substitute for good common sense and caution," her father warned. "Perhaps the best advice I can give you is to avoid being alone outside of our home and limiting your interactions with individuals of the cruder classes whenever possible."

As the carriage rumbled on, Major Smith thought about what Berta had told him. Perhaps Jencks' suspicion that Oscar could read, even to a limited extent, reminded him of his own illiteracy. Some people assumed that the black race was unable to learn and assume responsibilities and were therefore of a low class. Major Smith knew that was a fallacy; the only thing Oscar and other slaves lacked was the opportunity to improve their status. Awareness of his own deficiencies fueled Jencks' rage, so he took aim at the only available target-Berta. The man likely did not want to confront Oscar directly as doing so would reveal his own lack of bravery; the slave was taller and as strong as anyone in town.

Berta, whose tears had dried, listened intently to her father. He had enjoyed a life rich with experience thus far, and she knew he had a great deal of wisdom to share.

"I suspect that you were surprised at being criticized without cause, and it made you very angry," he said. "Be careful with that kind of anger, Berta. It can make you react in ways you later regret. Don't worry about your tears; they were tears of anger. I have heard that is a common reaction among women." Major Smith smiled at his daughter, adding, "I am fortunate not to have been the cause of such a reaction in you or your mother."

Berta permitted a glimmer of a smile in response to her father's attempt to lighten the conversation. "Thank you, Father," she said. "I don't understand what would make a person be so hateful and cruel!"

How could he explain to this sunny soul the existence of blighted ones like Jencks? Many would point to whiskey as the cause of his problems, but his type often revealed its true colors when fueled by liquor. He had seen Jencks' pitiful wife and their herd of ragged-looking children along the roadway, homesteading a piece of property not far from Daly's. They seemed to be underfed and lacking in proper clothing. Major Smith suspected that they frequently bore the brunt of the other man's mean spirit, and it made him sad to the bone. What children learned from life with their families often stayed with them forever.

After an interval of calm, Major Smith spoke again. "I don't think we need to alarm your mother with all that has happened today," he said. "But asking her some of these questions may help you with your own answers. She has many thoughtful insights into such matters."

He decided right then that he would also caution Oscar about showing proper humility when dealing with people in Crockett. Recalling his conversation with Judge Gossett, Major Smith understood that they certainly had enough problems without creating unnecessary new ones.

Berta, in the meantime, had moved to more pleasant thoughts about her piano and the new music the woman at church had let her borrow. A composer named Stephen Foster had written most of them, and they were very popular. New songs would be just the thing to get her mind off people like Jencks.

X

February 1862 - Smith Landing Plantation, Houston County

February is a time of transition in Houston County as the chill of winter wanes and the promise of nature's rebirth slowly emerges. The winter months of early 1862, however, had been an unusually harsh time in southeastern Texas and throughout many of the southern states.

News of the hardships endured by Texans serving in the Confederate Army in distant Virginia gradually made its way back to their homes by the postal service, which could only be described as erratic. Letters, when available, were shared by friends and relatives. On this particular day in early February, the winter doldrums were underscored by leaden skies and a constant drizzle.

Anna Jane rested on the divan in her parlor, watching as the flames swept over the new logs. Normally, a roaring fire would cheer her, but today she saw the flames as the consuming ravages of war, reducing everything in their path to ash. The somber calm of this scene was disrupted by the approaching sounds of a happy Berta, who bounded into the parlor closely followed by a breathless, but smiling, Hannah. "Oh, Mother, you won't believe what the postmaster from the store at Daly's just brought!" she exclaimed, waving an envelope. "A letter from Mr. John Wootters. I can't believe it!"

Berta was surprised that Wootters had written, but Anna Jane was not surprised in the least. Nevertheless, she clapped her hands and invited her daughter to share the young man's news. "Hannah, you come in too," she said. "I know you will want to hear what he has to say."

Hannah nodded and went to fetch hot tea as Berta opened the letter and began reading to herself. By the time she returned, Berta was weeping.

"I sure hope that Sergeant Wootters is doing better than you, child," Hannah said, setting down the tea tray. "Tell us what he's written that's making you worry so."

"Please tell us what he has written," her mother agreed. "Surely it's not a secret."

"His letter certainly is not a cause of worry," Berta said, regaining her composure. "In fact, the most he seems to be suffering from is a bit of boredom. There are no secrets, Mother, but I am not certain that Mr. Wootters is accurately describing his military life. He says that he has written other letters, but I haven't received them. I wonder if the letters I wrote were ever delivered since he doesn't mention having gotten any."

"Now, Berta, if you are so inclined, please share some of this information with your attentive audience," her mother said.

"He writes that they have had false alarms of impending battle, but they have yet to catch more than a fleeting glimpse of the Union troops. Their assignment has been a ten-mile sector of the Potomac River bank. Although the enemy can be seen on the other shore, they have shown no inclination for a fight. It seems that the main concern has been the lack of entertainment and that he misses hearing me play the piano."

As she continued reading, Berta again found herself on the verge of tears.

"Several of the company members have musical instruments and perform occasionally for our amusement," she read. Again, she paused.

"Just what is it about this letter that you don't believe?" Anna Jane asked.

"He describes their living quarters as mere shacks with 'gaps between the boards large enough for birds to fly through,'" she read. "I presume that he is making an attempt at light-heartedness. He maintains that he didn't know that the sky contained as much snow as has fallen on them and that some of his fellow soldiers have been ill.[23] He also mentions that Colonel

---

23 Polley, JB. "Hood's Texas Brigade," 1910.

McLeod took pneumonia and has gone to be with the Lord, which he says 'must be an improvement over the quarters of the First Texas.' I think life must be much harder for the troops than he wants me to believe."

"Thank the Lord that he is alive and seems well," Hannah said.

"Hannah is right; he does seem to be well," Anna Jane said. "We have all heard about the terrible battle at Bull Run, when the Federals seemed no match for the Virginia infantry.[24] Maybe the Union troops' enthusiasm for the fight is not as great as we had feared."

Berta, who was still trembling slightly, felt emotionally spent. Imagining John Wootters in a shack in the snow with Union troops just across the river was too much for her. She excused herself and went upstairs to lie down. As she climbed the stairs, Hannah noted that Berta had placed the letter in her blouse -- next to her heart.

*   *   *

Major Smith had not ridden the mare, Betsy, to Crockett that day as she was expected to give birth at any time. For this trip, which was primarily to learn what he could about the new Confederate government's activities and news about either the Sibley Brigade or the troops in Virginia, he had taken another mount. His obligations at the plantation were less pressing than usual; the fields had been prepared for the spring planting, and he had decided to not clear more land as the ability to deliver the crop to buyers remained doubtful. In the meantime, the plantation slaves were occupied with providing a continuous supply of firewood for both master's home and their own settlement, known as Cedar Branch.

On his return to Smith Landing that evening, he learned of the letter from John Wootters. He agreed with his daughter that the young man's optimistic tone was very deliberate; clearly, he did not want to upset Berta. Major Smith had already learned from other sources that the regiment had suffered a high number of casualties due to illness and that the death of Colonel McLeod was considered a great loss to the entire brigade.[25] McLeod had assumed command of the First Texas Regiment after Colonel Wigfall had been promoted Brigadier General to command the recently

---

[24] Foote, S. The Civil War, Vol. 1, p.71-84.
[25] Cutrer, T. "McLeod, Hugh," Handbook of Texas Online.

designated Texas Brigade. Considered a hero by many in Texas, McLeod had served in the War of Texas Independence and led the ill-fated Santa Fe Expedition twenty years earlier.[26]

All the news wasn't bad, however. Lodwick Downes told Major Smith that John Wootters had been elected to the position of Third Lieutenant by his company, demonstrating their confidence in his character and leadership.[27] Major Smith agreed with his family that this was an appropriate recognition of their friend's good qualities and ability.

He had been hoping for some information about Sibley's Brigade, which had left San Antonio in October for the long and dangerous trek to El Paso and the invasion of New Mexico.[28] There had been no recent word of the Brigade's whereabouts or activities, which only caused Anna Jane more anxiety.

Hannah's and Berta's best efforts to provide comfort, companionship and musical entertainment had little effect. Anna Jane remained listless and uninterested in activities that she once embraced. The only thing that could engage her was news about their son. As the sun set on this winter day, the seemingly good news about John Wootters was the only glimmer of hope available. Hannah noted that Berta had not offered the letter to her parents to read; to her knowledge, the young woman continued to keep it on her person.

Later that month, Betsy the mare gave birth to a male foal that Oscar confirmed had been sired by Magnus, the stallion given to Lucius for his service in Captain Pridgen's Horse Cavalry Company. Major Smith hoped that this new animal, like its sire, would have the strength and endurance necessary to fulfill his role at the plantation. The Smith family had not received any communications from Lucius since October, when he wrote of the company's imminent departure for El Paso. Their goal was to secure the territory of New Mexico for the Confederacy, and Lucius had been in high spirits about this mission.[29]

---

[26] Carroll, H. Bailey, "Texas Santa Fe Expedition." Handbook of Texas Online

[27] Appendix I. Register--J.H. Wootters elected 2nd Jr. Lt., Co I, 1Reg't. Inf. Texas Volunteers, Confed. Arch. Chap. 1, File No 76, p. 524.

[28] Taylor, J. Bloody Valverde: A Civil War Battle on the Rio Grande, February 21, 1862, p. 17.

[29] Ibid. p. 12.

Major Smith was confident that Captain Pridgen would provide the company with competent leadership; he was also impressed with Colonel Tom Green, commander of their Fifth Regiment.

With the departure of both Lucius and Elijah Chadwick, the plantation's former overseer, John had assumed their responsibilities for the daily management of the plantation. He had supervised the preparation of the fields for the next planting season which, despite the freezing days of February, were on the horizon for March. The preparation of the seeds and the fields was a high priority, but they would not expand the area being cultivated. While it was true that the future remained tenuous, idleness was not an option. Revenues from the cotton crop would be critical to the Confederate war effort.

Although the expected Union occupation of Galveston had not happened, shipping from the port was at a virtual standstill due to the naval blockade. Major Smith and other planters in Houston County were planning to send their crops of the 1862 season to Mexico under militia protection, and preparations for this planting season had fully occupied the ninety slaves in Major Smith's charge.

Other than planting and harvesting the cotton crop, the plantation provided food for its community of slaves and the Smith family. Beef production, other than a small herd of milk cows, had never become a major focus. As many other plantation owners had discovered, cattle did not seem to thrive in the warm, humid climate.[30] Anna Jane often related a family story about her ancestor, Johannes Kolb, who had emigrated from Pennsylvania to South Carolina, and brought with him a herd of fine cattle, expecting them to prosper in the absence of harsh winters. Much to his dismay, his cows steadily lost weight and produced less milk in the southern environment. He eventually abandoned this endeavor in favor of a grist mill, which he built and operated at his property on the Pee Dee River.

Hogs and chickens did not suffer from the ailments that affected cattle. Those, along with crops of corn, various greens and other vegetables would provide for most of their needs. These agricultural activities were overseen by Oscar. Hannah, as usual, was devoted to caring for Anna Jane, even as Berta, who seemed to be more of a young woman every day,

---

[30] Boles, JB. The South Through Time--Volume II. p. 524.

had increasingly become her mother's constant companion. Major Smith thanked God for having such loyal and loving women to take care of his wife, as his duties often took him away from home for the entire day.

*   *   *

Berta readily accepted her role of advocate of optimism and cheer for her mother, whose bouts of melancholy were punctuated by periods of contentment. She was aware that her role in the family involved something other than her own amusement, and the absence of Lucius increased the opportunities for her to interact and converse with her parents. Hannah always made sure that Anna's personal needs were taken care of, helping her to care for and maintain her appearance.

One afternoon, Berta found her mother sitting peacefully in her great chair before the fireplace, reading from the family Bible, which was so large it required a special stand. Anna Jane's red hair, now showing signs of graying, was combed and secured with a ribbon. She was wearing a pressed white blouse and was wrapped in a light shawl to further protect her from the occasional chill that moved through the room. The familiar strains of Für Elise drifted in from the music parlor, filling the room. Anna Jane stopped reading as Hannah entered the room.

"Miz Smith, would you want some tea and cornbread?" she asked. "I made a fresh batch, and it should be good with honey."

"Thank you, that would be delicious, Hannah," Anna Jane smiled. "My appetite seems to be improved. Please bring some for Berta as well. I know she'll want to have a bite when she finishes her practicing."

"Yes, ma'am," Hannah said. "That child sure does play that piano."

As Berta completed her playing and came in to the parlor, her mother gave gentle applause.

"Berta, I enjoy your playing so much, and your mastery of those pieces seems to be quite good," Anna Jane said, motioning for her daughter to join her. "I think your presence and your music help to lighten the burdens on my mind."

Berta took this opportunity to mention to her mother the concerns that had been weighing on her since the frightful experience with Mr. Jencks.

"I know you are very worried about Lucius, as am I," Berta said. "I am only reassured when I realize that he is a grown man with strong convictions. He told me that his faith in God's love and presence would always give him the strength to overcome his fear. I only wish my faith was so strong."

"I can only overcome my grief over Lucius' departure with help from our heavenly Father," her mother said. "I realize that my worry cannot be of any use to Lucius and that our Lord will always be with him, no matter what happens, and I certainly don't want these matters to cause you more distress."

"Mother, I think I am coming to terms with Lucius being away and this terrible war," Berta frowned. "But I have a much harder time understanding something that occurred on a trip to Crockett about a month before Christmas."

As Anna Jane sipped her tea, Berta recounted the experience at the mercantile store, sparing her no details about what Jencks said and how he had aimed a veiled threat at her entire family, all because he thought she was teaching Oscar to read.

"Darling, please don't let this upset you so," Anna Jane said, putting an arm around Berta, who was unable to stop herself from crying as she recalled the episode. "Some people feel personally threatened when slaves achieve a level of education, especially if that level exceeds their own. Those kinds of people often seek out others of an even lower status just to feel superior, and they consider slaves to be a culture of lower status. They don't realize that what slaves lack is opportunity, not ability."

Anna Jane knew full well that many slaves would benefit from education if it were made available to them. It was unfortunate, even wrong, she thought, that slavery was assumed to be a permanent status and did not allow for those with ability to better themselves. Freedom was not within their reach, except in rare cases where it was granted by their owners – and that was not permitted in Texas. Personally, Anna Jane thought that those with the will and capacity to elevate themselves to full citizenship through hard work and education should be able to do so. But she realized that the South, with its often narrow mindset, would likely always have two cultures, one black and one white. Even within those cultures, there were different classes of individuals based on a variety of factors and circumstances.

"What do you mean by a person's class?" asked Berta, who had been listening to her mother. "That sounds like something you'd find in European countries or in India, where they have a caste system, but not in America."

"That's right, in some European and Asian countries, a person's class is determined by birth," her mother explained. "They inherit the so-called 'class' of their parents and generally aren't able to change that status during their lifetime, except in rare exceptions."

She went on to explain that a society in which one's efforts and personal qualities, no matter how worthy, could not result in personal advancement or recognition went against the fabric of American culture. In America, she said, hard work and good character were rewarded, no matter one's class. As she so often did, Anna Jane crafted her explanation from a Biblical perspective.

The Bible, she pointed out, taught people to respect and honor God and to treat others as they themselves would want to be treated. To follow these commandments one was expected to respect and show kindness to all people, and to recognize that they also had to live by the standards set for everyone. Honesty, trustworthiness, loyalty, bravery and tolerance of the beliefs of others – all these were characteristics found in a higher class of individual.

"But Hannah and Oscar have these characteristics," Berta said. "Yet that awful Mr. Jencks, who seems to lack all of those traits, would wish to look down on them."

"Indeed my sweet girl, Hannah and Oscar and many others possess these qualities and are considered among the highest class of individuals in their culture," Anna Jane said. "That Jencks man, on the other hand, is a very low-class person, and those like him are best avoided. I don't know much about him or his wife, but I feel very sorry for anyone who cannot avoid being around them."

It was a pity, she noted, that their children with no educational opportunities, would likely not enjoy a better future than their parents. Perhaps someday there would be schools and organizations to help such children.

"Perhaps that's what I will do," Berta said, sitting up tall. "Someday, I may want to have a school to help educate children who lack those opportunities. It is very sad, indeed, that the Jencks children may be destined to grow up to be like their father. It seems very unfair that such a horrible man should determine what kind of life they'll experience."

Anna Jane marveled at what a thoughtful and strong-minded person her daughter was. She had no doubt that Berta would be a blessing to their family and to others, and she prayed for God to guide her in these matters as she grew to adulthood. Major Smith had mentioned the unfortunate incident to Anna Jane, but it seemed that Berta had grown stronger because of it. Yes, her daughter was innocent, perhaps sheltered, but she was not foolish. Thinking of Berta brought Lucius to mind again, and she felt a shadow cast its gloom. Rather than give in to the despair that would follow, she quickly asked Berta to play some of the new songs she had brought back from Crockett. So it was that the tunes of Stephen Foster once again rang through the Smith home.

XI

Summer 1862 – Smith Landing Plantation

One Sunday morning in early June, the Smith family remained at home instead of making the twenty-mile trip to Crockett as the small congregation in Daly's was not scheduled to have services that day. The demands of the plantation and other responsibilities required Major Smith's presence, especially in the absence of his overseer Elijah Chadwick. On this occasion, the family had its own prayer service after the breakfast which Hannah and Oscar had prepared and served in the dining area on the eastern side of the entrance hall.

The dining room had views of the Trinity River and of Hannah's special garden. From her chair in the parlor, Anna Jane had a view of the garden, which gave her great pleasure. On those days when she was feeling particularly weak, she would sit near the window and marvel at the garden's abundance. Hannah, who had an unusually green thumb, harvested seeds from a wide variety of flowering plants as well as edible greens and melons, always making certain that there was an adequate amount and variety to feed her charges.

That morning, as they were finishing their last cup of tea, Oscar appeared at the entrance of the room, looking somber.

"What is it, Oscar?" Major Smith asked.

"Major Smith, sir, we have visitors," Oscar said. "It's the postmaster from Crockett, and he has the preacher from the church with him."

A sudden gripping in his chest propelled Major Smith up from his chair, so sudden that he had to hold onto the back of the chair to keep from falling, and a dark veil clouded his vision. At that moment, a cloud must have passed over the face of the sun, for when he regained his vision, the room had noticeably darkened. In his heart, Major Smith knew why the visitors were there, and he sank back into his chair.

As a former military commander, he had also been responsible for notifying families when one of their loved ones died in the line of duty. Anna Jane and Berta remained transfixed, motionless at the table; they could hear Hannah sobbing in the entrance hall. The Baptist minister went directly to Anna Jane and Berta and embraced them together, while the postmaster extended his hand to Major Smith. The only audible sound was Hannah's crying.

The hush that had engulfed the room was interrupted by the sound of Major Smith opening the letter from Captain Redding S. Pridgen, Company H, Fifth Regiment, Texas Mounted Volunteers. He stared out the window, oblivious to the garden or the pine forests in the distance; he focused instead on infinity as he realized, just then, that life would never again be the same for his family. With an unexpected surge of energy, Anna Jane rose from her chair and came toward him, collapsing into his embrace, their combined grief keeping them tightly in its grip. Hannah had hugged Berta, who, convulsed with sobs, kept murmuring with disbelief that her brother was gone forever.

"Oh, John," Anna Jane whispered. "I have feared that such a message would arrive every day since Lucius rode away nearly a year ago. Now my worst nightmares have come true. If ever the Lord were to give us strength and peace, now is the time of our greatest need. How will I ever survive this day?"

"I have no words," her husband said. "I have also had such fears, but I pushed them to the back of my mind."

In a trembling voice, Hannah spoke up from the back corner and asked Major Smith to read the letter. He nodded, opened it and began to read.

"To my esteemed friends, Major John Smith and Mrs. Anna J. Smith," he read, his voice tremulous with grief. *"It is with great sadness and regret that I must relate to you the loss of*

*your son Lucius in the noble defense of our beloved Southland
and our freedoms."*

John was unable to continue reading as tears filled his eyes, and he
could no longer focus on the pages in his hands. After a few moments, he
collected himself and continued reading:

*Lucius was wounded during an attack, in which he
demonstrated great bravery and gallantry. This occurred
on the afternoon of February 21ˢᵗ at Valverde, a crossing of
the Rio Grande del Norte, as our brigade engaged our foes
near their Fort Craig. Our Company H had been directed
by Colonel Green to capture a Federal artillery battery,
and Lucius was among those who faced intense fire as they
succeeded in overcoming the enemy and seizing the weapons.
Sadly, our losses were great and none nearer to my heart than
my friend and companion, Lucius.*

*During their success on the field, Lucius was wounded. His
companions helped him to our camp, where he was attended
by Powhatan Jordan, the captain of Company A and an able
physician from San Antonio. By the next morning Lucius lost
his gallant struggle and, surrounded by his fellow troopers,
his spirit was summoned by our Maker."*

Major Smith paused here, took a breath and again focused on reading
the letter. The silence in the room was interrupted only by the morning
breeze ruffling the branches of a shade tree outside the window.

*On February 22ⁿᵈ, he and the other Texans lost in the
great victory were laid to rest with full military honors in a
Christian service surrounded by the survivors of the battle.
I regret the delay in writing to you, but we have only now
returned to San Antonio. Although our mission was not
the success we had hoped for, Lucius and the other gallant
troops of our Company H captured the cannons, which have
been returned to Texas where they will continue to aid our*

quest for freedom and independence. Again, please accept my deepest sympathies and be assured of my highest regard for your son and his valiant service. May our Heavenly Father receive him and his fallen companions into eternal rest and peace.

With highest regards and sincerest sympathy,
Redding S. Pridgen, Captain, Company H, Fifth Regiment,
Texas Mounted Volunteers, Confederate States of America.

As John finished reading, he could hear an insect buzzing softly through the open window and the call of a bird somewhere in the distance. Nature went on, as usual, ignorant of the grief that held this family in its clenched fist.

The minister rose and asked all present to join hands, offering to lead them in prayer. Anna motioned to Hannah and Oscar to join the circle and Hannah's large black hand engulfed Berta's delicate fingers in a gentle clasp.

"Almighty God, never has your flock, gathered here today, been more in need of your presence. In this time of great sadness, we long for You to restore our souls. We are confident in Your promise to welcome Lucius into Your everlasting presence and to have him dwell in Your house forever. Pour out Your blessings and comfort on each person gathered here as we pray in the name of Christ. Amen."

Only a mockingbird's song interrupted the silence that followed. The minister told them that he would hasten back to Crockett for the Sunday service, and he would also inform the congregation what had occurred. He assured the Smith family that the entire flock would share their grief, uphold their spirits to God and pray for them to receive divine comfort.

With a supply of cornbread and ham on hand for the return trip, the minister and postmaster departed. Hannah and Oscar accompanied them down the entrance road. The Smith family, meanwhile, remained seated at the dining table. Nobody said anything, each of them in the world of their own minds and their own grief.

"John, I have suspected in my heart that Lucius had passed from this life some months ago, and I have been inwardly grieving about this for too long a time," Anna Jane said, finally breaking the silence. "Now that I know it's certain, I can ask God to heal the empty space in my heart. Perhaps this dark tunnel through which I have been passing is finally coming to an end."

"I have not had such premonitions, and I am stunned by this message," Major Smith said. "I have never had thoughts other than that Lucius was safe. It may take more than this letter to convince me."

Berta, who had been sitting quietly, again began sobbing. She stood and excused herself, fleeing for the refuge of her own room. After an hour, Hannah knocked on the door to the parlor where Anna Jane and Major Smith were talking to ask if they wanted any fresh tea or a midday meal; they noticed that her eyes were swollen and red from crying. They replied that some food would be welcome, first they wanted Hannah to sit down and tell them of her feelings about what had happened that morning. Hannah, who had spent very little time in sitting in the parlor and conversing with white people, came more fully into the room but continued to stand.

"Oh, Miz Anna, I had suspected that Lucius had gone to be with the Lord, but I sometimes didn't believe those feelings," Hannah said. "It don't seem real. I know that somehow we will get past this, but I also know I will always miss him, just like I do my little Ossie. It's been near two years that my boy has been gone, and I still catch myself looking over to where he used to sit to see what he's up to. What I do know is that they are both now with the Lord in a better place than any of us has ever been. I feel sorry for myself, but I know I should not feel sorry for them."

Anna Jane nodded. She knew Hannah's words to be true and hoped that someday she, too, could accept her son's departure from this world. Sooner would be better for her family, especially Berta. Anna Jane did not think that her own delicate health would allow her many more days on this earth. The time she did have left would be best spent not plagued with grief. Concerned about Berta, she asked the slave to check on her before preparing their meal.

After regaining her own composure, Hannah knocked on the door to Berta's bedroom. When there was no response to her first knock, she gently pushed the door open and inquired within.

"Missy Abigail, is there anything I can get for you that would help you to feel better?"

"Oh! Hannah, please come in and tell me what I can do to stop crying and feeling so hopeless," Berta said. "You haven't called me Abigail in quite some time."

"Sometimes tears just have to flow until your eyes are empty, and then they quit on their own," Hannah said, smoothing the young girl's hair. "I called you Abigail because what you need is to act like that woman in the Bible, who was not only beautiful and smart but also very brave. Your brother won't be coming to this home again, but he would want you to be brave and not grieve for him."

This sent Berta into another fit of tears and sobs. It didn't seem possible that her brother would never again walk into their house or gallop down the road on his horse, that she would never again hear the tales of his hunting expeditions or other adventures or that she would never be able to tell him how proud she was to have him as a brother.

"I never really told Lucius how much I loved him and how important he was to me," Berta cried into Hannah's lap. "I wish I could ask him to forgive me for not being thoughtful enough to tell him those things."

"Miss Abigail, you can't ask Lucius those things," Hannah shook her head. "But you can always ask our Lord for forgiveness. He promises us that we will be granted what we want and need. Since you know that Lucius is with the Lord, he will likely know of your prayers, and since the Lord forgives you, surely Lucius will also." With that, she persuaded Berta to put on a good face and come back downstairs. Her mother and father were also suffering, she said, and would be happy to see her in a more cheerful state.

"I will do my best, Hannah, and thank you for being so kind," Berta said, managing a weak smile.

When Berta reentered the parlor, her parents were drinking tea and discussing their circumstances. Her father was arranging a visit to San Antonio; he thought a talk with some of the men from Lucius' company would bring him some peace of mind. The trip wouldn't take more than two weeks.

"Indeed, my dearest John, I want you to go," Anna Jane said. "Please remember every word that is said about our dear son and return quickly."

Seeing Berta at the door, Anna Jane invited her to join them.

"I am so glad that you seem to be more composed," she said to her daughter. "We have much to do to carry on with our lives."

*   *   *

Six weeks after the news of his son's death, Major Smith traveled to San Antonio to meet with those who had survived the trek back from their ill-fated expedition.[31] Summer evenings at the Smith Landing Plantation were the only respite from the oppressive heat. Two weeks after Major Smith's departure, Anna Jane and Berta were sitting on the veranda of their home hoping for a cooling breeze. The sounds of the impending night were rising – katydids buzzing, frogs croaking and the plaintive calls of whippoorwills – in a mounting crescendo. In the nearly two months since the visitors from Crockett had delivered their devastating news, Anna Jane had noticed a marked improvement in her own mood. The initial shock and grief had seemingly given way to a sense of acceptance and healing.

Berta continued to struggle with a sense of guilt over not telling Lucius how much she loved and admired him before he left for his final adventure. It seemed that her prayers for forgiveness were slow in being answered. As she sat with her mother, she marveled at the nighttime sounds and the melancholy effect they had on her. This music surely must be the same song that nature had offered since creation.

A person's life, unlike these vibrant sounds and rhythms, was only a brief audience for that symphony. As conductor of this musical masterpiece, God would ultimately bring it to a perfect conclusion. Going forward, she determined that she would no longer be as thoughtless as she had seemed to be toward her brother. Instead, she would ask God to help her express her feelings for her loved ones more fully.

The ladies' reverie was interrupted by the sounds of a carriage coming up the entrance road from the other side of the home and the calls of the driver to Hannah heralding the return of Major Smith from San Antonio. Major Smith had been accompanied on this journey by Oscar's son, Edgar, so that Oscar could remain at the plantation.

---

[31]   Appendix II. Item 10. Sibley's Brigade and the War in the West.

Major Smith greeted his admiring ladies and joined them on the veranda, while Oscar and his son took care of the carriage, the horses and his luggage.

"Oh John, we are glad that you are home safely!" Anna Jane said. "Please come and tell us all about your journey."

"It feels good to sit on a chair that isn't trying to bounce you into a ditch, but I must say that young Edgar is an excellent driver like his father," he smiled, settling into a comfortable chair. "The trip was as good as one could expect. San Antonio is a tedious distance away, and I was reminded that our cotton crop will be following the same path after the harvest in the fall."

Smith stretched his long legs, propping his feet on a stool. Once in San Antonio, he found accommodations at the Menger Inn, which was located next door to what was left of the Alamo. Passing by that site every day, he told them, reminded him of a previous generation of brave young men willing to make the ultimate sacrifice for freedom, just like Lucius and his comrades .

He had not been able to find Dr. Powhatan Jordan, who cared for Lucius in his final hours. According to Captain Pridgen, he had not seen Dr. Jordan since the Sibley Brigade's return to Texas and the doctor's whereabouts remained a mystery. However, a few members of Company H of the Fifth Texas Mounted Regiment were still in San Antonio, and Major Smith was able to meet with Elijah Chadwick, who had ridden into battle with Lucius on that fateful day.

"Elijah has returned safely," Anna Jane said. "That is something to be grateful for."

"Indeed it is", continued her husband, "But Elijah had more sad news to relate. Not only did we lose Lucius in the battle at Valverde, but his friend, Hosea Walling, was also killed. The tragic tale didn't end there. As Hosea died, so did his older brother, Robert, who was wounded and died of pneumonia a short time after the battle. The Walling family had lost both of its sons in the same battle."

It was more than Berta could stand.

"Oh, my God in Heaven!" she cried out. "How many more losses will we all be asked to bear?"

"Truly, grief will cover our land," Anna Jane said. "We will go tomorrow to pay the Wallings a visit."

"Elijah had much to say about our son," Major Smith went on. His eyes filled with tears and his voice faltered.

Apparently, Lucius had shown exceptional bravery in his final battle. In some way, one that he could not express aloud to his wife and daughter, he was proud that his son's life, if it had to end now, had ended on a note of bravery and honor. He hoped that Lucius would be remembered in such a way by those who served with him. He knew that any soldier or true man, in the best sense of those words, would want to depart this life known as a gentleman of integrity who faced death with a determined spirit and a clear conscience.

After hearing the details of the battle and how Lucius spent his last hours, Berta had had enough. Once again, she fled to the safety of her bedroom.

*　　*　　*

After a sleepless night, the Smith family rose early the next morning and gathered for breakfast. Hannah served the meal as Major Smith asked what the ladies had done in his absence. The list was filled with war-related activities. They'd been asked by the ladies at church to help knit one hundred pairs of socks and some sweaters to send to the Crockett Southrons in time for winter. Anna Jane admitted that the handiwork had been good for her spirits.

"I seem to be less aware of the foreboding melancholy that oppressed me in recent months," she said. "Perhaps knowing that Lucius is now with the Lord and my worry can no longer be of any use to anyone will ease my mind."

Perhaps the best news they had received was a letter from John Wootters. He had written a long one to his uncle, Lodwick Downes, who had been kind enough to share it with the Smith ladies. Lieutenant Wootters had also written to Berta in late April, but it had arrived only in the past two weeks. In March, his brigade had been ordered to move back from a position at the Potomac River. They were in the area of Fredericksburg when he wrote, and they were not pleased with the move as it seemed like a retreat. Their new defense line was the Rappahannock

River, and they had not engaged the enemy since their move. Berta did not understand why the brigade wanted to be closer to the fighting. Wouldn't they want to be further from the battlefield and out of harm's way?

"No, dear girl, I would expect that eagerness for engagement," her father said. "Especially of troops that have not truly been tested in battle. Did Lieutenant Wootters have anything else to report?"

Berta shook her head. Although she had written him several letters, she had received only one in return over the past six months. In that missive, he told her about the unseasonably cold weather and a snowstorm they had endured earlier in the month. Heavy rains followed, turning the roads into rivers of mud. He mentioned wanting to hear Berta play some tunes on the piano, and he seemed especially concerned about the safety of Gus, the pet pig that lived in the side-yard of the Downes & Long store. In Virginia, he said, Gus would likely have become bacon and ham as that, along with corn, was their main food. His letter, she said, was filled with news and musings, not feelings.

"Recall that the letter was written before the First Infantry had been engaged in any serious combat, and soldiers under almost any circumstances will continue to minimize the seriousness of their situation," Major Smith reminded her. "You do not need to chasten him for his lightheartedness; I expect that letters written by him after the battles of May and June will be much more serious."

Berta saw the sense in her father's words. She had followed his advice and written to John Wootters about the loss of Lucius and its devastating effects. She had not, however, told him of her own grief in failing to tell her brother of her love and pride in him. But, having vowed not to make that mistake again, she did tell Wootters how proud she was of his brave actions and how fervently the family prayed for his safe return to Texas and his home.

"I cannot imagine any person that would not appreciate and be strengthened by such sincere sentiment," her mother said. " I would encourage you to continue reminding him of those thoughts."

In an attempt to lighten the somber mood around the table, Major Smith changed the subject altogether. He reminded the ladies that, war notwithstanding, life went on, and should not be persistently plagued by melancholy. For the past year, he observed, Berta's formal education had been interrupted. And while he was pleased that she had continued musical studies with the pianist in Crockett, her academic and social development were also important. He and Anna Jane were concerned about the lack of other young ladies her age in the area. Berta should form friendships and feed her intellectual spirit. Unfortunately, with so much fighting in Virginia, continuing her education in that state would not be an option. So her parents decided that a solution much closer to our home would be ideal.

"God has blessed you with a keen mind as well as a loving heart," Major Smith told her. "To ignore your need for further education would be poor stewardship of the talents you have been given."

He had heard that the Masonic Lodge in Fairfield in Freestone County has opened a new school for young women known as the Fairfield Female College. It was just across the Trinity River, about a half day's journey from Smith Landing plantation. The school has close affiliations with the Baptist church and its president, Henry Lee Graves, a Mason from North Carolina, had an excellent academic reputation. Graves had served as president of Baylor University in Independence since its founding. There was also a separate Baylor Female College in Independence. Major Smith suggested that they visit these and other schools where Berta might want to pursue her studies in the future.[32]

"We should consider a visit to the schools in the next few months," Anna Jane said. "Selfishly, I would not want you to leave us for at least a year, and I do not want you very far away."

Berta was overwhelmed by her parents' thoughtfulness and generosity, especially in the wake of their loss. As much as she wanted to pursue schooling, she also knew it would take her at least a year to be ready to live away from home. That was something she'd never done, and it would be a difficult change for her. Perhaps in a year they would all be more comfortable with that plan. Until then, they would take the time to heal.

---

[32]   Shields, D.R. Fairfield Female College, Handbook of Texas Online

XII

1862-63, Houston County, Texas

On a Thursday in late November 1862, the Smith family traveled to Crockett as Major Smith needed to make arrangements for the large crop of cotton that had been baled and was ready for transport to the Mexican border. Anna Jane, whose strength and stamina had steadily improved over the previous months, had come to attend church services on Sunday and to visit with friends in anticipation of Christmas. Hannah was there to help Anna Jane; Oscar and his son, Edgar, drove the carriage.

Berta had been looking forward to the visit. She was eager for information about John Wootters, and she also hoped to deliver some Christmas gifts that she had knitted when she and her mother were making winter clothing for the troops in Virginia. While Anna Jane's mood had seemed to lighten, Berta's had remained darker than usual. Her parents concluded that a major factor was the absence of her tutors from the Smith plantation.

Travel by paddlewheel boat on the Trinity River had ceased with the Federal threat to Galveston. Berta's tutors had most likely enlisted or been called to serve in some capacity, so she was without their regular instruction. While the blockade had been in effect for one year, the presence of a Union army force had not been evident until October, when a squadron of eight Federal ships had taken control of the harbor. With the island city considered indefensible, the heavy artillery protecting it had been removed by the Confederate commander. Business and commerce were now nonexistent, and most of the citizenry had relocated to inland sites.[33]

Concern about her education led Major Smith and Anna Jane to travel with Berta to Freestone County to visit the Fairfield Female College. The roads leading to the town of Fairfield were reached by the ferry at the Smith Landing Plantation. The road linking the communities of Augusta and Daly's in Houston County to the river continued across the ferry to Fairfield, which was accessible except after prolonged rainfall. The Smith family would visit the college, which had two twenty-week sessions yearly with the next one beginning in early January. They felt that Berta was mature enough to attend the school as a boarding student, and that she would benefit from the intellectual and social stimulation.

Hannah thought that Berta's melancholy was also due to the lack of any recent letter from John Wootters. The Downes family in Crockett had received a letter in October, which they had shared. Major Smith had told Berta that Wootters had received one of her letters and written several back, but had not received any reply. Berta was dismayed by this as she had written often. She knew that mail delivery was, at best, erratic; it was apparent that only a few of her letters were reaching John Wootters.

As they traveled to Crockett, she gazed through the carriage windows at the wintertime scene. Although this area was generally known as the piney woods, a wide variety of trees grew throughout the forests. Whereas the land near the streams and low-lying areas was populated by hardwoods, the gentle hills were covered with thick stands of evergreens trees that seemed to reach far into the sky blocking direct sunlight. Rays beaming through this canopy gave the appearance of an ancient cathedral with towering arches and high windows casting illumination on penitent worshipers.

Berta thought about John Wootters and prayed that he be spared to return to his home in Texas. Her recent letters to him had implored him to be careful and encouraged him to ask God for protection. Berta had never really discussed her faith with him, suspecting that it would offer little comfort to one facing such grave dangers. But she wanted him to seek divine help and to remind him that God's ultimate grace and love were the only protection that could really meet all of their needs.

---

[33] Cotham, E.T., Battle on the Bay: The Civil War Struggle for Galveston.

His last letter had been full of optimism and described how the Texans had enhanced their reputation of being among the best fighting troops in the Army of Northern Virginia. But Berta and everyone knew that when the letter was written, the Crockett Southrons and their comrades had no idea what lay ahead of them. All of the Smith family members hoped to find out more about the fate of Wootters' company on this visit to Crockett.

Worrying about John Wootters interfered with Berta's ability to focus on other areas of her life, especially her desire to be a comfort to her parents. She had mixed feelings about the possibility of attending Fairfield Female College but realized that some change in her daily activities would be helpful. And while living away from home seemed a daunting prospect, she reminded herself that she would not be that far from home. She secretly hoped that her parents would insist she attend the college.

As they were passing through Daly's near the homestead of the unpleasant Mr. Jencks, Berta saw several children that she suspected were his playing near the roadway. "Father, would you please have Oscar stop the carriage?"

Major Smith had no idea why his daughter would make such a request, but without further question, he called to Oscar to pull up the team. As the horses came to a stop, the group of disheveled children scattered to the side of the road, where they stared at the well-dressed travelers with bewilderment and suspicion. The older children had drawn back furthest from the carriage, leaving only the smallest child nearby. Berta spoke softly to the little girl."

"Little Missy, are you and your brothers and sisters part of the Jencks family?" The child did not speak, but nodded as her brothers and sisters looked on.

"I want to be your friend," Berta said, opening the carriage door and stepping out to the side of the road. "I have some things I made for you and your brothers and sisters." She took a package from Hannah and presented it to the speechless child.

The older children whispered nervously to each other but did not come closer to investigate the package or the visitor.

"I hope you can find a use for these sweaters I have knitted," Berta said. "It is certain to be a cold winter. Please take them to your mother and share them with your brothers and sisters." Even as Berta left the package on the ground and turned back to the carriage, she could hear a small "thank you" from the little girl.

Once Berta had resumed her seat and said good bye to the children, Major Smith told Oscar to proceed without further delay. The carriage lurched forward. Looking back out the window, Berta saw the older children pulling at the package. She watched until the figures grew smaller and smaller and finally faded from sight.

"Anna Jane, I hope you and Berta have carefully considered this apparent act of kindness," Major Smith said. "While I am sure the children and their mother will be pleased with the gifts, I am uncertain how old Jencks will react. It will likely depend on his sobriety at the time. Hopefully they can avoid discussing where the clothing came from."

"Berta has become quite adept at knitting and I didn't see any harm in trying to extend a hand of charity to these children," Anna Jane scolded her husband. "From the looks of them, they will certainly be able to use whatever clothing we can give them."

Major Smith could see little benefit in discussing the potential ramifications of this act of charity, so they continued riding into the town without further conversation. Hannah did note that during the remainder of their journey, Berta had a smile on her face. She did not need to say anything to show how satisfied she was with her accomplishment.

*   *   *

On arriving in Crockett, the Smiths went straight to the new hotel in town to situate Anna Jane and Berta. Major Smith then walked over to the Masonic Lodge, where he expected to obtain information about the status of the Texas Brigade and plans for delivery of the cotton crop, which was now in storage. Lodwick Downes, Andrew Gossett and others had much to tell him, as news of the First Texas Regiment had filtered back to their community from the occasional letters and by telegraph. They confirmed that the only way to move the cotton was over land to the Rio Grande River in southern Texas, where it could be loaded through Mexican merchants on ships sailing under European flags. A militia group would be leaving with the first shipment of product within the month.

Lodwick Downes, who seemed to have aged greatly in the past year, greeted Smith warmly on his arrival at the lodge. The store owner had noticeably slowed his pace and seemed more stooped than in previous months, which Smith attributed to burdens resulting from the lack of commercial activity in town. These cares, reflected on his lined face, seemed to ebb somewhat as he clasped Smith's hand.

"John, my friend, It is so good to see you again," Downes said. "I have much news to share with you from my nephew, John Wootters. I also hope your family has come with you on this visit as I have a message to deliver to your daughter."

"Anna Jane and Berta are at the hotel, and we will be in town through Sunday," Smith responded. "I know that Berta will be anxious to see you and hear about the word from your nephew. She received a letter from him some time ago, but that was before the intense action the First Texas Regiment has had in more recent months. Tell me what you have learned about our Crockett Southrons and the war in the East."

Downes told him that a wire had come to Crockett two days ago containing news about the Confederates in Maryland and a terrible battle at a town called Sharpsburg. The letter from John Wootters to his uncle had been written after their brigade had fought a battle in August near Manassas, Virginia. It concerned the second battle at that location, and it had been written before Robert E. Lee led his army north of the Potomac River into Maryland and the recent disaster.[34]

After the great victory at Manassas, Lee determined to move the army across the Potomac and into Union territory. This move was viewed with concern by many Southerners, as it was a distinct change from the more defensive strategy that Confederate President Jefferson Davis had discussed. This war was not a design of conquest, he noted, but rather an attempt to force the Federals to let the southland go in peace. Instead, Abraham Lincoln had then declared all slaves to be free in his Emancipation Proclamation as well as his intention to enforce that proclamation in all territory under Federal control. Not surprisingly, it angered and motivated many who previously had been less enthusiastic about going to war.[35]

---

[34] Appendix II. Item 11. The 1st Texas Reg't, Hood's Brigade--1862. The Peninsula Campaign, Second Manassas, and the Maryland Campaign.

[35] Foote, S. The Civil War: A Narrative, Volume One, pp. 687-700.

The only good news Downes had to report was that Wootters had, thus far, survived; many of his friends and fellow soldiers would never return home. At least seven of their company had been killed, including the commander, Captain R. W. Cotton,[36] while many others, Wootters' friend Gus Aldrich included, were wounded. The First Texas Regiment commander, Lieutenant Colonel Philip Work, reported losing 186 of 226 men in this single battle. Overall, more than 550 out of 850 were killed or wounded. Fortunately, Lee was able to withdraw back across the Potomac River, or the entire army might have been lost. And while further information had yet to trickle in, the results of the battle at Shiloh in April[37] and more recently at Sharpsburg made things look grim for the Confederacy. Wootters was promoted to senior second lieutenant the day following the battle at Sharpsburg and was now the commander of their company.[38]

Major Smith was stunned into silence. He could not imagine so many losses to a single group of men. It sounded as though the survival of any had been a miracle, and he was thankful that Wootters had been one of the fortunate few. He thought Wootters must have fought with great valor to have been given command of the company. He also hoped Downes had more encouraging news to share and said so.

"The pall of grief that has beset Anna Jane since the loss of Lucius has only recently begun to recede," Major Smith said. "Such terrible news could likely have a dampening effect on her."

Downes reassured his friend that the letter's contents were more optimistic than what he'd just heard. He would send it with Major Smith so that both Berta and Anna Jane could read it, and then retrieve it from them on Sunday after church. Major Smith then shared with him the possibility of Berta going away to the young women's college in Fairfield and how he would visit with Judge Gossett on the subject during this visit. He confessed that he and Anna Jane both thought it would benefit Berta to occupy her mind and to be around girls her own age, as she, too, was becoming all too familiar with melancholy.

---

[36]   Mainer, T. Houston County in the Civil War, p. 17-19.

[37]   Appendix II. Item 12. General Albert Sidney Johnston and the Battle of Shiloh.

[38]   Appendix I. Regimental Return of the 1ˢᵗ Reg't Texas Vols. for the month of October 1862: JH Wooters(sic) Promoted from 2 Jr to 2 Sr Lieut Co I, 1ˢᵗ Reg't Texas Vols. September 30/62.

Major Smith was settled into a comfortable chair at the Masonic Lodge when Judge Gossett stopped in for his daily visit. He made straight for this friend, but his usual smile and enthusiasm were absent, which told Major Smith that something was not quite right.

"It is good to see you, John," the judge said, shaking his hand. "I only wish the news about the Confederacy was as hopeful."

Major Smith nodded and told Gossett that he knew about the results of the two most recent battles.

"Our state has paid a higher price for our freedoms than anyone could have imagined," the judge said. "The reality of Lincoln's intent to free slaves and the certain reluctance of the European nations to rally to our cause makes the outlook bleak indeed."

Both men were quiet for a moment as the reality of what was sure to happen going forward sank in. The likelihood of any peaceful resolution seemed to have vanished; more Southerners than ever seemed determined to continue the struggle. How things would turn out remained to be seen. And Major Smith, with only one child left, was concerned about Berta's opportunities.

"I remember you mentioned an interest in Fairfield Female College, and I have recently received more information about their activities which I'll share with you," Gossett said. "Doesn't your daughter possess excellent musical talent?"

As it turned out, one of the wounded Confederates from the battle of Shiloh was an adventurer from Europe, who came to aid the Confederate cause. He had recovered from his injuries sufficiently to take a position at the Fairfield College as instructor of musical arts. According to Gossett, this Rudolph von Godski claimed to be descended from a noble family in Poland. Whether or not that was the case, he was, in fact, reputed to be an accomplished pianist. Perhaps Berta would benefit from his instruction?

"This is interesting news, especially since we plan to visit there in the next month," Major Smith said. "The college has much to recommend it with its ties to Masonry and the Baptist church and the fine reputation of its president, Dr. Henry Graves. I hope that Berta will be amenable to attending."

*   *   *

When John Smith returned to the hotel, he found Anna and Berta reflecting a much more somber mood that just a few hours earlier.

"What has caused my pretty girls to be so unhappy?" he asked. "Are the hotel rooms not to your liking, or did you find that mice had already occupied them?"

"We have heard about the terrible circumstances of our Crockett Southrons and their regiment in Maryland," Anna Jane said, shaking her head. "The news gives us no reason to smile."

"True, true, but I do have some good news to share," he said, taking a seat by the fireplace. "Our friend John Wootters has not only survived the ordeal, but he is now commander of their company. Lodwick Downes has asked me to bring this letter he had received, as it has a special message that is likely of interest to Berta."

With these words, Berta sat back in a large chair and began to weep, her shoulders shaking from the force from sobs. Hannah, who was also crying, took the girl with in her strong arms and held her tight. Their relief was palpable.

"Now, this letter was written well before the army moved into Maryland, and while its optimism may not still be appropriate, it doesn't demand excessive tears," her father said. "I thought you would find it of interest as Wootters specifically asked his uncle to share it with you."

"Read the letter, child," a now-smiling Hannah said. "I want to know what the lieutenant has to say!"

Berta took the letter and opened it with a trembling hand. Dated September 1st, it was more than two months old. She briefly wondered if any of her letters had found their way to Mr. Wootters, especially since the troops seemed to move frequently. She cleared her throat and began to read:

My Dear Uncle,

I am writing this note more hurriedly than I would have wished as I have much to tell since my last letter. You have most surely learned about our brigade and its success earlier in the summer, even if you have not received the letters I wrote from Richmond. The complaint that we had journeyed all the way from Texas and had no one to fight was answered in May, when we were sent against the Federals at a port called Eltham's Landing on the York River. Although it was not a major battle, it gave us a chance to show General Johnston what Texans can do in a fight. At the end of June, after General Lee had taken the command, we had another chance at a place known as Gaines Farm, where General Hood was called upon to save the day against a stubborn Union defensive line. Late in the afternoon our men charged over a quarter-mile of rough ground with loud rebel yells, despite their guns. This must have put the fear of God in them as their line broke and the federals fell back in defeat. The only thing that saved them was nightfall, but by the next morning their General Porter had removed his troops across the Chickominnie (sic) River burning the bridges in defeat."[39]

Berta's tears had subsided, but her voice softened to the point of a whisper as she continued her reading:

"The Fourth and Fifth Regiments had the greatest losses, but our First paid its price as Colonel Rainey, our commander, was wounded. We are now led by Lt. Col. Philip Work. Our Crockett Southrons lost four men – Boykin, Morris, Manning and Montgomery, who will be greatly missed as they had each become my close friends. Our Lt. Sheridan was wounded, as was my good friend Lt. Wall, and will not be able to continue with the company. Willie will be returning home, but he has left one finger in Virginia as a result of his wound. He may have arrived in Crockett by the time you receive this, so please tell him that we wish him well and, if his finger regrows, he is welcome back here at any time."

"How can they have such a cavalier feeling about such bloodshed and tragedy?" Berta turned to her parents. "What has happened to their minds?"

---

[39] Reference is to the Chickahominy River in Virginia.

"It's only natural that men, when faced with the likelihood of death, remove that thought from their minds," he explained. "It is a way of confronting fear and keeping that feeling from preventing them from failing to act bravely."

Berta shook her head; she simply didn't understand. But she continued reading.

> "I suspect you already know of what I have written as I sent other letters from Richmond, where we spent a month trying to recover from our losses. During that time we became aware of the burden that has fallen on all of our Confederate brothers as the hospitals in our capital are filled with injured men, especially a very large one known as Chimborazo. The First Texas' numbers were far below last spring, and we gladly received a new company from Trinity County. They arrived in early August just as we were directed to march north from Richmond."

During a pause, Oscar appeared quietly in the doorway to the parlor. The slave informed Major Smith that the team and carriage had been put away in the stable, and if all the tasks were done, he and his son, Edgar, would retire for the evening. Once again, Berta returned to the letter.

> The next day we crossed the Rapahinik (sic) River to join Gen. Johnston's divisions, and the new Trinity troops were amused at their first combat action. General Lee has prohibited men from foraging at the expense of locals, but some troops were tempted by a field of ripening corn and set about to obtain a meal. As they entered the field they met a Union scouting party with similar intentions, and the result was a fist fight suitable for any bar room and roasting ears bombardments were hurled. The Texans quickly took the field but our brigade quartermaster felt obliged to buy 100 acres from its owner. The Roasting Ears Fight was not a great benefit, as we were ordered to continue toward the Bull Run Mountains the next morning. The divisions succeeded in clearing a gap known as Thoroughfare, and over the next two

days the federals took a great beating. Our brigade attacked a field called the Chinn Ridge, where we met two regiments from New York that were not prepared for the fight. These Zuvies (sic) in their bright red and blue uniforms were nearly wiped out. Their fallen covered the field and have been rightly described as appearing like the fields covered with bluebonnets and paintbrush flowers in Texas.[40]

"Is it possible that a human being's spirit can become so hardened that a scene of death and destruction can be so described?" Berta said. "I just don't know if I can continue to read of such horrors."

"Please finish the letter, Missy Berta, so we can know what he says to you," Hannah said. Instead, Berta handed the letter to her mother, who read on:

"I must close this as the postmaster is calling for any letters that are to be sent before we leave this place in the morning. Please tell my friend Miss Berta Smith, that I have received one of her letters and I am saddened about the loss of her brother Lucius. I am certain that he served bravely and that his actions would make any man proud. He must have stood valiantly with his comrades until God called him to real peace. Also tell her that I thank her for her words of encouragement and reassure her that I and my fellow soldiers are well aware that our faith is the only source of strength sufficient to sustain us as we complete our duty. Her letters are very welcome as others I have received are of such trivial content that I suspect the writer is unaware of what is happening in the war. We are indeed fighting not only because of our own pride and for our safety but to secure freedom for those of a gentle nature as she possesses. Please give my love to all of our family and ask them to write when they are able.

Your fond nephew, John Wootters."

---

[40] References are to the Rappahannock River in Virginia and to the regiment of New York Zoaves.

As Anna Jane folded the letter, returning it to the frayed envelope, the room was silent. A few minutes later, Major Smith spoke.

"You have heard words from one who represents the best that our southland can offer," he said. "We can only pray that he and his comrades remain safe and, if such is not to be, then that our Heavenly Father will receive each of them into eternal peace."

As each silently offered a prayer, Major Smith told his wife and daughter what Judge Gossett had shared with him: Fairfield Female College had engaged a new music instructor and the Smith family should visit there soon. They had discussed such a trip on several occasions, and now it seemed the time was right. They would go in December. Berta was looking forward to it.

*   *   *

On Sunday during church, Berta could not stop thinking about John Wootters and the letter he had written. She didn't know him very well, but now she wondered if her initial impression of a gentle and thoughtful soul was wrong. The appalling loss of life that he seemed to readily accept was beyond her grasp. She had recurring thoughts about the role of divine intervention in the cataclysmic conflict, and she was certain that everyone in church and at such meetings across the north and south were offering similar prayers.

Having read the Book of Job in the Bible, Berta had concluded that many issues were simply beyond human understanding and that the only valid prayer request was that God grant each individual the ability to endure and to have faith. She could not, however, keep from asking God to spare the life of John Wootters and bring him safely home.

Once the service was over, she went looking for Lodwick Downes to return the letter. He suggested that Berta continue to reassure his nephew that there were many reasons for him to survive, that he was held in the highest regard and esteem, and his safe return was the subject of their daily prayers. Berta felt a brief urge to ask Downes about the effectiveness of prayer, but instead thanked him profusely and assured him that her prayers and letters would continue. The return to the plantation saw the Smith family in an improved mood. They all were optimistic about their planned visit to Fairfield in the coming weeks.

*   *   *

January 1863 would always be one of the most memorable of times in Berta Smith's life. It was the month she became a student at the Fairfield Female College. Their visit in December had allayed any concerns they had; Berta was especially excited about the piano instruction she would receive. The new music instructor's reputation had spread rapidly. He was, it seemed, an accomplished pianist from a Polish noble family, the House of Sobieski. The opportunity to study piano with him appealed to Berta, and she sensed, at the time of her visit, that the school would become like a second home to her.[41] Her initial impression of the college was boosted by the warm reception she received from the other students. The prospect of being with other girls with whom she had much in common was something she could look forward to.

Even before she matriculated, Berta, along with many other Texans, was in a mood of excitement over the remarkable triumph of the Confederates at the battle of Galveston on New Year's Day. The Valverde Battery, guns captured by the heroic but fatal charge of Lucius Smith and other Texans in New Mexico one year earlier, had contributed to the victory.[42]

Most of Berta's new classmates had family members and friends serving the Confederate cause. Dr. Graves and his faculty members did their best to help the students focus on their studies and other activities, and the prevailing atmosphere of the college was one of optimism and enthusiasm. Even in her first weeks at the college, this clearly had a positive effect on Berta's attitude. She returned to the plantation for the last weekend of the month to pack up some additional clothes, sheet music and other items from her bedroom, and it was obvious to everyone in the Smith home that Berta's heart and spirit were lighter. They could tell just by the way she walked from room to room. They also knew she would step even more lively when she discovered the surprise that awaited her,

*　　*　　*

The carriage came to a stop at the front veranda of the Smith Plantation home. Hannah, who had made the trip to accompany Berta back home from the college in Fairfield, slowly exited the carriage. Oscar secured the

---

41　Appendix I. The Houston Chronicle, September 28, 1930.
42　Appendix II. Item 13. Battle of Galveston.

horses first and then helped Hannah and Berta up to the front entrance, where they were greeted by a smiling Anna Jane.

"Welcome home! I hope you had a good trip and I can't wait to hear about your first weeks at college," she said. "Come in, come in, I have something for you."

"The college is a wonderful place in so many ways," Berta said, holding her mother in a warm but gentle embrace. "Dr. Graves and the faculty are interested in helping us learn and helpful when we need their attention. Our accommodations are just fine and the servants are very helpful with our laundry and keeping our rooms in good order."

Berta noticed that her mother seemed a little unsteady, but continued her description. The building and its surroundings were delightful, she said. Not only was it an elegant structure, it was also well heated, as there was a fireplace in her sitting room. The grounds, which were neatly kept, would be breathtaking with the spring flowers in full bloom. But the best part was the company of all the girls at the college.

There were only about thirty of them, and one named Martha Meriwether, who was a year ahead of Berta, lived close to Smith Landing plantation. There was a larger number of younger students in the lower school, which was known as the Academy, and they all lived in the Fairfield area. According to Berta, the girls in her classes, some of whom came from as far away and Louisiana and Mississippi, were very pleasant.

One thing she had noticed, she told her mother, was how strict Dr. Graves was with the girls' meal times and how insistent that they all follow their schedules with promptness and punctuality.

If one of us is late for dinner, the door is locked and that person misses the meal," Berta said. "When that happens, some of the other girls will smuggle food out of the dining room and take it to the one being punished. But we are very careful to not be caught."

It seemed that Dr. Graves runs a tight ship. With so many girls in one place, her mother pointed out, it was likely necessary to have rules and to follow them.

"How is the music instructor I have heard so much about?" Anna Jane asked. "I gather his injury at Shiloh has not prevented him from teaching."

"Count von Godski, as he insists on being called, shows no signs of his disability other than a slight limp," Berta smiled. "He really is a very serious and excellent pianist, and I know he will greatly help me improve my playing."

Berta also thought Count, who was very proud of his mustache, sometimes acted like a dandy. If she looked at him too closely, she found it hard to keep from laughing. As for his taste in music, he was partial to pieces by Frederic Chopin, perhaps because of the Polish roots he shared with that composer. Berta hadn't yet tried to play any of his music; she found the pieces very difficult to play, but beautiful. When Count von Godski played them, she could sit and listen for hours.

"Your Father and I have missed you, but it is reassuring to know that you are so happy and busy with your studies," said Anna Jane, whose fatigue was beginning to show. "The college certainly agrees with you, and I am sure that if you are careful to complete your studies and practice your piano pieces, you should not have very many occasions to have to forego your dinner. Now go unpack your bags because I have a surprise for you: a letter from John Wootters, delivered this week!"

*   *   *

Berta held her breath as she held the letter from John Wootters. She felt lightheaded, she felt dizzy, she felt a flushed sensation travel up her neck to the top of her head. Leaning on the bannister, she walked upstairs and directly to her room. Her first reaction was one of confidence: the company commander had responded to her notes with a personal letter. She recalled how strong and handsome he was, what an impressive figure he had presented the day he left with the Crockett Southrons. Quickly dismissing those girlish thoughts, Berta allowed insecurity to wash over her as she carefully opened the sealed envelope. Would he write descriptions of the terrible realities of war? What would the message reveal about him? She had not been able to forget the image from his earlier letter of the dead soldiers strewn across the fields like wildflowers. Many of those soldiers had been someone's brother or son, whether fighting for the north or the south. She took a deep breath and focused on the page in her hand:

> *My dear Miss Smith, I am writing you from our camp near the town of Fredericksburg, in what is said to have been the gentle countryside of Virginia. At this time, it is cold and*

barren except for the tents of our regiment and the trodden fields of what were farms. I want to express appreciation on behalf of the Crockett Southrons for the warm stockings and sweaters that you and the other ladies made for our dwindling number. We have even received a supply of shoes, which were badly needed as our only means of transportation is by our feet.

Berta's eyes were now free of tears as she tried to imagine the scene described for her. She had not considered how many of the 110 men that had marched from Crockett a year and a half ago were still alive, or still at their duties. It was certainly a smaller band than she remembered. She moved closer to the window to read by the fading light:

It is likely that one could imagine that there are no acts of kindness to be found in an army's occupation, but I have just learned of such a case following the terrible battle at Fredericksburg.[43] The Federal general called for an attack that was doomed to failure and resulted in the loss of many of their troops. Our regiment and others in General Longstreet's command had been building a defensive position on high ground near the town. For reasons we could not imagine, their forces made a direct attack on the position with the results that we the defenders certainly expected. That night, a South Carolina sergeant, who must have been appalled by the suffering of the federals injured on the field, risked his life to take water to the men lying between the battle lines. The Union solders did not fire at him as he ministered to their wounded, when he would have been an easy target. My only regret is that I did not have such an opportunity or would likely not have been so brave as he was.

Berta could not continue after reading these words until her tearful sobs could subside. After an interval she resumed her reading:

---

[43]   Appendix II. Item 14. Battle of Fredericksburg.

I have written several letters but as you may not have received them I will write again that I thank you for the words you sent of your prayers for our safety and belief that only God's grace can give us the strength to perform our duties. We are aware that many on the opposing side of the battle share our faith. We can only do our duties with the desire to support our comrades and to defend the freedoms we hold so dear. One can only admire men who will sacrifice so much for this cause even though we hope for a very different outcome.

Please continue to offer prayers on our behalf. We will also be praying that you will be able to face the hardships in your path. Please give my love to your family. I hope to be able to return to give all of you my warmest regards.

Your friend far away.
Lt. John Wootters

Berta sat in wonder at what she had read. She had many questions, more than before she'd read the letter. Sometime later, she heard Hannah knocking on the bedroom door.

"Missy Berta, your supper is ready and your momma and poppa are worrisome about you," she said. "They want you to come downstairs when you are able."

"Oh, Hannah, I didn't realize how long I had been lost in my own thoughts," Berta got up and opened the door. "Please tell them that I am coming now."

*   *   *

At the dinner table, Berta recounted her description of the activities at the college for her father, who agreed that the decision for her to attend was a good one. He was particularly interested in what had brought her piano instructor to the Confederate army and seemed pleased that her studies were both challenging and enjoyable.

Berta related much of what Wootters had told her about the Crockett Southrons in Virginia. The conversation with her parents left many of her questions unanswered, and she realized that the mind and heart of a soldier facing such dangers were not something she could fully understand. She was glad to be returning the next morning to her college and to activities that were far removed from the agony of the battlefield.

XIII

Late Summer, 1863 –
Houston County, Texas

The summer after Berta's first session at the Fairfield Female College was hard for her; as much as she enjoyed being home with her parents, she also missed being with her school friends and in the classroom. During those moments of yearning to be back at school, she turned to her music, her parents' company and the wilderness around Smith Landing Plantation, all of which brought her great joy.

Although the property extended several miles from the river, it was the one-mile wooded area adjoining the river that she found particularly enchanting. The gentle Cedar Branch meandered through this section, carrying its clear water to the powerful and often murky Trinity River; numerous trails coursed through the hardwood forests bordering the river. Thanks to her botanical studies at the college, Berta was much more aware of the plants and flowers that grew in the area. The forest floor contained numerous palmetto palm bushes as well as ancient-looking ferns and mosses; interspersed among the gigantic oak trees were magnolias with enormous white blooms and pecan trees heavy with nuts and possessive squirrels.

The variety of creatures living in the forest – raccoons, possums, deer, all manner of birds and creeping things, and the occasional black bear – seemed endless. Berta marveled at how these animals and plants were perfectly content with their place in the world. She couldn't help but wonder what it was about humans that made them constantly question their place in God's divine plan, and in idle moments, she would speculate about her own future, wondering what God intended for her and whether she was prepared for it.

She would often walk on the bluff and observe the river below. Once bustling with traffic, the Trinity was now largely quiet and empty. The packet boats that had made frequent visits to Houston County and occasionally to their dock before the war were now absent, victims of a war that also seemed so far away. Down river in Galveston, the port remained blockaded by a federal naval force. Although the city had been free of the occupying Union troops since January, business activities remained moribund due to the blockade.[44]

On this afternoon, as Berta passed the front veranda she saw the garden and, in particular, the rose bush that her friend, Betty Graves, had given her in May. She was pleased to see that it had a number of blossoms and a promising array of buds, and she reminded herself to take a supply of the flowers back to the college, for both Betty and her father, Dr. Graves. He would likely remember her confusion when he asked her about the plant at their final meeting of the spring session. At the time, she had been confused and uncertain about the idea of love and how she felt about it. Perhaps human nature resembled the river – languid during the dry season, a raging torrent after heavy rains – and the apparent chaos that was such a disruption to her world. Could a person be both gentle and violent? Was it possible for John Wootters to be a sensitive and kind person, but also someone who was capable of glorifying suffering and death? The answer would not come to her. She wondered if it ever would.

As she crossed the veranda and entered the house, she felt a sense of security and comfort surround her. The entrance hall offered a shady refuge from the afternoon heat and still atmosphere. Occasional breezes swept up from the river, circulating cooler air through the house and dispersing the warm air through small openings near the tops of the large windows. The entrance hall had rooms that branched off from either side, rooms that were used for dining or visiting, a library and a music room that accommodated her piano. During the summer months, the kitchen area

---

[44]   Appendix II. Item 13. The Battle of Galveston

was kept cool from the lack of cooking, as those activities were confined to a structure separate from the main house.

Hannah supervised most of the domestic activities, including the meals, which were signaled by a large bell whose ringing could be heard across the property. The bell announced meals not only for the family but also for the more than ninety slaves who worked in the nearby fields and lived on the plantation. Because the Union blockade had halted all transport of the cotton crop to markets, the slaves had redirected their efforts to clearing the forest for firewood, lumber and future farmland and to the production of corn and other crops and livestock, such as hogs and chickens. They lived about one mile inland from the river, on high ground near the church that had been provided by Major Smith.

*   *   *

Berta entered the music room and noted that someone had placed a rose stem in a vase on the piano. The rose bush was flourishing, producing delicate pink blossoms that added color and cheer to the house as well as the garden. Hannah always made sure that one stem was in a vase on the piano and another in the nearby parlor where Anna Jane spent much of her time. Berta played the piano several hours every day and had dutifully worked on the Beethoven sonatas and Chopin pieces over the summer. Since beginning her studies with Count von Godski, her skills had improved significantly. Major Smith and Anna Jane were very pleased with her evident talent.

In addition to taking afternoon walks and practicing piano, Berta spent much of her time reading. She was fond of novels from Europe, especially books by the Bronte sisters, and she loved to pore over the large family Bible. Over the past year or so, she had become interested in the history of the ancient Hebrews and their subsequent Jewish generations as well as the more familiar New Testament scriptures. The community of Daly's had established a small Baptist church, which was more convenient for regular worship than the church in Crockett. Her parents were pleased that she was enthusiastic and curious about her faith.

Lieutenant John Wootters was never far from Berta's mind, and she spent hours writing letters to him. She had not received anything from him recently, but a letter from early in the summer sent to his family in

Crockett had described the dissatisfaction that his company felt at their assignment to the southern Virginia and North Carolina border area. They had been sent there to get food and other supplies that the Army of Northern Virginia needed.[45] While they had succeeded in acquiring substantial supplies of pork and corn, local farmers weren't always eager to give up their crops or livestock. The diet of the Confederates was so meager, Wootters observed, that if the Union troops didn't kill them, starvation probably would. In an attempt at levity, he observed that the plump Union troops were much better targets than the gaunt Confederates. He had written that the greatest disappointment for him and his company was missing out on the battle at Chancellorsville, one of the greatest achievements of General Robert E. Lee and his Army.[46]

By the end of the summer, there had been no further messages from Wootters; Confederate supporters were aware of the disastrous events at Gettysburg, Pennsylvania, and the loss at Vicksburg, Mississippi, which gave control of the Mississippi River to the Federal forces. Further support of the Confederate armies east of the river would not be available from the states west of it, and future communications would be even less dependable. The telegraph carried some information that could only add to the gloom that pervaded Texas.

Hood's Brigade had suffered severe losses at Gettysburg; the First Regiment reported twenty-four men killed and fifty-four wounded. The town of Crockett was shocked by the deaths of the Jones brothers and William House, who had been with John Wootters at the flag ceremony two years previously.[47] Berta was relieved by the news that Wootters had not only survived but had been promoted to first lieutenant and continued as their company commander. She vowed to continue praying for his safe return to Texas as well as for the preservation of his mind and spirit.

*   *   *

As the summer drew to a close, the Smith family remained anxious about the possibility of a Union invasion. Texas had been largely spared

---

[45]   Breiner, T.L. "Pork Belly Politics".

[46]   Catton, B. "Never Call Retreat" p.144-156.

[47]   Mainer, TN, Houston County in the Civil War. P 23-4.

the destruction of warfare, but rumor had it that the presence of Union forces was eminent. Despite these great uncertainties, Berta seemed lighter in spirit and demeanor than she had in some time. Hannah, whose insights were most always accurate, was sure that John Wootters' continued safety and survival accounted for the spring in Berta's step.

Anna Jane and Major Smith also noticed their daughter's unusual radiance. They would be celebrating her sixteenth birthday on Friday, September 4, which coincided with her return to Fairfield for the next college session. Anna Jane, with Hannah's help, had made sure Berta would be appropriately clothed in the frilly and blousy skirts that were the fashion among the daughters of planters' families. Fancy cloth was scarce, but Anna Jane had been able to reuse and redesign older dresses to accommodate her daughter's wardrobe.

Major Smith and Oscar had recently returned from a visit to Crockett with a supply of new ribbon and a message that was both amusing and concerning. He told the family of a conversation overheard at the Masonic Lodge having to do with a certain local family and a gift of sweaters. Although it had taken nearly six months, the ne'er-do-well Jencks, who had previously accosted young Berta about teaching Oscar to read, had observed that his own children were wearing sweaters that he couldn't remember buying. When his youngest, who hadn't yet learned of the expediency of lying, identified the red-haired lady and the old slave as the source of the clothing, even Jencks was able to solve the mystery.

Jencks had confronted Oscar during one of his trips to Crockett and asked him who had given Berta permission to provide his children with such gifts. The somewhat abashed Oscar answered him in a way that Smith's friends at the lodge thought so amusing that they insisted he get a first-hand description of the event from Oscar. So, during their return trip, Major Smith asked him about his run-in with Jencks.

"I was just loading the wagon with parts for the plow that broke, when up comes that white man and he seemed in a rage about something," Oscar said, frowning. "I didn't even see him coming when he started yelling at me. He said, 'Hey, boy, who done tole dat red-headed girl she could give dem clothes to my chilluns?' I didn't know what to say, so I just looked at him and the longer I looked the madder he got. I couldn't think how to answer, so I said that the Lord told her to do it."

Smith couldn't help but laugh at this description of the conversation. "What did he say when you suggested that divine inspiration was behind it?"

"I don't think he knew what I said because he got even madder and said, 'Who is DiLaud and where in the world is dis Dilaud fellow?'" Oscar said. "I was so confused that I said that I didn't know where the Lord is. That just made his face turn even more red, and he still didn't know what I was saying because he said that he wanted to know who this 'Dillard' fellow is and that he and Missy Berta better stop meddling in his family's business."

That was exactly the story Major Smith had heard at the Lodge. What's more, it hadn't taken long for most of Crockett to find out and to have a good laugh at Jencks' expense. And that worried Major Smith, as it was unwise to have such an unpredictable and angry person as an enemy.

"I think it's best for you to avoid any dealings with Jencks, and the next time we have a reason for you to be in Crockett you should send Edgar," Major Smith said. "I doubt that Jencks will connect Edgar to our plantation, and there's no need to make more trouble."

Later that evening as the Smith family was having a celebratory supper in honor of, Berta's birthday and the beginning of a new year at the college, her father related in a stern tone what he had heard in Crockett and from Oscar that afternoon.

"People like Jencks can pose significant dangers to you, Oscar and anyone else he associates with our family," he said, looking directly at Berta. "Please avoid any interaction or association with that man or his family, as even the most innocent gesture will just fuel his hatred. You or anyone else in our family should not leave our property without an escort. Although the sheriff has said that if Jencks causes any more trouble he will 'lock him up and throw away the key,' you must assume responsibility for your own safety."

Berta nodded and looked down at her plate. She was sad to have caused problems for her family and even sadder for the children who had to live with the foul-tempered Jencks, but she would soon be leaving for Fairfield. From that safe distance, it would be no problem to avoid any unpleasant encounters.

XIV

December 1863 – Fairfield, Texas

The autumn of 1863 was a time of resolution for the Confederacy and for Berta who was now in an advanced class of the Fairfield Female College. More than a quarter of the young women expecting to return for the fall session had been unable to do so because of the economic hardships faced by the planters of Texas and throughout the South. Students whose families lived in Louisiana and Mississippi, where the war had become a constant threat, were facing very troubled times.

The faculty and other workers at the College did their best to create an air of stability for the students, but all felt the impending doom that was enveloping the Confederate states. Since the fall of Vicksburg, with the relative isolation of the western areas and the failure at Gettysburg of General Lee's planned invasion of the northern states, only the most optimistic Southerner expected the secession movement to succeed.

Although less widely recognized than the battles at Gettysburg and Vicksburg, the Union army's triumphant Tullahoma Campaign in Tennessee would have profound effects on the outcome of the war. The widely hailed victory of Texans at the Battle of Sabine Pass in September 1863 helped to restore some morale and enthusiasm across the state. The overall outlook for the Confederacy, however, was grim, as the Texas troops could not reach the battlefields in the east due to effective Union blockades.

On her return to college in September, Berta found that her friend and confidante, Betty, had been warmly received back home by her family after her elopement in May. Her husband, William, had been assigned to Walker's Greyhounds, a division made up of twelve regiments from Texas commanded by Major General John George Walker, and had gone immediately to northern Louisiana to try to support the Confederate efforts at Vicksburg.

Betty had resumed her duties at the academy, teaching young students who came daily from their homes in Freestone County; she also continued to nurture the rose garden. Both Betty and Dr. Graves were pleased that Berta brought them souvenir flowers from the plant Betty had given her and that Berta had aptly named 'the rose of love.' In all her sixteen years, Berta had never heard anything quite so romantic as the love story of Betty and William. She marveled that something like it could happen outside of the pages of her treasured European novels.

Still, Berta struggled to understand Betty's distinction between loving with one's mind and with one's heart. She had sought an appropriate opportunity to question her older and wiser friend, and on a particular autumn afternoon when the crisp air represented a distinct change in the seasons, she got her chance. One of the reasons for her interest in visiting with Betty was the confusing feeling she had for John Wootters and the fact that a bond seemed to be developing between them. How could she have such feeling about someone she had not seen in more than two years? They had both experienced so many changes since then that they might not even recognize each other.

*   *   *

Certainly Berta was pleased that her child-like shape had developed into a more womanly figure; she felt confident in her growing attractiveness and maturity. The changes in her thoughts and feelings were a surprise to her as she was becoming aware of a growing desire within herself to nurture and care for others.

Her optimistic spirit had been tempered by the deaths of little Ossie and her dear brother, Lucius. The potential brevity of life and the reality of the separation resulting from death were thoughts that troubled her. Nearly everyone she knew, including her own family, had suffered hardship and upheaval, as lives were disrupted and torn apart by the war between states. It was enough to change her views, not only of the world but of herself.

As Berta approached the rose garden on that autumn afternoon, Betty offered her a smile and a greeting, but the younger woman did not respond with her usual cheer.

"I'm so glad to see you, but I fear that the number of roses in your garden is diminishing as quickly as our hopes for an independent South," Berta said. "I am afraid we are entering a winter that will last much longer than a single season."

"I must say that my cheerful confidante has taken on a cloak of gloom," Betty note. "It doesn't seem natural or fitting for you, Berta. Has something happened?"

"Only the letter received not long ago from my friend John Wootters, who is serving in Tennessee. Or perhaps he is back in Virginia with Hood's Texas Brigade," Berta answered. "He describes events that are so terrible I don't know how the human spirit can bear them. I am sure that his messages temper the reality of the situation. He likely does not want to review in his own mind or for me the actual horrors he has seen."

"Indeed, I understand and share your anxiety about the future," Betty said. "I pray daily that my dear William will return. Whatever you say about the terrible circumstance of the battlefield is certainly true. One cannot have seen those horrors without it having some long-lasting effect on one's mind and spirit. We can only ask God to bring them back and over time make them whole again."

Berta nodded, thinking again about the suffering John Wootters must have witnessed throughout the war and never told her. Sometimes, it was too much to bear. Betty distracted her with a question about Wootters, as she knew the pair had been writing for quite some time. The sun shone brightly as they walked through the garden and only the occasional chill of a breeze reminded them that the cold of winter was around the corner.

So Berta told her how she had met Wootters' family on arriving in Houston County from North Carolina, how his brother, James, had come to Texas to work with their uncle at his merchandise store in Crockett, and how their families had become friends. She recalled how her family attended the Baptist church in Crockett, and it was there she often saw Wootters and became aware of his knowledge of her faith.

"Although he was a grown man, my mother felt sympathy for him because his parents had both died when he was very young and he was raised and educated by relatives on the eastern shore of Maryland," Berta said. "Occasionally I would play piano for our church services, and Mr. Wootters seemed to appreciate it and encouraged my efforts."

Berta joined Betty in cutting dead branches from the bushes. As they continued working, Betty noted how interesting it was that he would notice her friend's musical talent. But Berta, who seemed lost in thought, continued talking. He was one of the first men from Crockett to join the Confederate army in the summer of '61, she pointed out, and he was also chosen to receive the company flag at a ceremony. His words that day had been thoughtful and brave; it would be impossible for Berta to forget them. She admitted to writing him letters that, at first, reflected her own naiveté about the war, and she worried that he may have thought them childish and frivolous.

"After Lucius died, I became very upset when I realized that I had never told him how much I loved him and how proud I was of him. And then he was gone forever," Berta said, choking up a little. "I resolved then never to make that mistake again. That's when the nature of my letters to Mr. Wootters began to change."

She wanted him to know how proud she was and how she respected the commitment he'd made to fight for his country; she wanted him to know that she prayed daily for his safe return. And while he wrote back that he appreciated her sincerity and concern, Berta continued to send him words of encouragement, interspersed with pleas that he not take any foolish risks, as his life was in enough danger already.

"I'm sure your messages have been very reassuring and important to him," Betty said.

"I really am very proud of him," Berta said. "He has been steadily promoted up the ranks and is now first lieutenant and commander of his company.[48] There is no question about his bravery and leadership, but I am concerned about the effects that so much death and destruction must have on his mind and spirit."

After a pause where the only sounds were the buzzing of insects in the garden, Betty smiled and took her friend's hands.

---

[48]   Appendix I. Roster, Co. I, 1 Regiment Texas Volunteers, Texas Brigade, Field's Division, Longstreet's Corp, Army of Northern Virginia, July 15, 1863.

"My dear Berta," she said in a near whisper. "Have you ever considered that you may be in love with Lieutenant Wootters and that what you call friendship may have progressed to something more substantial?"

Berta looked at her friend with skeptical eyes. Of course that wasn't possible. How could she be in love with someone she hadn't seen in two years and then when she wasn't much more than a child? He could have changed so much that she might not even want to continue the friendship. Berta shook her head. No, that wasn't the answer. She was certain.

"I appreciate your opinion, Betty, since you are the person with whom I would be comfortable having a conversation about love," she said. "You had mentioned last spring before your marriage that you and William were very much in love. Ever since then, I have struggled to understand what you meant."

Betty's gaze drifted to the mounting clouds in the eastern sky and how they reflected the light of the setting sun. She paused briefly to catch her breath and blink away a small tear before continuing.

"William and I knew that we were in love, and we have publicly declared and vowed to honor that love forever," Betty said. "To describe how we knew it was love isn't easy to do. I will do my best to share some of my feelings and ideas. You can form your own conclusions."

Berta could not immediately respond to her friend's reaction, but she was reassured when Betty took her arm and walked with her to a nearby garden bench. In this shady spot, she continued. She spoke of the Biblical meanings of love, the love of God, sacrificial love and the unconditional love that Christ had for his followers and for all people. But an easier way, she noted, to describe love as a bond between a man and woman was the ability to love with mind and heart. Loving with the mind implied rational thought, while loving with the heart was a more emotional experience.

"I think that an enduring love has to involve an agreement between one's mind and one's heart," Betty said. "Without that agreement, it's difficult to imagine a substantial foundation for one's life."

Berta listened with rapt attention as understanding dawned on her. Her feelings for John Wootters, which were coming straight from the heart, had not been tempered by much thought. She realized that now, and she decided to pray for guidance.

"I will nevertheless continue to write him letters of encouragement," Berta announced. "Now, wise friend, we need to store these garden tools and put these few rose stems in some water as we will be expected at supper very soon."

*   *   *

Fairfield provided a secure home for Berta, where she could improve her musical skills and general education. Count von Godski had departed the college for adventures in California, but Berta's playing continued to develop. She was now frequently the pianist at the Baptist church in Fairfield, where her own faith was nurtured. Her greatest pleasure at the college, however, came from the friendships she had with the other students. As there were no significant opportunities for social interactions outside the college, the young women amused themselves when not occupied by their studies. In the afternoon they would play games on the college grounds or stroll among the gardens and wooded areas of the property.

Dinner time remained a formal affair for the students. They were expected to arrive promptly at the designated time, dressed in their elegant dresses and white gloves. The workers at the college included seven slaves that Dr. Graves had assigned to help the young women with the housekeeping chores and their clothing, which was always kept cleaned and ironed and in appropriate condition. During the evening hours, the girls would occasionally amuse themselves by holding balls, during which they danced to their own music. Not having male dancing partners, some of the taller girls would dress the part and dramatize the roles of gallant escorts, even fashioning mustaches after the style of Count von Godski who, even in his absence, was a source of amusement.[49]

The evening entertainment would be interrupted by the bedtime ringing of the bell, after which one of the teachers would make rounds to assure that all were in bed. Occassional late-night visits would be cut short by the teacher on duty. For Berta, the coming of the Christmas season marked the end of the fall session at the college and the return to the Smith Landing Plantation, where she hoped a new letter from Lieutenant Wootters would be waiting for her.

---

[49]   Burks, C. "Fairfield Female College."

XV

1864 – Fairfield, Texas

T he Union victory at Vicksburg in July 1863 had isolated the western Confederate states from the battlefields in Tennessee, Georgia and Virginia. The blockade of the Mississippi River and the Gulf of Mexico by the Union Navy helped to prevent any movement of troops from west to east. In Texas, the year had begun with the Confederate re-capture of Galveston and ended with the dramatic defeat of the Union invasion at Sabine Pass, but frustration was running high due to the state's inability to get past Union blockades and contribute to the southland's effort.[50]

While messages from John Wootters continued to be sporadic, Berta learned of his promotion to captain of his company in March 1864.[51] He reported that the boredom of the brigade's long winter camp near Knoxville, Tennessee, and the uncertainty of future assignments had ended when the Texas Brigade, now under the command of Brigadier General John Gregg, received orders to return to Virginia at the end of March. General Lee was preparing for whatever the new commanding General of the Union Army, Ulysses S. Grant, might order.[52] The Texas Division and all of General Longstreet's Corps would rejoin the Army of Northern Virginia in an attempt to thwart General Grant's strategy to capture Richmond.

---

[50] Appendix II. Item 17. The Battle of Sabine Pass.
[51] Appendix I. Roster of Commissioned Officers, Provisional Army Confederate States, Promoted Mar. 13, 1864.
[52] Appendix II. Item 22. Union Army Generals

In early 1864, a large Union force was threatening the city of Shreveport, Louisiana; their success would open a direct route for an invasion of Texas. Following the defeat at Vicksburg the previous summer, the Walker Greyhounds and other Texas units had spent months marching in Arkansas and Louisiana without encountering significant combat. The mud, mosquitoes and hardships of the swamps and marshes had claimed the lives of many of the troops.[53] Morale was at a low point until February 1864 when they were placed under the command of Brigadier General T.N. Waul and assigned to the command of Major General Richard Taylor.[54] Their mission was to counter the invasion of the Federal army, which was now advancing up the Red River toward Shreveport.

The staff of the Fairfield Female College tried to remain cheerfully optimistic, and the young ladies in the now smaller college class continued their routine of studies. More than half of the students expected for the spring session had been unable to return.

Berta had assumed new duties, assisting her closest friend and confidant Betty Graves in teaching of the younger students at the academy. She followed her usual study program, which included piano exercises, and often provided music for the Fairfield Baptist Church. One morning in mid-May, Berta arrived in the classroom to help Betty and found she wasn't there. She instructed the students to continue reading their lessons from the previous session.

Half an hour passed and still there was no sign of her friend. Berta grew increasingly concerned; it wasn't like Betty to miss a class. Moments later, a faculty member appeared in the doorway, her face ashen. Berta felt a terrible knot of anxiety form in her stomach.

"Miss Smith, would you please come into the hallway for a moment?"

Once out of earshot of the students, the teacher spoke in a hushed voice.

"The most terrible circumstance has come upon us, and you must know that Miss Graves will not be attending your sessions this morning."

"Oh dear Lord, what has happened to Betty?" Berta felt tightness in her chest and throat.

---

[53] Appendix II. Item 18. Walker's Texas Division, the Red River Campaign and the Battle of Mansfield

[54] General Richard Taylor was the son of former U.S. President Zachary Taylor.

"I don't know for certain, but there was a commotion at the front entrance just as everyone had left the dining room. A messenger from the Fairfield post office apparently delivered a letter to her, and I'm told that she collapsed and was being assisted to her bedroom by her parents."

Berta's mind flashed to the memory of the postmaster and minister arriving at Smith Landing. She knew immediately the contents of the letter-- that dreaded message of regret from the Army. Covering her mouth with her hand, she could only utter, "Her dear William."

Later that day she learned what the message said. William had received a mortal wound in his service with the Waul's Brigade of the Texas Division in the battle at Mansfield, Louisiana. He had been taken to the nearby Keatchi Women's College, which had been converted to a hospital for the wounded Confederates. Despite their efforts, he died in the company of his fellow soldiers and was buried with full military honors with one hundred other members of Walker's Texas Division in a cemetery at the college.

Berta was initially overwhelmed, not only by her own grief and remembering the loss of her brother Lucius but also by her awareness of how much her dear friend Betty must be suffering. Betty had apparently collapsed before being assisted to her living quarters, where she remained sobbing uncontrollably.

Dr. Graves did his best to reassure Berta and her classmates that Betty was being attended by her mother and there was nothing else for them to do except to keep her in their prayers. Berta prayed that William would be received into the heavenly home promised to those who loved the Lord, and she prayed that Betty would somehow be able to find the peace that could heal her mind and her heart.

The next day, with the permission of Dr. and Mrs. Graves, Berta knocked on the door of Betty's room.

"Betty, my dear friend, it is Berta," she said. "With your permission, I would like to come in." After a few minutes with no response, Berta again spoke, this time more loudly. "Betty, if my presence does not add to your burden, it would help relieve my grieving heart to see you and hear your voice."

Berta heard movement from behind the door, and in another moment it opened slowly to reveal Betty, her eyes red and swollen.

"I am in no condition to be presented to any polite company," she said. "But if seeing me will relieve your mind, please come in."

On entering the bedroom, Berta offered her friend a rose from the special bush that, to her, represented William and Betty's love. The young women clung to each other. It was clear that Betty, whose hair and clothing were always arranged with the utmost care, had not changed her clothes since receiving the dreadful message.

"I have been so anxious about you as have all of your friends," Berta said. "Just to see you standing upright is a blessing to my saddened soul. Although your heart may be broken, the pain is shared by many who have been lifting you up in our prayers."

Betty, tear-streaked and disheveled, sat down on a divan, the rose resting on her lap. She gazed at the flower, twisting the simple gold band on the fourth finger of her left hand; the shadows under her eyes accentuated the pallor in her cheeks.

"I just don't know how I can go on," she said, her eyes filling again with tears. "The past day has been more than my mind can bear. I can't see any prospect for happiness."

"Few people can understand the grief that you feel," Berta said. "Many of us are sharing a small part of your pain, and we are praying for you to receive the peace that our Lord can provide."

"Indeed, Berta, you know that our Lord assures us that we will never be given a burden that we are unable to bear," Betty said in a quiet voice. "He promises that we will have the strength to overcome any grief we experience. Time will eventually heal my wounds. I know that William's pain is over and that he will have eternal peace. Someday I will join him in God's presence."

Betty's gaze wandered to the soft clouds drifting past her window, and Berta noted with some relief that her breathing was slowing down. She knew that her friend would never completely recover from this, that she would likely carry the scar on her spirit forever. But she hoped that Betty would recover enough to live a rich, fulfilling life.

"Please know your friends are outside praying for your mind and heart to heal," Berta said. "When you are able to join us, the grief will be much lifted from our hearts and from those of your family. We are here to love and support you in this desperate time."

Berta got up to excuse herself and saw that Betty was holding the rose close to her heart, a sad smile on her face. "We all love you," Berta said.

*   *   *

The following day, college activities continued as usual, but a sense of gloom pervaded everything, from classroom sessions and study periods to recreational time. In place of the usual games and laughter, small groups of friends quietly discussed the disaster of war and the irreplaceable loss of loved ones. Many of the girls could identify with Betty as they had lost family members or friends in the war; some had lost their homes. Also absent was the irrepressible optimism about the future that girls their age typically embraced.

The evening meal was heralded by the usual ringing of the college bell. On this occasion every student was prompt in attendance as Dr. Graves blessed the food. Before the dishes had been placed on the table, the door at the back of the room opened and there stood a well-groomed Betty. Applause broke out across the room, as every girl stood up and clapped. Dr. Graves came forward to embrace his daughter and help her to her usual seat at the head table. As everyone sat back down, Betty rose from her chair and silence fell on the entire gathering. Even the servers stopped what they were doing as Betty spoke.

"My dear friends and family, I want you to know of my regret for any grief or anxiety that I have caused during the past days, and I want to express my heartfelt thanks for your prayers and friendship during this terrible time," she said. "Although I know William will not be returning to me, I have asked God to help me understand my feelings, and I am certain that he has sent me the love and affection of my friends and family to help calm my troubled mind. It gives me strength to know that we will all lift each other up as we go forward to face an uncertain future. Again, I thank you for your friendship and for this Fairfield Academy and College, which reassures me that we will continue to have a place to serve and learn in this world."

As she took her seat, the meal was served and conversation resumed, albeit at a more subdued level. It was clear to everyone present that although life would go on, it would never be the same for Betty, for this group of young women or for the southland.

*   *   *

The spring session at Fairfield College concluded in late May, and the girls prepared to return to home for the summer. Back at Smith Landing Plantation, Berta wondered what the future held for her and her family. Then, in mid-July a telegraph message arrived in Crockett informing them that Captain John Wootters had been wounded at Bermuda Hundred[55], Virginia en route to Petersburg and that he had been taken to Richmond for medical care. [56] His friends and family in Houston County did not know the extent of his injury, nor did they know how he was currently faring.

Not surprisingly, the news of Captain Wootters' injury and hospitalization caused Berta no end of distress. She was concerned that he might lose an arm or leg, as she was aware that amputation was often the expedient solution to badly injured limbs. Equally troubling was the fact that many soldiers and veterans who suffered those kinds of injuries often took to drinking to dull the constant pain. But what bothered her most was the relief she felt at hearing that John Wootters had been wounded. To her, the news wasn't necessarily bad; rather, it meant that he would no longer be able to serve in active combat. He was almost certain to survive the war, and would be returning to Houston County perhaps sooner than expected. It was, in some ways, the best news Berta could have wished for.

The news about her mother's health, however, wasn't quite as positive. Anna Jane had suffered a prolonged illness earlier in the summer and been so weakened by it that there had been some concern she wouldn't survive. But she had gradually regained her strength and was now able to join her family for longer periods.

On one particular evening, they were sitting on the veranda overlooking the approach to the front of the house and the Trinity River. It was late in the season, and the flow of the current was slower than usual; the spring rains were a distant memory. It seemed unlikely that the packet boats from Galveston could manage the shallow water. Indeed, it had been so long since anyone in Houston County had seen them that the subject never came up. Back on the veranda, Berta asked her father about issues that were on her mind.

---

[55]   Appendix II. Item 21. Bermuda Hundred.

[56]   Appendix I. Report of the 1st Regiment Texas Infantry. JH Wootters, June 17, 1864, Wounded right arm, severe. Register of General Hospital No. 9. Richmond, Virginia. Admitted June 17, To Howard Grove, June 19, 1864.

"It's nearly time for me to return to Fairfield College, and I want to thank you and Mother for sending me there," she said. "I miss my dear classmates and teachers and hope that the college will continue despite this terrible war."

"We would do anything to see that you continue," her father smiled and nodded. "The reports we have received from Dr. Graves indicate that you have benefited greatly from these experiences."

Her mother nodded in agreement. "You seem to have talents not only in your music but also in your academic studies," she said. "Dr. Graves says those talents should be nurtured beyond what he can offer at Fairfield. But the future is so uncertain we can only take one year at a time."

Major Smith frowned, his mouth a grim line. He and Anna Jane weren't optimistic about the future; in his heart, he knew it was only a matter of time before the Confederate troops were defeated and the Federal government declared all slaves to be free citizens. When that happened, he feared chaos would follow, which would benefit neither landowners nor slaves. Many of their slaves and their families before them had served the Smiths and the Pounceys for generations, and both Anna Jane and Major Smith felt obligated to help these dependents survive and succeed, whatever the future might hold. Smith Landing Plantation could not survive without the workers that tended the crops and livestock nor without those slaves, like Hannah, who tended to the family's personal needs. To that end, Major Smith would arrange for them to own land in their own right, as surely the laws in Texas would change to allow freed slaves to own property.

"I have discussed these matters with my friends in Crockett who have legal and judicial experience, and we will be preparing documents with provisions regarding the transfer of some property to each of the families who want to remain in this area," Major Smith said. "Those who are able will continue to plant and will share in the value we receive for our crops. And over time, they can pay for their land."

It seemed a logical approach to the situation. Things were uncertain and changing from day to day. It could be dangerous for their slaves to have no place to call their own, Major Smith noted, as a defeated southland could also be a very hostile one, particularly in regards to freed slaves. Those who chose to leave could be subject to laws they did not understand. He already planned to meet with Oscar and Edgar and the heads of other slave families to lay out his plan and discuss their reaction to potential changes that lay head. A number of slaves had disappeared from plantations near Crockett, and the militia had been on alert for the possibility of any major disturbances.

"Hannah and her family are very loyal to you and Mother, and many of them already consider the church and the cemetery that you provided for them to be their own domain," Berta said. "I am sure that once free, some will want to remain here, where they have the security of a home of their own."

Berta also had an idea brewing. Although her run-in with the cranky Jencks in past years years had stayed with her. It had also inspired her to teach the slaves to read and write, if for no other reason than to prove that they could.

"Although I am certainly not as mad at him as I once was, I still don't like him at all," she told her parents. "But I must confess that it would give me pleasure to see his expression if Oscar was to read him one of Shakespeare's soliloquies from Hamlet."

"Now Berta, I am sure that some level of forgiveness may be available to you for harboring such thoughts, but the penitence would likely be long and arduous!" Major Smith said, attempting to smile. "I am confident that Oscar would have enough sense not to do such a thing, even if he were able to recite the part from memory. And I would urge you to temper your zeal for spreading knowledge, at least until we have a better idea about the future."

*   *   *

A few weeks later Berta returned to her beloved college for the fall session and immersed herself in her studies and the duties that marked her year as a member of the senior class. She had been at the school for only a few weeks before she was notified that Edgar, Hannah and Oscar's son had arrived with a message for her.

Such visits made her anxious, as they were usually precipitated by bad news. On arriving, Edgar told her that Hannah and her parents had sent him with a copy of a letter sent to Captain John Wootters' family in Crockett. Edgar didn't know exactly what was in the letter, but that his mother told him that Miss Berta would want to know of it without delay. He had ridden his horse to the limit of its capacity to comply with her request.

Relief flooded Berta, as she had imagined the worst: that the emergency involved one of her parents. Opening the letter, she nearly fainted on reading the first lines. It was a copy of a terse telegraph message received in Marshall and carried to Crockett by a messenger as the wires between the towns were temporarily disrupted. It read: "Capt. John H. Wootters is on leave from the 1st Reg't. Tex and reassigned to the Trans-Mississippi Dept. for the purpose of recruiting duty in Texas. Will report directly to Gen. Edmund Kirby Smith on his arrival in the state. By Order of the Secy War, James A. Seddon."[57]

John Wootters, it seemed, was at long last coming home.

---

[57] Appendix I. Inspection Report P, No. 51; enclosure 13. – Inspection Report of the Texas Brigade, Field's Division, 1st Army Corps, commanded by Col. F.S. Bass. Absent commissioned officers accounted for: By what authority - J.H. Wootters, Capt 1 Regt. Tex – Report dated: Exterior Line Richmond Defenses Chas City Road Jan 17, 1865 – Recruiting in Texas – Secy War, August 1864.

XVI

Winter 1864 – Smith Landing Plantation

O n September 2, 1864, the Confederacy's faint hopes of maintaining its independence vanished with the fall of Atlanta to the Union Army. That victory also virtually guaranteed President Lincoln's re-election, and two months later, the Radical Republicans gained a veto-proof majority in the U.S. House and Senate.[58] The Confederate forces had not been able to slow the progress of Union troops in either Tennessee or Georgia, and as the ranks of Union soldiers grew in number, the ultimate outcome appeared inevitable.[59]

As the Federal policy was to use emancipation as a military and political strategy, it was clear that social disruption across the South would proceed as rapidly as the invading Union forces. Major John Smith had considered these matters, along with their inevitable outcome, and made plans to transfer ownership of some property to his slave families. Many of the slaves at the Smith Landing Plantation welcomed this solution. The Cedar Branch community had become an entity centered on its church; the stability of the plantation and security of its residents and their homes seemed assured.

---

[58] Appendix II. Item 19. Presidential Election of 1864 (from the Library of Congress)

[59] Catton, B. Never Call Retreat. pp. 383-395.

With Hannah's devoted attention, Anna Jane managed to keep up her strength and stamina despite the cold winter weather. At the Fairfield Female College, Berta was nearing the close of the fall session, and everyone involved seemed pleased with her developing skills as a teacher of the academy's younger students. It was apparent to the faculty that Berta had considerable talent working with the children. Her piano studies continued to progress but at a slower rate, as her schedule did not allow her as much time to practice.

Among the things she most treasured were the friendships she had formed with her classmates. Only seven girls remained in her senior class, and although they had very different personalities, their unique camaraderie and sharing a love of the College gave them great comfort. With activities and friendships to fill her time, Berta was less anxious about the lack of communication from Captain Wootters, particularly since he was no longer on the battlefield. Moreover, she knew the journey from Richmond, Virginia to his new assignment in Texas would be arduous, so she did not expect to have any news from him for some time. She nevertheless continued to pray for his safety.

Back in Houston County, Major Smith was satisfied that life could move forward, for his family and his property despite the hopeless outlook for the Confederacy, and he remained fully engaged in the daily operations of the plantation. Although the economy of Texas and the entire Confederacy was in a disastrous condition, the plantation was nearly self-sufficient and able to provide for the needs of those who lived and worked on it. The Confederate currency was useless, merchandise goods were essentially unavailable for purchase at any price, and cotton production had come to a complete standstill as there was no market for the product. Warehouses throughout Texas and northern Louisiana were filled to overflowing with bales of cotton.

Across East Texas, information and news was slow to arrive. The telegraph was the only dependable source of communication, and even that was only occasionally so. There had been no further word concerning Captain John Wootters since August, when his family and friends were informed of his re-assignment to recruiting duty in Texas. The extent and effects of his injury were unknown.

At Smith Landing Plantation, Edgar had taken on more of the supervisory duties as his father, Oscar, showed signs of slowing down with age. Major Smith was pleased with Edgar's leadership and his ability to encourage productivity among the workers without treating them harshly, as was suspected at neighboring plantations. Major Smith had always considered his slaves an asset of his property and believed that a valuable asset should be treated well.

Dusk arrived early on those December evenings, and the campfires in the slave community would glow brightly. On one particular night, Smith was standing in the roadway discussing the next day's plans with Edgar when a rider appeared at the distant end of the drive. Smith assumed that someone had lost his way while looking for the branch in the road that led to the Trinity River crossing. But as the figure slowly emerged from the shadows, they could see that he wore the military uniform of the Confederacy. It was then that Smith recognized the soldier.

"My God in Heaven, if it isn't Captain Wootters!"

Even as he spoke the words, Smith felt a twinge of uncertainty. The soldier's face was both familiar and unknown to him, and yet it must be Captain Wootters. What other Confederate captain would appear at his home on a chilly December night? The soldier's right hand and wrist were tucked inside his jacket, and he was holding the horse's reins with his left hand; he was lean to the point of appearing gaunt, and his face was covered by a well-trimmed beard, which contrasted sharply with his pallor.

"Truly, Major Smith," the mounted figure replied. "It is Captain Wootters, or what is left of him."

"Please come into my home as no one could be more welcome than yourself," Major Smith said. "I cannot tell you how pleased I am that you are back in Texas. Come inside and Edgar will take care of your horse." The slave took the reins from Captain Wootters as Major Smith gestured to him to come inside.

"Edgar, tell Hannah that we have a special guest for dinner," he said. "Anna Jane will be delighted that you are here this evening."

Wootters slowly dismounted and extended his left hand to Smith who clasped it in his two outstretched hands.

"Excuse my left hand, Major Smith, but the grip in my right hand is not sufficient to express the warmth of my greeting," Wootters said.

"That doesn't matter," Smith said. "What matters is that you are here. Please come inside our home where you can warm your arm and your spirits."

The two men entered the hallway from the veranda, but before they could advance beyond the front door, Hannah burst in from the rear entrance. She made straight for Captain Wootters, weeping openly, and encircled his gaunt body with her abundant arms.

"Oh, Dear Lord, thank you for answering our prayers!" she cried. "My goodness, Captain, you look like you could use a good meal and you have come to the right place for that. You can't know how hard we've been praying for your safe return."

"Hannah, it's been so long since I have been in Texas that I wouldn't recognize you if our friend Berta didn't tell me about you in her letters," Wootters said, at last smiling. "It is good to be back home, and I would much appreciate a warm supper."

They entered the parlor where Anna Jane usually sat in front of the fireplace and found her standing, a broad smile lighting up her face.

"Oh, Captain Wootters, it is so good to see you," she exclaimed. "I hope you are visiting long enough to tell us all about yourself and how your injury is progressing. Please come in and make yourself comfortable. I know Hannah will be setting a place for you at the table."

"Indeed, Mrs. Smith, a warm room and a good meal are just what my mind, body and soul have been longing for," Wootters replied. "I can't think of a more delightful place to enjoy them than in your gracious home."

Major Smith offered the young man a comfortable chair and asked Oscar, who was in eager attendance, to bring them a spot of bourbon, the special reserve that he kept in the library for honored guests. Turning back to Captain Wootters, he asked him to recount what had occurred over the past months and what he was planning to do now that his new assignment had sent him back to Texas.

* * *

In the brighter light of the parlor, the Smiths could more clearly see their visitor, and the changes in his appearance were stark. Other than his much leaner figure and right arm, which was supported by a sling, his face showed lines of worry and the sparkle in his normally bright eyes had dimmed. There was no evidence of the smiling face they had first encountered at the mercantile store three and a half years earlier. And when standing, he stood erect, as if expecting to review the troops and give them the orders of the day. John Wootters was indeed a changed man.

Oscar offered the visitor a portion of the special whiskey, and Wootters sipped it gratefully, staring at the fire before turning back to the Smiths.

"So much has changed in my life in the past half year that I can barely recognize myself or my homeland," he said. "There may not be enough pages in an entire library to describe all that has occurred, but of greatest interest to me is to know how the Smith family is faring and how Berta is getting along at Fairfield College."

Anna Jane nodded and went on to tell him that her daughter was well and making a good record at the school. The college was certainly the bright spot in her life, she noted, as it seemed to lessen the melancholy Berta felt when at home, which her mother was sure had to do with continuing sadness over the loss of Lucius and anxiety about Captain Wootter's own welfare. Berta had grown into a very capable young lady.

"Her skills at the piano are improving nicely, and she often mentions the need to practice so she can play pieces for you," Anna Jane said. "She remembers your interest in her music and your encouragement."

As Wootters listened to the news about Berta, he thought that nothing would please him more than to hear her play again. He hoped the opportunity would present itself soon. Unfortunately, it would have to wait a little longer. His orders were to first report to General Edmund Kirby Smith in Marshall, which he had already done, and then proceed to Galveston to meet with Colonel Ashbel Smith. After visiting briefly with his family in Crockett, Wootters would make his way to the port city.

He expressed concern to Major Smith about the state of the Confederate Army in Texas and General Kirby Smith's ability to inspire loyalty and make good, strategic decisions. General Smith had a long and distinguished military career, and had served the Confederacy well in the early years of the war at First Manassas and in Tennessee. As commander of the Trans-Mississippi Department, he had been instrumental in stopping the Union Army's Red River Campaign.[60] Since then, however, he had made

---

[60]   Shehan-Dean, A. Struggle for a Vast Future: The American Civil War.

unpopular – and unwise – decisions that had led to unrest among the Texas troops.

"The number of desertions from our Texas regiments is increasing daily, and those who stay are often disregarding the orders of their superior officers," Wootters told Major Smith. "There have been reports of soldiers stealing equipment and supplies from the storehouses to sell or barter for their own benefit, which demeans the sacrifices that have been honorably made by so many. General Hood would never tolerate such behavior."

Smith could see the tension building in Wootters' face as his eyes narrowed and the lines across his forehead deepened. Hoping to diffuse the mounting tension, Anna Jane beckoned the men into the dining room in her most cheerful voice. Once they were seated at the table, the conversation turned to Wootters' physical well-being and the responsibilities of his new assignment in Galveston. He had been wounded on June 17th, a day etched forever in his memory. The Crockett Southrons, along with what was left of the First Texas, were moving towards the city of Petersburg, after spending several days awaiting orders at the town of Bermuda Hundred, near where the James and Appomattox Rivers join east of Richmond in Virginia.

Biding one's time was a frequent activity for soldiers, he told them, and after the terrible battle of Cold Harbor, there was some uncertainty as to what Ulysses S. Grant and his army would do next.[61] When it became apparent that his objective was to capture Petersburg, General Fields' Texas Division was directed to go there and join the troops of General PGT Beauregard's command.

On that fateful day the sunlight was beginning to fade, as the Crockett Southrons were in camp for the night, when a Union sniper's bullet ended Wootters' service to that company.[62] His arm was flung into the air with an uncontrollable force that brought him to the ground and, in that instant, Wootters knew that he'd been hit. A searing pain coursed through his arm; soldiers around him fell to the ground, expecting further gunfire, but none came.

---

[61] Appendix II. Item 20. The 1864 Overland Campaign--The Wilderness to Cold Harbor.

[62] Appendix I. Report 1st (First) Texas: J.H. Wooters (sic) Capt., Co. I, 1Regiment Texas Infantry, Appears on a Report of casualties in the 1st Regiment Texas Infantry for A.D. 1864. June 17, 1864 Wounded right wrist-severe.

"I felt a terrible pain in my arm and then nothing," Wootters told them. "It was just numb, and I couldn't move my hand. Unfortunately, those problems have largely persisted."

Lieutenant Aldrich, another soldier from Crockett, helped secure Wootters' damaged arm and took him to a more protected location. The next few hours were a blurred memory, but soon he found himself on horseback and heading toward Richmond about ten miles away.

Anna and John's attention was so focused on Wootters that they didn't realize Hannah had come into the room carrying a tray of additional servings. She placed the tray on the table and stood quietly as he continued talking.

"We were directed to the Receiving and Wayside Hospital, and by daybreak it seemed this would be my new abode,[63]" he said. "As the sun rose over Richmond that morning, I knew I had likely spent my last day with the comrades with whom I had shared breakfast every morning for three years."

The receiving hospital, he later learned, had been a municipal tobacco warehouse; in wartime, however, it was receiving up to 3,000 patients every month.[64] Anna Jane shook her head, unable to imagine so many wounded young men lying in makeshift beds so far from home. From there, as he could not rejoin his unit, Wootters was transferred to Howard's Grove Hospital.[65] Once a picnic and recreation area, Howard's Grove had been converted to a hospital with more than sixty buildings and accommodations for up to 1,800 patients. It was nearly a city unto itself, with its own water supply, laundry, bakery, storehouses and other facilities.

Wootters continued his tale, as Major Smith and Anna Jane sat in grim silence, the remains of their dinner growing cold. Over the next few weeks, Wootters had received attentive and excellent medical advice from the surgeon-in-charge, Dr. T.M. Palmer. He reported to Dr. William A.

---

[63]   Appendix I. Arch., Chap. 6, File No. 108, page 719. JH Wooters (sic) Appears on a Register of Receiving and Wayside Hospital, or General Hospital No. 9, Richmond, Virginia, Admitted June 17, 1864, Disposition Howard Grove, June 19, 1864.

[64]   Information about General Hospital #9 in Richmond, VA during the Civil War. From Civil War Richmond.

[65]   Information about Howard's Grove Hospital in Richmond VA during the Civil War. From Civil War Richmond,

Carrington, medical director of Virginia Hospitals, who earlier in the war had served as the surgeon of the Seventh Virginia Regiment.[66] Even though the physicians and surgeons in attendance were highly skilled, they were limited in number; nor were there enough attendants to care for the patients.

The Richmond newspapers often published pleas for ladies to visit or to lend their servants to assist in the care of the men.[67] One of the services these ladies rendered was to assist the wounded in writing letters. Because of the injury to his right arm, Wootters could not hold a pen; however, a Richmond matron helped him write a letter to the family of E.M. Oliver, one of the privates who fought with him in Company I and had died in battle.

The painful duty of informing the Oliver family of their loved one's death was the last official function Wootters provided for Company I and the First Texas Infantry. Of the original 110 men who marched away from Crockett on that warm day in July three years ago, only nine remained alive and uninjured.[68] "The sadness and the knowledge of that fact will stay with me forever," Wootters said.

On the afternoon of his arrival at Howard's Grove Hospital, Dr. Palmer examined Wootters' wound; his arm and hand still had no sense of feeling. Following the examination, Palmer told the young soldier that the future mobility of his arm remained in doubt, as the ulnar bone, while intact, was chipped and the radius had been crushed; the latter would likely not heal.

It was miraculous, in fact, that the shot had not severed any major arteries and that his nerves did not appear to be affected. This last was a point of optimism, as Palmer would not have to amputate the arm. He did, however, need to perform surgery to remove bone fragments and damaged tissue. Only time would tell how much function Wootters would eventually regain in his arm and hand, but surgery would certainly help things along.

*   *   *

---

66   T.M. Palmer CSR, M331, National Archives, Civil War Richmond.

67   Richmond Examiner, 5/17/1864, Civil War Richmond.

68   Mainer, T.N., Houston County in the Civil War, p. 31.

At this point in Wootters' narrative, the Smiths had lost all interest in the meal. Their full attention was directed to their guest. Major Smith placed an additional log on the fire and motioned for Hannah to sit on a side chair so that she could continue listening.

"I told Dr. Palmer that the past six weeks had shown me that the outlook for our Confederacy was bleak," Wootters said. He stood and briefly paced around the dining room, rubbing his weakened right arm. "The battle at Cold Harbor resulted in a slaughter of their troops that would be appalling to anyone, regardless of what we have experienced in past years.[69] Any commander who regards the lives of his troops so cheaply as seen in these actions of the Union Army poses problems that the southland will not be able to overcome."

When Wootters took his seat at the table, there was no trace of a smile on his handsome face. "Dr. Palmer later indicated that I was probably not familiar with the order of President Lincoln for the conscription of 500,000 men by the Ides of March. Of course I knew nothing about such information,[70]" he said, looking directly at Major Smith. "We agreed that it was best to not share that news with the men in the field as it could be very discouraging to our effort."

Major Smith understood and nodded in agreement. Instead, he expressed his family's thanks that Wootters had seen some progress in his health and urged the younger man to eat his fill, as he had lost much weight in the past three years. It would also not do to disappoint Hannah, who liked nothing better than to see people enjoying her cooking.

"When we received a copy of the wire indicating that you were returning to Texas for recruiting purposes, we couldn't help but wonder where you could possibly find enough men to form a single regiment," Major Smith said to Wootters. "The eastern states must be equally or even more depleted of men than Texas."

His assumption was correct. As Wootters went on to tell them, his arm had improved noticeably by early August, but had not progressed beyond that. While he was determined to rejoin his company, Dr. Palmer advised

---

[69] Appendix II. Item 20. The Overland Campaign: From The Wilderness to Cold Harbor.

[70] "The Draft for Half A Million of Men", New York Times, February 1, 1864, The New York Times Complete Civil War. p. 300.

him against it and within twenty-four hours, Wootters had received a summons to report to the General Headquarters of the Army of Northern Virginia. It seemed that Dr. Palmer had practiced medicine in Richmond for years before the war and was highly regarded among that city's elite. Wootters suspected the good doctor was behind his new orders.

Fortunately, the hospital staff were able to procure a proper uniform for him; he was, in fact, still wearing it. He was to meet with a senior general, and he was, under no circumstances, to complain or question anything that was said or prolong the conversation in any way. This last order brought a smile to Major Smith's face. Hannah, who had been serving berry cobbler, stopped abruptly to listen.

"I was ushered into a room at the headquarters, where a number of staff officers were meeting, and was stunned to see General Lee sitting at the table," Wootters continued. "I saluted him, which required that I use my left hand to prop up my right wrist, and General Lee introduced me to the group as a member of Hood's Texas Brigade which had tried to give him orders."

General Lee continued by saying that Wootters' unit had ordered him to take a position at the back of the brigade when he was attempting to lead us in an attack on the Union line at the Wilderness.

"What did you say when the General took you to task in front of the other officers?" Anna Jane asked. "What did you do?"

"I was stunned and could only remain at attention, feeling my pulse beat at a might pace," Wootters said. "I did manage to say that it was the best order ever given, and we had no regrets about it."

It was then that General Lee admitted the intelligence of the Texan's plan, while also indicating that he would be the one to give any new orders. For now, he told the officers, Wootters would not return to his company at Petersburg and would instead be reassigned to recruiting duty in Texas. Furthermore, Wootters was to deliver two messages: one to General Edmund Kirby Smith announcing his presence and assignment, and another to Colonel Ashbel Smith with the Second Texas Infantry in Galveston concerning the injury to his own right arm. After issuing those orders, General Lee told Wootters he was dismissed, and wished him a safe passage and a successful journey.

Colonel Ashbel Smith was a highly respected physician who had served with General Lee in the war with Mexico and whose medical advice was highly valued. It seemed that Colonel Smith had also suffered an arm injury – his in the battle of Shiloh – and might have some personal experience to share. The group sat silently as all were stunned by what they had heard.

"I must say, Captain Wootters, when General Robert E. Lee issues an order and it is signed by the Secretary of War, it would be unlikely that anyone would question the directive," Major Smith said.

"I agree, sir, but I must confess that leaving my troops is much more difficult for my mind to accept than anticipating a direct assault on any enemy position," Wootters said. "I must, however, agree with you that an order from General Lee would be willingly accepted by any soldier who has served with him. If he were to order us to walk on water, I suspect all of his troops would try to do just that."

As Hannah finished serving the cobbler, Oscar stoked the fire, which began to burn more brightly. With his story told and the whisky warming him from the inside out, Wootters finally reached a degree of contentment.

"I don't recall ever having such a fine meal, certainly not since being in the army or even before leaving Crockett," he said to his hosts. "You are more than kind to provide such a feast."

"Captain Wootters, we are so thankful that you are back in Texas, and we hope that you never have to face such horrors again," Anna Jane said, going slightly pale. "I will pray that this violence has not left scars on your mind and spirit and, if so, that the Lord helps to heal them. While you and Major Smith finish your conversation, I will excuse myself as I am very tired."

With Hannah's help, she left the men to their own deliberations. After a second helping of berry cobbler, Major Smith showed the young captain to his bedroom and facilities for the night, with the invitation that he was welcome back any time and for as long as he wished.

*　　*　　*

After Smith retired, Wootters went back to the dining area where Hannah was clearing the last of the dinner dishes and requested a few minutes to visit with her. After offering her guest a third helping of cobbler, which he accepted, Hannah sat down and waited for Wootters to speak.

Throughout the evening, she noticed that he seemed alert, not relaxed. But he captured the last berry in a spoon, the tension in his face softened as he exclaimed, "Hannah, that is the best meal I have ever had!"

"Captain Wootters, I didn't know you had such a sweet tooth!" Hannah said, returning the smile. "I'd give you more but that is the last of the cobbler. I'll make more if you are staying over for a few days."

"Unfortunately, I will be leaving tomorrow," Wootters said. "After seeing my family in Crockett, I have to continue on to Galveston."

"Captain Wootters, how long have you been back in Texas?" Hannah asked. "And what have you seen before coming here tonight that is so worrisome?"

Wootters arose from his chair, the tension in his body immediately evident.

"I have been in Marshall meeting with the commander of the Texas troops in Texas," he answered. "What I heard has been as hard for my mind as the sniper's minie-ball was for my arm."

Virtually nobody in the Texas command was aware of what was happening in this war, he told her. From the commanding general who imagines continuing the war after the Confederates in the east are annihilated to the privates who were deserting their posts and plundering the supplies, they all seemed to lack any awareness. And that lack of awareness failed to honor those who had served and died for the Confederate cause.

Hannah was surprised by these angry words; John Wootters had always presented himself as a mild-mannered and calm sort. Seeing the look on her face, he apologized for his outburst.

"You don't need to apologize for your feelings, Captain," she said. "Sometimes it's best to let them out where you can see them."

Wootters sat down again and looked directly at Hannah.

"What I really wanted to ask you was about my young friend Berta," he said. "As you see, what I have experienced in this war has hardened my heart and spirit so that being around me may be something that her gentle nature can't accept."

Ever observant, Hannah noted that his eyes appeared to moisten and his voice wavered slightly at the mention of Berta's name. She nodded and kept her tongue.

"Berta is very special to me, as she was the only person who wrote to me and seemed to understand what I was experiencing," he said. "Her words gave me hope that there would be something, or someone, surviving this war who had the strength to carry on to the future. I don't want her to be frightened of me."

Hannah smiled broadly, her white teeth shining in the dim light of the dining room.

"Although Miss Berta is still young to me, she is very much a grown woman and has changed greatly in the past three years," she said. "About the only things that are the same are her red hair and her sweet disposition. She has a very smart mind and thinks about everything more than anyone I ever met. Of all the people she knows, I think she has more concern about you than anyone, and I know that she prays for your safe return every day of her life. Now I don't know everything that is in her mind but I am not sure she is as delicate as she seems."

"No person should ever have to know what we have endured in this war," he said in a low voice.

Hannah, who had taken a seat in front of him, looked directly into his eyes told him exactly what she thought. He needed to take some time to heal, physically and spiritually, before he could plan what to do with the rest of his life. It would be good, she thought, for him to stay close to his fellow soldiers, who had seen and done what he had seen and done. She suggested that this might lead him to some peace of mind.

"White people can't really understand what it's like to be a slave, but other slaves do understand," she said. "One of the ways our people keeps up their spirits is by visiting with each other about the hardships and bad things they've seen. Soldiers have shared the same bad times, just like slaves have. You are going to be all right, Captain Wootters, but it's going to take time."

And with that, Hannah announced that she would see him in the morning at breakfast and he should bring a hearty appetite to the table.

Captain John Wootters went to sleep that night in a most comfortable bed. While the turmoil and concern that often kept him awake still lurked in the corners of his mind, he thought for the first time in ages that there might be a path that could lead him out of the darkness.[71]

---

[71] Appendix II. Item 22. Union Army Generals

XVII

May 1865 – Fairfield, Texas

A s the fateful year of 1865 began to unfold across the South, spring did not bring with it the usual air of hope, rebirth and anticipation. It was apparent that the dwindling numbers of men in the Confederate ranks could not hold back the advancing Union forces. In Texas, frustrations were running especially high, as the state's 60,000 troops were unable to help their comrades east of the Mississippi due to the blockades by the U.S. Navy. Morale was low, desertions were on the rise, and the economic impact on the civilian population was reaching crisis proportion.

Anxiety was rampant throughout the Confederacy. Most people were aware that the South's military and economic capabilities were exhausted. Then on April 9th, nearly every city, town and village received the dreaded, but expected, news that General Lee had surrendered the Army of Northern Virginia to General Grant at Appomattox Court House, Virginia. As it had become clear in recent weeks that General Lee could no longer defend against the siege of Petersburg, his army evacuated the Petersburg and Richmond defenses and moved westward on the second day of April. Their attempt to escape across the Roanoke River was thwarted, and the 28,000 poorly fed and under-equipped Confederates were no match for the 100,000 well-supplied Union soldiers.

With the agreement of his senior generals – Ewell, Gordon, Longstreet and others – General Lee agreed to meet with General Grant on the morning of April 9th. General Grant, showing his great respect for the Confederate leader and his troops, allowed General Lee to select the place of his surrender, and he chose the home of Wilmer McLean in the town of Appomattox Court House. That afternoon, the two leaders met and the surrender terms previously declared by General Grant were accepted. The terms were as generous as could be anticipated: "the officers and men will be allowed to return to their homes, not to be disturbed by United States authority so long as they observe their paroles and the laws in force where they reside." The officers were permitted to retain their side-arms and personal equipment. Grant also allowed the defeated Confederates to take their horses and mules, and provided Lee with food rations his starving army so desperately needed.[72]

At the formal ceremony on April 12th, the Confederates were permitted to surrender with honor and respect as the 28,000 soldiers stacked their arms. Although the war in Virginia was over, it was uncertain how troops in other parts of the southland might react, however, leaders of other principal commands began surrendering their troops soon thereafter, due, in part, to their respect for General Lee and the lack of appetite for continued bloodshed. Two weeks later, General Joseph E. Johnston surrendered his troops in the southeastern Confederate states at Durham, North Carolina, and on May 8th, General Richard Taylor, commander of the Department of Alabama and Mississippi and the Army of Tennessee, surrendered at Citronelle, Alabama. The only significant Confederate force still active at the time of the Fairfield's graduation ceremony in mid-May, was the army of the Trans-Mississippi Department, commanded by General Edmund Kirby Smith.

The Southland's uncertain future cast a pall of gloom as Fairfield Female College prepared for its closing ceremonies. The spirit of gaiety that would usually accompany a graduation was nowhere to be found in Freestone County, and as the spring session drew to a close, the seven members of the senior class were a pensive and somber group. They remained bonded by the experiences that they shared, and the responsibility for writing and delivering an essay for the graduation ceremony fell to Berta Smith, who had been named class valedictorian.

It was a task that weighed heavily on her; she wanted to express her love and appreciation for the many individuals associated with the college as well as for her classmates. The seven senior girls had dubbed themselves The Mystic Seven, reflecting their close friendships. All were aware of the

---

[72] Foote, S. The Civil War. Volume Three, pp.907-956.

great uncertainty they would face on returning to their homes and families after graduation. The one comfort sustaining them was the friendship they shared; as the time of separation drew nearer, they seemed to cling to each other in a bid for reassurance.

Major John Smith and Anna Jane would attend the graduation ceremony, accompanied by Hannah, Oscar and their son, Edgar. The Smiths had arrived in Freestone County the afternoon before the graduation and stayed at an inn for visiting Masons. The evening before the ceremony, Hannah went to Berta's college home to help her pack for the return to the Smith Plantation the following day.

On arriving, Hannah was directed to Berta's room on the second floor. She reached the top of the circular stairway and entered the parlor connecting to the bedroom. There was Berta, sitting at a desk with tears in her eyes.

"Missy Berta!" Hannah cried out. "Why are you so sad? Are you feeling all right?"

"Oh, Hannah! I am so glad to see you," Berta said, rushing into her confidante's comforting embrace. "I have been so worried about reading this message tomorrow at the ceremony, and I'm sad to think about my college days coming to an end. I will miss my friends and teachers so much."

"Of course it's natural to grieve when you leave something you love," Hannah said, smoothing back Berta's hair. "One thing you can't do is keep time from passing. We get older every day, whether we want to or not."

"You always know how to make me see things clearly, no matter how frightened or sad I may be," Berta sniffed and wiped her face. "I hope my mother is feeling well and that the trip wasn't too hard for her."

Hannah nodded and reassured her that Anna Jane was just fine. Both of her parents were so proud of their daughter that nothing could spoil this day for them, not even economic and political turmoil. And Berta, too, should let nothing distract her from the joy of her graduation ceremony. But the younger woman, it seemed, had something else on her mind.

"I am so happy that Captain Wootters has returned to Texas," Berta said casually. "Have you seen him since he visited just before Christmas?"

"No, child, he is very busy with his duties in Galveston," Hannah said as she began the job of packing Berta's trunks. "He has only passed through our neck of the woods without visiting."

"He wrote me a short letter last month saying that his arm was improving and that he was so thankful for Colonel Ashbel Smith[73]," Berta said. "He said he was hoping to come for our graduation but he wasn't sure about his assignment. I do not expect him to be able to attend, as it sounded as if he has been very occupied."

"He will come if he can," Hannah said. "Now you don't need to keep reading your paper, but you do need to help me pack your trunk so we can leave tomorrow."

Berta, now smiling, agreed that she was finished re-reading her essay and turned her attention to the packing job at hand.

*   *   *

Warm sunshine greeted them on the morning of the graduation. The sky was clear, and all signs pointed to a pleasant day for this ceremony. The morning activities included tours of the college for the families of the younger students and a music recital, which the senior girls would perform for those in attendance. The instructors had selected Berta to give the final performance, and she had decided to play two piano compositions by Beethoven. The first was Bagatelle in A Minor, better known as Für Elise, one of her favorites; the other work was the second movement of a sonata often referred to as the Pathetique, which reflected in many ways her own sadness about the state of the Southland.

The audience was awed by the sensitivity and skill she showed in her presentation of these pieces. The applause was loud and appreciative, so much so that Berta responded to calls for an encore performance.

On returning to the piano, she played variations on a tune that, when played in a slow metric, was not immediately recognizable. But after the first stanza of the work, she broke into a lively traditional rendition of "I Wish I Was in Dixie's Land," which elicited a rousing cheer and singing from the audience. The response to her music lifted her spirits, and Berta thought for the first time that morning that she would be able to complete the day's activities, including the reading of her essay, with a smile on her face.

*   *   *

---

[73]   Appendix II. Item 23. Colonel Ashbel Smith, M.D.

The graduation ceremonies were held early in the afternoon at the front entrance of the college before an audience that was smaller than in previous years. Parents, family members, friends and guests were in attendance. Dr. Graves and other faculty, as well as the college overseers, sat on the veranda, which was decorated with patriotic bunting and flags. As usual, the students were seated at the front of the audience, grouped by seniority in chairs on the lawn facing the building's entrance. After the requisite prayers, welcomes and salutations, Berta was introduced and came to the podium with a sense of trepidation.

Berta began her essay[74] with a quotation and paraphrase from Charlotte Bronte's Jane Eyre at the point when the main character's spiteful aunt is dying and reveals the letter written three years earlier to Jane from her uncle, John Eyre, promising her a better future.[75]

"Earth is a scene of continued change," Berta said. "The fabrics of human genius rise in beauty and dazzle the admiring world, but like all things earthly they fall, crumble into dust."

"This occasion is one of moment to many," she continued. "To our friends of this vicinity, we gladly thank you for the favors we have enjoyed at your hands. The time has come when we must return to our cherished homes and, we ask a place in your memories and with you, leave our blessings and ardent wishes for your happiness."

She went on to thank the college and its founders, and to express gratitude on behalf of the senior class for the privilege of having received such a thorough and important education.

The clouds that had partially blocked the sunshine had drifted to the south, and the bright rays brought a glow of perspiration across her brow. As she dabbed her face with her handkerchief, some thought she was drying tears, as many in the audience were also feeling the emotion of the moment. She concluded her presentation by addressing her fellow seniors, the Mystic Seven.

"Beloved classmates, begging your kind hearts to bear with us, we must bid a last farewell. Though our bodies be far removed, our spirits shall linger, the time for parting comes, and it is with deep and heartfelt emotion that I think of it."

---

[74] Appendix I. Valedictory Essay, May, 1865.
[75] Bronte, Charlotte. Jane Eyre, Chapter XXI.

Not to ignore the crisis of their beloved Confederacy that was foremost in her audience's minds, she added: "God only knows when shadows gather thickly around and disappointments hide from your anxious view the long wished-for headland toward which you press. We know that the bright sunshine succeeds the storm, and the future is before us radiant with the light of hope. Now run, my bursting heart – say farewell to your companions of my college days. Dear friends, instructors and classmates, we extend to you all a heartfelt good bye."

Berta left the podium to thunderous applause interspersed with the occasional sigh. Those in attendance knew they were witnessing the end of an era in the history of their country and their own lives. As she walked to her seat, her gaze was directed to the periphery of the audience where, standing in the shade of an oak tree, was a group of men wearing the Confederate Army uniform. Looking at them more closely, she realized that the man at the edge of their group was her friend, Captain John Wootters, but his appearance seemed so changed that she couldn't be sure. She looked again, with greater effort, and saw that it was, indeed, John Wootters. Had she not been about to sit down at that moment, she might have fainted from her surprise.

Light-headed, her heart racing, Berta remained seated a bit longer when the students were called to receive their certificates of graduation. By the time the ceremony had ended, she was feeling more herself. She went to greet family and friends, and acknowledge their congratulations before focusing her attention on the person who had been central to her thoughts, yet seemed like a stranger to her mind.

Berta made her way to the edge of the crowd as she saw John Wootters moving in her direction. She was suddenly seized by a sense of panic. He was unsmiling and sporting a beard, and he seemed taller than she remembered. He had an air of authority and strength in his stride, but as their eyes met, a radiant smile lit up his face. At that moment, Berta experienced an unfamiliar feeling, one that she would later compare to her feelings after the church service in Crockett four years earlier. Wootters approached her with outstretched arms and pulled her toward him. Berta stood motionless for a long moment.

"Oh, John, it is so very good to see you," she finally said.

At those words, she felt a tightness in her throat. Her arms encircled his neck and, after a gentle hug, they looked into each other's eyes. Neither said anything for what seemed like several minutes. Then they both began to laugh, softly, as Berta found herself able to speak again.

"Oh, Mr. Wootters, it is fortunate that I was unaware of your presence before making my presentation," she whispered. "I might have been speechless at an inopportune time. I am very glad you could be here today."

She stepped back and took a visual measure of him. "I have been very concerned about your well-being, and seeing you looking so fit and handsome is truly a blessing and answer to my prayers."

"I cannot tell you how thankful I am to be here today," he said, noting that it had been nearly four years since he'd left Crockett. "I not only was able to hear your words which were the most beautiful and gentle messages that I have ever heard, but your piano pieces earlier this day were exquisite and encouraging. Certainly the music of heaven couldn't be more pleasing to my ears."

This lavish compliment made Berta's cheeks flush bright pink. She appreciated his kindness, she told him, but he was much too generous with his praise. Of greater concern was his health and recovery from his injury. And while he was handsome and elegant as she had imagined he would be, he was also considerably leaner. The war years had taken their toll on his body as well as his spirit.

"Please walk with me to the flower garden and tell me what you have experienced since your visit with my parents last winter," Berta said, taking his good arm. "I have, of course, heard what you told them as they were amazed by the events following your injury. We are all so thankful and relieved with your return that words can scarcely describe my happiness."

She led them in the direction of the rose garden, where there was privacy as well as shade. She attempted to tuck her hair back into place – a few strands had come undone as she returned Wootters' embrace – but gave up after repeated attempts. They passed her special rose bush, and she broke off a stem with a large pink blossom, placing it in the lace handkerchief her mother had given her as a birthday gift. It was a treasure she carried with her on special occasions.

"When I had stopped for that pleasant visit with your parents, I was en route to Galveston," he said. "My visits to troops in Tyler, Huntsville and Hempstead made it clear that recruitment to the chaotic condition of our troops was not possible."

"Your surprise visit was certainly the high point of the season for my parents," Berta said. "They could hardly speak of anything but how honored they were that you paid them a call. Nor could Hannah."

That visit had also been a high point for Wootters. As he noted, the meetings with the troops and officers across the state were disappointing. Even as he continued to emphasize the importance of maintaining the honor and integrity of our forces, he could see the lack of discipline was pervading the ranks. After being in Galveston a short time, news came of General Lee's surrender and that other Confederate generals had followed suit. Only Colonel Ashbel Smith's leadership was able to prevent outright mutiny among the remnants of the Second Texas Infantry in that city.

That Berta and Captain Wootters appeared to be renewing their acquaintance did not escape Hannah's sharp eyes. She wisely suggested to Major Smith and Anna Jane that they all retire to the rooms Berta occupied during the school year and make certain that everything was in order for the return trip home. As the crowd attending the graduation ceremony gradually dispersed, Berta and John continued their stroll through the rose garden.

"You have had such experiences in the years since you and the Crockett Southrons marched away from town on that July day four years ago that it would likely take a lifetime to relate them all, and I suspect there are many you would rather not discuss," she said. "You mentioned that the past few months have been distressing to you. What have you seen that caused you to say that?"

"You are quite correct in saying that much that has happened is difficult to revisit, but many of those experiences are so tightly secured in my memory that they are not likely to ever fade," he responded. "What has grieved me in the past few months are the actions of many so-called soldiers who seem determined to shun all order and discipline and to only take whatever they can for themselves. Rioting and plunder do nothing to honor the memory of the brave soldiers I have known."

Somewhere in the garden, an agitated mocking bird cried loudly to discourage a squirrel from coming too close to its nest. Here, there was peace, and Berta wanted very much to envision a more hopeful future than what the present world seemed to offer.

"I have no right to burden you with my own anxieties, and I apologize for having done so," Wootters said, suddenly aware of having bared so much of himself to the young woman. "This has been a beautiful occasion, and I share with your family a great sense of pride in your accomplishments."

"Hearing about your experiences, both good and bad, would never be burdensome to me," Berta said. "I look forward to hearing as much about them as you are willing to share. I am just thankful that you have returned and seem so well physically. Nothing could detract from my happiness at this time."

They talked about Wootters' plans after that day. He was, he told her, on his way back to Houston at the direction of General Kirby Smith, who was en route to hold a court of inquiry to investigate the causes of the disorder and lawlessness that had become so prevalent. Once that was finished, he would accompany Colonel Ashbel Smith and William Ballinger, a Galveston attorney, to New Orleans to arrange for peace terms for Texas. The group would then return to Galveston, where they hoped General Kirby Smith would sign the terms and officially end the war in the state. Beyond that, Wootters planned to arrange business activities he could pursue after the war was over.

His hope was to start a cotton brokerage business; he had already met with several individuals who were interested in joining him in such a venture. They would manage an office in Galveston, and Wootters would meet with planters in East Texas to encourage them to market their products through his firm. He was confident that demand for cotton would continue to grow. During his absence, his older brother, James, also known as J.C., had continued to manage the mercantile business. Following the unexpected death of their Uncle Lodwick's partner, Colonel Long, the elder Wootters had married Long's widow, Emily, and they now had two children of their own. During the war, J.C. had served for a short time with the Thirteenth Texas Cavalry, after which he had returned to his work in Houston County and served one term in the Texas Legislature. Wootters' sister, Sarah, who was six years his senior, lived in Crockett with her husband, W.H. Moore, and their children.

As the afternoon wore on, the sun moved behind a stand of tall pines and the shadows seemed to dance about the garden. The temperature cooled a bit as clouds began moving in. Captain Wootters and Berta sat down on a bench. Berta laid the rose wrapped in her lace handkerchief on her lap.

"It is very sad that your parents died so young and did not have the opportunity to see their children become such valued citizens" she said. "You and your brother and sister were very fortunate to have such caring relatives."

"Truly, we were blessed in many ways," Wootters nodded. "But I have always regretted losing them and having to rely on the kindness of others. Now it seems that I will be dependent on my comrades-in-arms and others close to my heart to be able to move ahead with my life. You have helped me to know that our ultimate purpose in life is to understand and live the plan that God intends for each of us. Tell me what you anticipate doing, now that you have finished your courses here."

Berta told him that she would be returning to Houston County. She wanted to be of help to her parents, especially to Anna Jane whose health continued to be quite fragile. Her father, she said, had already taken steps to provide land that could be owned by the family-owned slaves who had, over the years, contributed so much to making the Smiths' lives comfortable. Berta had no doubt that once they were free to leave, some certainly would. But a number of them had already indicated they would remain close by to raise their own families in the area. And then she told Wootters her biggest secret.

"This summer I plan to begin teaching some of the slave children to read just as I have been teaching the younger students at the Fairfield Academy," she revealed. "It seems unfair to expect people to be able to function as freedmen when they lack many of the skills needed to succeed in any capacity."

Wootters was surprised by these plans, but decided not to pursue that conversation. He did, however, promise not to reveal her plans to anyone.

"I don't think anyone would fault you for your feelings," he said. "You are the child of gentle people, and despite these harsh times, you have all persevered."

As they walked towards the college building, Berta took the rose and the handkerchief in which it was nestled, and placed them in his hand. "Please take this bloom as it comes from a particular bush that is very special to me," she said.

Nearing the driveway, they saw the Smith family standing near the loaded carriage, with Edgar ready to guide the horses back home. After greeting Major Smith, Anna Jane and Hannah and her family, Wootters said his goodbyes to Berta, but with the expectation that it would not be for long. He waved until he could no longer see the carriage and then took the lace handkerchief, inhaling the faint rose fragrance. Smiling to himself, he carefully placed the handkerchief in his coat pocket. It had, indeed, been a very pleasant day.

XVIII

Late Summer 1865 – On Texas Roadways

I t was late in the season when John Wootters returned to Houston County from Galveston, where he had spent much of that summer. The previous few months had been eventful and, he hoped, would prove beneficial to his future. The journey by horseback from Galveston was long and tedious, but he was taking it slowly so as not to push his mount beyond its limits.

The months after his return to Texas had affected him perhaps as much as the previous three years of combat duty with Hood's Brigade. Some of his embittered fellow soldiers would conclude that the only thing he had gained from those experiences was this aging horse and three uniforms. One of the uniforms was as worn as the horse, but he had received a new suit for his trip to New Orleans with Colonel Ashbel Smith. As he made his way through the towns of Houston, Huntsville and Trinity toward his destination in Crockett, he had ample time to reflect on the events of the past several years. He could only smile to himself and be grateful that the prospects for the future, as far as he could tell, seemed reasonably bright.

He would never be able to erase the memory of so many comrades who had served in the First Texas Regiment with him, especially those in the Crockett Southrons. How naïve they had been when they so proudly marched out of town on that July afternoon in 1861. He marveled at their enthusiasm while training on the field at Howard's Grove in Richmond and their disappointment and boredom on the Potomac defense lines later that winter. Their first real action at Gaines' Farm the next spring showed them the death and injury that would be their ever present companions.

Little did they know what lay ahead at Sharpsburg when it became apparent, to those that survived, that there would be nothing glorious about this war. This idea was further reinforced at Gettysburg, Chickamauga and the Wilderness. That the soldiers serving on both sides were brave was clear in those battles; for the Union Army, that courage shone through further at Fredericksburg, Spotsylvania Courthouse and Cold Harbor. Following those debacles, it became obvious that no amount of Confederate zeal could overcome the vast resources of the Federal government. With the Union willing to sacrifice its men in mass charges despite extraordinary losses, eventually the southern defenders would not be able to persevere. Their bravery, persistence and devotion to their comrades, however, would never be forgotten.

*   *   *

As the summer months had been warm and largely dry, John Wootters took every opportunity to provide water for his horse and enjoy shady respites on this journey. The most hopeful event of recent months had been his visit with Berta at her graduation in May. Although he had passed through Houston County several times since then, his visits had been brief due to the urgency of his duties. He had promised himself and Berta that, whenever possible, he would not continue to be such a stranger.

Indeed, his visit to Fairfield had been a revelation. Not only had the young girl become a beautiful woman, but she was also certainly a lady of substantial intelligence and insight. He had learned of her significant faith from her letters, but he had not been aware of the extent of her musical talents and the depths of her mind.

After taking his leave from the Smith family in May, he had proceeded to Crockett for a visit with relatives and then on to Houston, to assist General Kirby Smith with his inquiry into the rioting and mayhem that had occurred there.[76] He had been dismayed by the desertions and looting going on in that town, but before General Kirby Smith arrived, Wootters had received a message directing him to report to Colonel Ashbel Smith in Galveston. He was to be an aide for a special mission to New Orleans.[77]

---

[76]   Cutrer, T.W. "Smith, Edmund Kirby," Handbook of Texas Online.

[77]   Silverthorne, E. "Smith, Ashbel," Handbook of Texas Online.

Wootters was aware that both General Kirby Smith and the governor of Texas, Pendleton Murrah, shared the idea that Texas might be able to continue down the secessionist pathway despite the collapse of the rest of the Confederacy.[78] Murrah had asked Colonel Ashbel Smith and William P. Ballinger, a highly regarded attorney in Galveston to journey to New Orleans to determine what terms of peace could be expected for Texas.[79] Colonel Smith had specifically requested that Wootters accompany them as an aide.

The Texas delegation expected that the Union commander in New Orleans would only discuss terms of surrender and then only with his Confederate military counterpart. On their arrival they learned that the expectation was accurate. The Federal commander, General Edward R. S. Canby,[80] had indeed refused to meet with their delegation. However, he did offer General Kirby Smith's chief of staff the same terms as had been extended to Generals Lee, Johnston and Taylor. On June 2nd, when their boat returned from New Orleans, General Kirby Smith formally signed the documents of surrender. The most destructive era in American history was officially over in Texas.

*   *   *

On June 19th, General Gordon Granger and two thousand Union troops arrived in Galveston to establish Federal control in Texas. On that day from the balcony of Ashton Villa, General Granger read aloud the General Order No. 3, which officially freed all slaves in the state.[81] No

---

[78]   Wooster, R.A. "Murrah, Pendleton," Handbook of Texas Online.

[79]   King, C.R. "Ballinger, William Pitt," Handbook of Texas Online.

[80]   General Edward R.S. Canby led the Federal troops of the Department of New Mexico and after forcing the retreat of General Sibley's Brigade following the Battle of Glorietta Pass, he was reassigned to the east. By 1864, he commanded the Union troops in the Battle of Mobile, Alabama and its capture in April 1865. He had accepted the surrender of General Richard Taylor in May 1865 at Citronelle, Alabama.

[81]   "General Order #3: The People of Texas are informed that, in accordance with a proclamation from the Executive of the United States, all slaves are free. This involves an absolute equality of personal rights of property between former masters and slaves, and the connection heretofore existing between them becomes that between employer and hired labor. The freedmen are advised to remain quietly at their present homes and work for wages. They are informed that they will not be allowed to collect at military posts and that they will not be supported in idleness either there or elsewhere."

one in Wootters' family had ever owned slaves, but he had expected to become an owner once he started his life as a planter. He had learned from Major Smith and Anna Jane that slavery was not necessary for a viable agricultural economy. Wootters suspected that the economy might be more effective without the oppressive presence of that institution.

Major Smith had agreed to help him establish a plantation of his own and, while in Galveston, Wootters had been able to obtain property near Daly's in Houston County where he planned to begin his farming activities. He had also made arrangements to start a cotton brokerage operation. He and a new acquaintance, Mr. Duble, who had experience in the warehouse and brokerage business, had agreed to form a partnership. Wootters was convinced that they could successfully compete for the business of planters in the Trinity River area.

While in New Orleans, Wootters consulted with physicians about his injury, and they had told him to expect continued improvement in the function of the nerves in his hand and arm, even as some of the medical professionals expressed concern about possible persistent inflammation in his arm bone. Injuries such as this one could affect one's heart and kidneys, and it would be difficult to know whether or not this inflammation was present as he had little sensation of pain in the injured arm. Since amputation was the only suggested alternative treatment, Wootters was willing to wait for signs of further improvement.

The late afternoon sun offered little relief from the heat. With drops of sweat falling into his eyes, Wootters instinctively raised his right hand to wipe his face and realized that there was some feeling in the thumb, which although hardly more than a tingle, was at least an encouraging sign. Perhaps he would soon be able to write a letter to Berta with his preferred hand.

Indeed, his thoughts kept returning to Berta, with her lovely face and fiery red hair. She was constantly in his mind. After hearing her speak at the graduation, he understood that she was also living through a difficult time of transition. Although his experiences had been of the harshest sort imaginable, hers had caused her great anxiety. She had lost her brother, young Ossie and Betty's husband, William. Berta seemed to have responded to these experiences by gaining strength from her faith. Although she was still affected by them, her faith seemed to have grown, and she clearly was able to move forward with her life. Wootters thought he had much to learn from the Smith family, and he considered that Berta's parents could have been like the parents that he had never really known. He appreciated Major Smith's interest in helping him learn the skills he would need to successfully manage an agricultural enterprise.

As he neared the town of Trinity, he came upon a boy who was trying to persuade a young heifer to follow him through a gate to a path leading away from the road. Wootters stopped to observe the predicament of the youth and to allow his horse to have some water from a nearby tank. When he asked the boy if he needed some help the response was that he sure did and that he couldn't understand why the animal so disliked that particular path. Wootters suggested that the heifer probably didn't know what was at the end of the path and whatever was there would not be an improvement over where she had already been. As he and his horse approached the heifer, she promptly went through the gate; the youth said that he was much obliged for the help. John smiled as he thought that he really had not done anything to help. In fact, the heifer had concluded that being in close proximity to a horse was less desirable than whatever was down the path. It made him recall Berta's interest in teaching slaves to read, but he had significant misgivings about how such an effort would be perceived by much of the white population.

Noting the significant number of freedmen walking along the roadways, Wootters realized that the freedom to determine their own destination was a new experience for them. Although he had dealt with many slaves during his years at the mercantile store, none had paid him as much attention as Hannah. She had, in fact, given him sage advice during his visit in December, and he had often thought back to her words. Truly, Hannah had exceptional abilities and insights; with educational opportunities, she would have been able to have significantly improved her life.

Wootters expected the coming generation to see a vastly different world than his own, and he was thankful to be present for its unfolding. Sharing that world with Berta seemed like a goal he must pursue.

As he entered the town of Crockett, he was eager to visit with his brother and sister and their families and with his aging uncle. He hoped to find lodging, depending on his now worthless Confederate money or the generosity of the owners of the inn or at the Masonic lodge. Once ensconced, he would post a letter to Berta announcing his return and hopefully would be invited to pay a call at Smith Landing plantation.

* * *

Although the almanac indicated that summer would soon be ending, the heat in the Trinity River bottom-land showed no sign of easing. The corn fields, brown and barren as their crops had been long ago harvested, were awaiting rainfall. Once the soil was more pliable, the fields would be plowed and prepared for future use. As planters throughout the area knew, the end of the summer farming season heralded the beginning of autumn with the promise of cooler temperatures to come.

There was also another beginning on the horizon: the new school that Berta would provide for children in the Daly's area. She had anticipated and planned for this venture since returning home from college in May. At Fairfield, she had learned much about teaching young students, and she looked forward to helping children discover the pleasure of reading and learning. As to where she would conduct the lessons, she was fortunate that Reverend Joseph Pritchard had volunteered the use of the church building for that purpose. Berta felt very blessed, indeed.

On this particular afternoon, she had been at the church building preparing a room for the dozen students she expected to attend her class the following week. Oscar was driving the carriage back to the Smith plantation as he had been instructed to do by her father. As the carriage ride was proving too bumpy for her to concentrate on a book, she took the opportunity to revisit in her mind the events of the summer.

Graduation and the reality of not returning to Fairfield Female College had been more challenging than she had expected. Although she would miss her friends and especially her mentor, Betty Graves, her days had been filled with activities. She had spent time knitting and sewing with her mother over the past months, and was pleased to note some improvement in Anna Jane's strength and stamina.

She recalled Reverend Pritchard's visit to their home not long ago. As pastor at the Baptist Church in Crockett and a part-time pastor of the mission church at Daly's, the Reverend Pritchard held services at Daly's on late Sunday afternoons twice a month; the congregation was too small to have a full-time minister. However, more people were building homes in the area, and the numbers at his afternoon services were increasing. Berta suspected that one of Reverend Pritchard's reasons for visiting their area was her parents' frequent invitation to dine at their home before his return to Crockett. Hannah always prepared his favorite meal – fried chicken, greens, cornbread and gravy – and he never seemed to lack an appetite.

A man much admired by all who knew him, Pritchard had served the church in Crockett for as long as Berta could remember. He was a jolly, avuncular minister whose message of forgiveness and kindness was more appreciated than the harsher version of Christianity found occasionally at other churches. His large size indicated that he had missed few meals in his lifetime; he was easy with a smile and knew the names of every member of the congregation and their children.

Over dinner at her parents' home one evening early in the summer, Berta was telling the Reverend Pritchard about her interest in teaching young children to read and how she longed to open a school for local youngsters. That conversation led to another regarding the need for education for children in the Daly's area as none was presently available. It was then that the Reverend Pritchard suggested that the church building would be an appropriate location for such a school, as the facility went unused several days of the week.

On another of his visits, the conversation had included comments about the handiwork that she and Anna Jane undertook to amuse themselves and to provide attractive items for their household use. Much to Berta's chagrin, the Reverend Pritchard brought up the episode between Oscar and Jencks, which he found entertaining, and wondered if Berta had made any more clothing for those children. In deference to her father's warning, she had not. Nor was she planning to in the future. Major Smith had used that occasion to once again emphasize to Berta the importance of never leaving home alone; hence, Oscar's main duty had become driving her to Daly's and to other destinations when needed. This wasn't something she regretted; riding in the carriage would allow her to wear better clothes to school in place of riding attire.

Now, with summer nearly gone, Berta was eagerly anticipating the start of school in one week. First, she wondered what to wear the first day of classes, and decided that since the students at Fairfield College were expected to dress nicely for class, she would continue that tradition at her own school. Presenting herself neatly would establish a level of decorum for the classroom that she would expect to be reflected in the efforts of the students. She wondered briefly if the Jencks children would attend her school, but was not surprised when their names did not appear on her roll.

Berta was aroused from her reverie as the carriage came to a stop at the front veranda. Hannah was there to greet them, and her broad smile indicated that she must have something special on her mind.

"Missy Berta, there was someone here to see you this afternoon," she said. "You must have passed him on the road."

"Who might be paying a visit on such a warm afternoon?" Berta asked, stepping out of the carriage.

The clerk from the store at Daly's had just departed after delivering a letter addressed to her. Glancing at the letter, Berta saw that it was from Captain John Wootters, and she felt a sudden knot of anticipation in her chest. She opened it and read:

> *My dear Miss Smith, your friend and obedient admirer has returned to Houston County from his duties and would beseech you to grant him the privilege of visiting with you at your convenience. Please reply to the undersigned by return post to the Masonic Lodge at Crockett where he will be anxiously awaiting and hoping for a favorable response. Your humble and expectant friend, Cap't. J. Wootters.*

As Hannah suspected the origin of the letter, she was standing by with evident curiosity, waiting to hear its contents. Once Berta finished reading it, Hannah smiled broadly and instructed the younger woman to respond right away.

"You write him back, and I'll have Oscar take it to the post office at Daly's right this minute," she said. "Tell him that I am making the biggest batch of berry cobbler he's ever seen, so he better show up hungry."

Unable to refuse such a directive, Berta wrote back, inviting Wootters to call at the plantation the following Saturday. If his schedule permitted, she wrote, he would be welcome to stay for supper and that the entire Smith family would look forward to his visit.

XIX

Spring 1866 – Houston County, Texas

The early spring mornings were still cool, but soon after the sun rose above the treetops, the air turned sultry. Oscar knew this meant that catfish would rise to the surface from the depths of the lake at Elkhart Creek. With some fat pork belly for bait tucked into his basket, he was eager to hook a giant fish that was likely to be found near his favorite fishing spot. He had already driven Miss Berta to the school at the church in Daly's and was now on his way to the lake. For a brief moment, he considered driving to the nearby town of Augusta, which he had never visited. But as Augusta was regarded among freedmen as a place best avoided, the desire to go fishing won out.

After leaving the church, he turned down a road along the creek that led to the lake. Oscar smiled to himself as the carriage rumbled toward the water. One who had never been a slave could not appreciate the excitement of being able to decide on their own what they wanted to do on a particular day. His only responsibility was to drive Miss Berta and her mother whenever they needed to be away from the plantation. In return for this service, Major Smith had deeded him the homesite at Cedar Branch, where he and Hannah lived. While Berta was teaching her class, he was able to do whatever pleased him, and nothing interested him more than trying to catch that big fish. He had seen its back and fins rising above the waterline and thought it must be as long as a man is tall.

Oscar often marveled that slavery had really, finally ended; it was something he and his forbearers had been born into and from which they had all prayed for deliverance. That he could move about at will and that his descendants would choose the direction of their own lives filled him with a wondrous new sense of happiness. While some of the younger men in the Cedar Branch community had left for parts unknown, he was thankful that their son, Edgar, had decided to stay close to home and work in the fields that Major Smith had sold to him.

Major Smith had even agreed to help Edgar acquire an education in the future, if and when such an opportunity became available. Edgar had expressed an interest in preaching the gospel and realized that his effectiveness would be greater with the appropriate training. In the meantime, under Berta's tutelage and with Hannah's help, he was learning to read. Oscar was proud that his son had such lofty aspirations and the will to work for them.

Oscar and Hannah's desire to remain close to home surprised nobody, as Hannah had occasionally said that she wanted to be laid to rest near their son, Ossie. That desire was further encouraged by rumors that bands of hostile Ku Klux Klansmen had been seen throughout the area. These white men had been known to kill unsuspecting freedmen under the cover of night, and their white-hooded garments, used as disguises, made them even more terrifying. Oscar did not want to do anything that would attract their attention; appearing in an unfamiliar place like Augusta might do just that.

As he continued towards the lake, Oscar noted that the creek was somewhat higher than expected as they had received more rain this spring than usual. Although it would be much lower later in the summer, the creek always had some flowing water. Several miles below Daly's, the creek formed a lake before continuing on to the Trinity River about half the distance to Crockett.

The lakeshore was partially obscured by dense grapevines that grew in profusion near the water. There were trails made by deer and other animals leading to the lake so that one could easily reach its banks. This was widely known as an excellent fishing spot, and local people could often be found there trying to lure the resident catfish to the water's surface. In April and May, the bushes that protected the shoreline provided large quantities of a reddish fruit that women from the area would turn into mayhaw jelly. As he neared the lake, he noted that the crop had not been completely harvested. If the fish weren't biting, he would instead gather fruit for the jelly and berries for future cobblers.

Oscar was very content to spend the remainder of his days with Hannah in their home. He realized that without an education, one's prospects were very limited unless he had skill in a craft or the ability to learn one. The demand for able-bodied workers was said to be great, and a number of the younger freedmen had already left for larger towns. While he remained concerned about what the future held in store for that younger generation, he knew that at least it could be the potential for a better life. He also knew that it might hold the prospect of trouble for which many were unprepared.

* * *

As the sun passed the noon hour, Oscar walked the short distance back to the carriage. He had left it not far from the lake, where the road ended and became a narrow trail. The large catfish had not appeared, but he was pleased nonetheless with the number of fish he had caught. These and a basket of berries represented a good day's effort, and he whistled merrily to the horses as they made their way back to Daly's.

Once there, he found a shady spot beside the general store near the church building. It was here that he usually stopped the carriage to wait for Berta to finish her work in the school room. As he sat there recalling his successful day, who did he see walking in his direction but Jencks, with a scowl on his face sour enough to curdle milk. Oscar sat still and quiet as Jencks walked by, grateful that the man had not stopped to torment or provoke him. Minutes later, Berta emerged from the church building, and he urged his team forward. After helping her into the carriage, he proudly showed off the abundance of mayhaw berries and the good catch of fish; Berta would later recall Oscar saying that he thought he had enough berries for Hannah to make as much cobbler as Captain Wootters might want.

The return trip to the plantation was most pleasant, as a cool breeze tempered the heat of the afternoon sun. As she considered the abundance of fish and berries, Berta wondered if John Wootters enjoyed visiting with her as much as he enjoyed Hannah's cobbler. The thought of his occasional visits made her smile, as it had been apparent from their conversations that his agricultural and business ventures were proving both satisfying and successful. The thought of some future visit from him awakened in her a sense of excitement. She also reasoned that if the prospects of berry cobbler would tempt him to come more often, she would ask Hannah to show her how to make the dessert on her own.

*   *   *

Late that afternoon, Anna Jane and Berta were sitting on the front veranda discussing the day's activities, and knitting socks and sweaters for the new Dorcas Aid Society to distribute to families in need of winter clothing. This effort had been particularly pleasing to Reverend Pritchard, as there were many children who would need warm clothing. The women of the church in both Crockett and in Daly's had responded enthusiastically to his request for help with the knitting. Berta cherished this time as it gave her the opportunity to visit with her mother for long periods, which had been less frequent when she was at college.

As they spoke of Berta's teaching and other news, Anna Jane expressed concern that her daughter's piano skills were suffering from a lack of practice. Berta spent more time preparing for class and visiting with her mother, and her music was being neglected as a result.

"It's true that I haven't been playing the piano as much as in the past, but unless I am learning new pieces, I don't need to spend as much time playing as I did at college," Berta admitted. "The time I spend with you is very important to me, and I wouldn't want to exchange it for any other pastime."

"Have you considered what you want to do in the future with your music?," Anna Jane asked. "Your father and I had always imagined that you would want to study at one of the conservatories or colleges in the East when the war was over. You really do have skills that all of us, especially your instructors, feel should be nurtured."

Berta blushed at the compliment. She wanted to correct her mother's statement by adding that she wouldn't attribute her musical efforts to inherent skills; it was only after hours of practice that these so-called skills were evident.

"I am thankful that I can create music from my excellent instrument, and doing so is one of my greatest pleasures," Berta said carefully. "I have asked God to guide my thoughts about these matters, and I feel in my heart that He has opened other opportunities that make it difficult to know what is the correct path to pursue. I feel that He wants me to also use what skills I have to teach people who wish to learn." She was also quick to add that remaining close to home in order to help her parents also brought her great happiness.

Anna Jane smiled at her daughter and marveled at how her last child seemed to have suddenly grown into a thoughtful young woman. She could only hope that she would live long enough to see the story of Berta's life unfold.

"In the past year, I have also learned that my heart has great concern for my friend Captain Wootters," Berta continued. "He is in the process of establishing future directions for his life, and I want to be available to help him if I'm able."

At that, both women stopped their knitting and looked at each other, as though seeking some unspoken meaning in Berta's words. She cleared her throat and told her mother that she did not think leaving home and her family was part of God's plan for now. It did not seem, she said, the best path to follow.

"Berta, my dear child, you are truly a thoughtful and spirit-filled young lady, and your father and I respect your ideas and plans greatly," Anna Jane said. "Of course, I am delighted that you want to remain near us, but I do not want my own selfish desires to stand in the way of your dreams. Tell me, are Hannah's suspicions correct? Has your interest in Mr. Wootters has progressed beyond friendship to love?"

At those words, Berta's tendency to blush betrayed her.

"Mr. Wootters has been away for so long that I am not certain we really know each other," Berta said, choosing her words carefully. "It makes me very happy to see him back in Texas and showing evidence of recovering from his injury. But although my heart holds him in a very special place, my mind has yet to understand the course his life will take. I am confident that he will find the correct path for his future; it is possible that such a future may include the two of us, but right now I just don't know."

"You have been such a blessing to all of us," Anna Jane said, hugging her daughter. "I will also pray for both you and Mr. Wootters in your understanding of these matters."

The sun had sunk below the tree line, and evening shadows had overtaken the veranda. As it was too dark to continue sewing, Berta and her mother moved indoors to the music room to look for the sheet music of a scherzo that Berta had not played in some time. Anna Jane seemed more energetic than usual and was helping sort through the pages of music with great enthusiasm. There was a knock on the door, and Hannah entered, announcing that a visitor had arrived to see Major Smith.

"Hannah, you know Major Smith won't return from Crockett until this time tomorrow," Anna Jane said. "Who is it that is surprising us with the visit?"

"It's that young deputy sheriff who we see sometimes down at the store at Daly's," Hannah answered. "You'll know who I mean. He's the one who looks too young to actually be a deputy."

"Please show him in, and I will explain that he must wait until tomorrow to see Major Smith, unless he goes to Crockett before then."

In a moment Hannah returned, followed by the deputy. He had forgotten to remove his hat and was fidgeting nervously. When he entered the parlor, Anna Jane stood up and extended her hand; that seemed to put the young man somewhat at ease. He jerked his hand back abruptly and took off his hat, as if suddenly remembering his manners.

"Hannah tells me that you are here to see Major Smith," Anna Jane said. "I am sorry that he isn't here this evening, but if you are going to Crockett you may see him. He is there on business. but he should return tomorrow if you want to wait and see him then."

The deputy stammered as he tried to answer Anna Jane, who was smiling somewhat impatiently. "I...I...I...would rather speak to y...y...you in confidence i...i...if that is possible," he said.

"Of course," she said, turning to Hannah. "Why don't you finish setting the table, and we will be through here very soon, I am sure. Deputy, do you mind if my daughter hears what you have to say as she may remember more clearly than I?" The deputy nodded in agreement and shuffled his feet as Hannah closed the door behind her.

"Now, what brings you to our home on such an unexpected visit? I hope nothing is amiss."

"I am here because of a most disturbing situation, Mrs. Smith, and we need your help in resolving it," he said. "A man named Jencks from the Daly's area has filed a complaint. He is well known to law enforcement, as he has often been the cause of controversy and an occasional resident in the county jail in Crockett. He has just this afternoon made an accusation against the freedman named Oscar who lives on this plantation."

"What on earth could cause that devil Jencks to complain about anything except his own rudeness?" Berta gasped, forgetting herself.

Taken aback by the young woman's direct manner, the deputy told them that Jencks claimed the new calf from his black and white cow was with the herd yesterday but today had disappeared. He believed that Oscar had taken it because he had seen Oscar riding down the road to the Elkhart Creek lake today. The road to the lake ran by his property line, and he hadn't seen anyone else in the area. Moreover, he planned to file a complaint stating exactly that in Crockett; Oscar would be required to come to town to answer the charge.

"If you know anything about this situation, you may be able to help resolve it," the deputy said.

"How could Oscar possibly have taken a calf from that horrible Jencks?" Berta said, her face flush with anger. "After he left me at the Daly's church for my school class, he went to the lake to fish and gather berries, and before returning to our plantation he waited at the church building to bring me back home. If he had a dead calf in the carriage I certainly would have seen it and even more so if it had been alive! I don't think Judge Gossett or any other reasonable person will think Oscar is the culprit."

The deputy continued to fidget with his hat, as if embarrassed. He hadn't wanted to bring this news to Smith Landing plantation, but there were procedures, and they had to be followed. He agreed with Berta the accusation was likely groundless, and urged both women to provide any information they could to help resolve the matter quickly.

"I will be in Crockett tomorrow, and hopefully the situation can be dismissed quickly," he said.

With raised eyebrows, Anna Jane thanked him for his visit and his advice, and asked him to relay the message to Major Smith if he happened to run into him in Crockett that evening.

"I might add that Oscar and Hannah, as well as this family, will be having catfish for supper," she said. "I assure you there is no likelihood that we will be having veal."

After the deputy made his exit, Berta and Anna Jane agreed that under no circumstances should Oscar leave the security of the plantation and that legal measures would have to be forthcoming from the County Court before the deputy would be re-admitted to the property. Moreover, Oscar and Hannah did not need to be told of the visit until Major Smith could advise them. Berta resolved to have Edgar drive Hannah and her to Crockett the next day so she could inform her father of the situation and hopefully meet with Judge Gossett about the matter.

*　　*　　*

After a restless night, Berta arose early and informed Hannah and Edgar of her wishes. They left for Crockett shortly after breakfast. Berta had some additional plans, which she decided to not share with her mother, and as the three travelers crossed the creek at Daly's, she asked Edgar to stop at the general store. Berta asked the proprietor if he could recall any people traveling towards the lake on the previous day, any strangers he did not recognize. Regrettably, the answer was 'no.'

She thanked him and asked Edgar to then proceed in the direction of the lake. When asked why they were taking this detour, she said that she wanted to see the spot where Oscar thought a certain monstrous catfish was hiding out.

Hannah and Edgar silently thought that this was a most unusual request but proceeded as Berta directed. It was easy to identify the homestead property inhabited by the Jencks family. Beyond it was wooded land unclaimed and uninhabited by any settlers in the area. A considerable amount of Houston County was unclaimed land; from the road the area did not look very amenable to agriculture in Berta's eyes.

Berta had heard about this area from her brother, Lucius, who had enjoyed many hours of exploring the sand canyon. About a mile past the boundary stream, Berta was startled by the raucous cries of a flock of ravens. An upward glance revealed a similar number of buzzards circling. Noting the number of birds, she asked Edgar to stop the carriage and wait while she and Hannah made a short foray into the wooded area.

Hannah protested mildly that she was too old to venture into the woods, but decided that she had better accompany her younger charge, just to keep her out of trouble.

A short distance later, the two women came upon a clearing and saw the beginning of a washed out sand formation. Within one hundred yards was a small canyon, and on coming to the canyon rim, Berta saw something that truly offended her sensibilities.

In the bottom of the canyon about thirty feet down were the remains of a black and white calf, with at least twenty turkey vultures, also known as buzzards, feasting on the remains. An equal number of ravens perched further back, adding their disdainful cries.

"Oh Hannah, I have never seen such a horrible sight," Berta cried out. "That poor calf must have gotten too close to the edge and fallen to its death. Let's go now as I have an unusual request to make of Edgar."

Hannah, of course, had no idea why this discovery startled her young friend, whose face was now nearly the same shade of red as her hair. On returning to the carriage, Berta made a request of Edgar that gave Hannah pause. What she wanted was for Edgar to follow the trail to the calf's carcass, cut off its tail and bring it back to the carriage.

Hannah was too stunned to speak, much less to inquire as to the purpose of this bizarre request. She sat silently in the carriage and prayed that Berta hadn't completely lost her mind and that if she had, the loss was only temporary. After Edgar returned, tail in hand, the trio proceeded to Crockett.

*　　*　　*

On arriving in town, Berta found her father at the office of Judge Gossett, where they were discussing matters related to the Masonic lodge.

"What a surprise to see you here at the Court House when I didn't even expect you to be in Crockett today!" Major Smith said. "What is the occasion of your visit?"

Berta told him about the unexpected visit from one of the sheriff's deputies, the missing calf and Jencks' accusation, which was preposterous because Oscar was the last person on Earth who would steal anything, especially a calf. She had come to Crockett to counsel with her father and Judge Gossett, and felt fortunate to have found them together in the same place. She planned to give the sheriff a thorough explanation of what she thought had actually happened. Major Smith agreed that Oscar was most certainly not guilty, but that the accusation alone could make his life more difficult.

Gossett, who had been sitting quietly, listening to the conversation and thoughtfully stroking his ample chin, nodded.

"This could be a problem for Oscar, especially if there was a jury trial involved. Fair trials for freedmen like Oscar may be difficult to obtain in our present circumstance," he said. "The best alternative for Oscar would be to avoid any legal proceedings at all by discussing this with the sheriff."

Major Smith looked over at his daughter to find her smiling. "Berta you seem happier than I would expect, considering the gravity of this situation."

"That's because there is more to the story than I have told you," she said, her dimples deepening. "I decided to investigate with Hannah, and we found the calf."

Berta then proceeded to tell her father and Judge Gossett about how she and Hannah had seen the birds, followed them and eventually found what remained of the calf.

"There wasn't much left of the poor beast, but I did ask Edgar to fetch me the tail so I could show it to you and the sheriff when I told him my story," she said. "The evidence is still in the carriage as I didn't think it appropriate to bring it into such a proper building as this."

"Young lady, you have very likely saved your man Oscar's hide," Judge Gossett exclaimed. "It would appear that neither Jencks nor the deputy spent much time looking for the calf, when blaming Oscar was such an easy remedy." He urged her to go with her father to the sheriff's office and explain what had happened. And when they were finished, they would report back to Judge Gossett.

"Your bravery is remarkable for one so gentle-appearing," the judge said "But celebrating your accomplishment would be unwise."

Berta and her father thanked him for his advice and set off to find the sheriff's office.

* * *

It took some time, but Berta relayed the true story of the "stolen" calf, much to the surprise and consternation of the sheriff and the deputies present in his office. By the time she finished, she was reassured that no charges would be filed against Oscar. The sheriff also supported concerns expressed by Judge Gossett for Berta's safety in this matter, while Major Smith pointed out that he had expressed such warnings in the past.

As they were returning to Smith Landing Plantation, Hannah and Edgar were very curious about the tail of the deceased calf. Major Smith explained what had happened, warning them that any interaction with Jencks or others like him was best avoided. Thanks to Berta's bravery and initiative, a situation potentially dangerous for Oscar had been thwarted.

*   *   *

Two weeks later, John Wootters attended a Masonic lodge function where he encountered Judge Gossett. The older man asked about Berta, as he was aware of their friendship, and Wootters told him of her various educational activities and charitable efforts as well as her devotion to her family. The judge, in turn, revealed the story of the calf's tail and cautioned Wootters that this information was not for public consumption for fear of some retaliation from Jencks.

For the first time, it dawned on Wootters that residing alongside Berta's gentle mind and spirit were an iron will and formidable sense of duty; she was indeed a match for any imaginable hardship or circumstance. In that moment of realization, he understood that the opportunity to spend the rest of his life with her might be the greatest single blessing God could ever bestow on him. He would pray that his own mind and spirit would continue healing so that he could be worthy of such a companion.

XX

Autumn 1866 – Smith Landing Plantation

The planting and harvest seasons of 1866 had been months of intense activity for John Wootters. He had worked day and night, supervising the clearing of land and the planting of a cotton crop on his new acreage near Daly's. He was also engaged in his fledgling cotton brokerage venture, which was showing good initial prospects. A number of acquaintances, many of whom he knew from his Confederate Army days, had agreed to market cotton crops through his new firm.

Houston County was home to many survivors of the war who, as former comrades-in-arms, were a close-knit group. Some had served in Hood's Brigade, including three of his best friends: Willie Wall and the Aldrich brothers, Gus and Colin. Lieutenant Wall had been one of the original officers of the Crockett Southrons and one of its first casualties. A severe hand wound had resulted in the loss of a thumb at Gaines' Mill in 1862. That had ended his active military career, but his health and enthusiasm for life had apparently made a full recovery. Wootters had recently learned that Will and Miss Nettie Cooper were to marry on December 6th.[82] On learning that he would be asked to participate in the ceremony, Wootters promised himself that he would purchase a dress suit as soon as he was able.

---

[82] History of Houston County, p. 609.

As for the Aldrich brothers, Gus had been wounded in the battles of Gettysburg and Chickamauga but had recovered enough to remain active in their company. He served as commander of the dwindling Crockett Southrons after John was unable to continue, and was present at Appomattox when General Lee surrendered. Gus' younger brother Colin, who had served as mess sergeant for the Crockett Southrons, was one of the few men of their company to not be injured throughout the war. He quickly readjusted to civilian life and had recently married Miss Betty Kyle, whose family lived in Augusta.[83]

Gus and John Wootters had recently attended a social event at the home of Dr. Francis Lewis Meriwether and his wife, Ethalinda. They were a well-regarded couple, and they seemed to enjoy hosting parties at their plantation, especially for the younger, unmarried people of the area. These socials were characterized by piano music, often provided by Dr. Meriwether and Ethalinda, with enthusiastic singing and dancing. Their daughters, Martha and Frances, were friends of Berta and had also attended the Fairfield Female College.[84]

When Wootters attended these events, he would notice that Berta was a vivacious and beautiful part of the celebrations. He would feel a twinge of irritation to see her surrounded by friends, as he knew that people were drawn by her radiant smile and inclusive nature. He even suspected that he was slightly jealous when those friends included overly attentive young men. Wootters made a special effort to be present at these gatherings.

Even so, agricultural activities and business ventures occupied much of his time and efforts, the latter requiring him to travel to plantations and communities in the area where there were prospects for his brokerage firm.[85] The management of his property near Daly's had benefited from Major Smith's frequent and insightful advice and from the opportunity to employ freedmen living in the Cedar Branch community.

During the summer and early autumn, he visited the Smith plantation as often as possible to consult with Major Smith and to visit Berta. He never turned down an invitation to stay for supper, as the meals provided by Hannah and her daughter, Addie, were not only delicious, but also

---

83 Ibid. p. 226.
84 Ibid. p. 472-73.
85 Appendix I. Letter from Berta Smith to John Wootters.

much better than what he could provide for himself. Although Wootters had erected a small cottage on his property, it was far from commodious. The expansion of these living quarters to a more developed home would be a project for the winter months. He did not want to delay this activity. If he were ever able to persuade Berta to marry him, he needed to offer her better accommodations.

*   *   *

In late October, after the final harvest welcomed the first chill of the season, Berta received a letter from John Wootters that made her smile. Unlike the usual brief notes she was used to receiving, this carefully written missive formally requested an afternoon visit to her home and indicated that he would be anxiously hoping for a welcoming reply. She informed Hannah and Anna Jane of the request.

"This is an unusual note from Captain Wootters," she said, her face lighting up with a smile. "Now that he has completed his successful harvest, he must want to adopt the airs of a gentleman planter with such a formal request!"

"You know he has something more on his mind than an extra helping of berry cobbler," Hannah shook her finger at the younger woman. "I sure hope you plan to make him welcome!"

"Truly, Berta, your father and I want him to feel very much at home here, and I am sure that you will write him to accept his visit," Anna Jane was also smiling. "I know that he and your father have had much to discuss in recent months, and I suspect that he may have something to ask about other than the preparation of cotton seedlings."

In truth, Anna Jane knew that her husband had already had a conversation with Wootters about a marriage proposal and had advised him that such a marriage would certainly have their blessing. He had also told the young suitor that his daughter had very definite ideas and a mind of her own, and that her parents' influence might not carry much weight.

Berta discussed the anticipated visit with Hannah and Oscar as she wanted to welcome her guest with more gentility than usual. Hannah would provide his favorite items for dinner, but dessert would be a berry cobbler prepared by Berta. It was one of the many skills she'd acquired during the summer months.

Although both Hannah and her mother had suggested that Captain Wootters was likely planning to propose marriage, Berta wasn't convinced about the purpose of his visit; she was even less certain about her response. After all, she had spent only brief intervals with him in recent months, and those had usually been on his visits to discuss his cotton farming with her father or at the occasional social event.

She had noted, however, that his demeanor had changed over the past year. Wootters had become more like the cheerful, optimistic person she remembered from previous years, and their friends all seemed to hold him in high regard. He was clearly a leader among the young people in their circle of acquaintances. Berta had also heard about his concern for the well-being of his former comrades and the efforts he devoted to helping them recover, both physically and spiritually, from the war.

Although she had long been aware of the love that she had for him in her heart, she was reassured by the gradual reconciliation of her mind to this idea that he was, indeed, the one whom God had provided to be her mate. Even so, it did occur to her that he may have a very different purpose for this visit. What if he merely wanted to celebrate the successful completion of his first year as a planter? What if he had other plans for his life other than staying in their community? She decided that trying to predict a life for the two of them was beyond her and that she could only rely on the Lord to answer her questions and provide directions for their lives.

As the day of Captain Wootters' visit neared, Berta made certain that the event would be a memorable one, whatever its purpose. The front parlor, which doubled as her music room, was suitably arranged and decorated with the last blooms of the year from Berta's special rose bush. She herself would be wearing an elegant dress and playing her favorite piano music. The hallway, dining room and parlor would be cheerfully illuminated by an extra supply of candles to be lighted at the appropriate time. She would welcome her guest and have time to visit with him before her parents joined them at the dinner hour.

As she was reviewing the evening's arrangements in her mind, Berta sat at the piano playing the gentle notes of Für Elise. The late afternoon sun shone through the pine trees and into the windows, illuminating the sheet music on her piano stand. It reminded her that the piano and her attempts to produce music had been one of her greatest pleasures in life.

A slight breeze fluttered the curtains, and she heard a faint sound, a distant honking that could only be a flock of geese making its way from the distant north to their winter home in Texas. She felt her throat tighten with emotion as she was reminded that the God who directed those creatures and their companions on vast migrations also directed her own life's journey. At that very moment, she was certain that John Wootters was the person with whom she was meant to spend her life.

A soft knock on the door brought her back to the present. It was Oscar.

"Miss Berta, you have a guest," he said. "I believe you are expecting him."

Berta stood up quickly, perhaps too quickly because she felt a rush of faintness and had to hold onto the piano. John Wootters walked into the room behind Oscar.

"Miss Smith, I hope we didn't disturb you as I may be a bit earlier than you had been expecting."

"No, I was just daydreaming, and the sound of wild geese passing by aroused a bit of unexpected melancholy," Berta shook her head. "I am so pleased that you are here. I hope everyone has made you feel welcome."

"Indeed they have," he smiled. "Edgar has taken my horse to the stable where he will be glad to have some much needed rest. We have had a busy week, and he has covered more miles than he would prefer."

As she sat back on her piano bench, Berta found herself looking up into the most gentle and caring expression she could have imagined.

"Please, Captain Wootters, won't you sit down?" she motioned to a chair in the sitting area. "Would you like some tea? Oscar will be happy to bring some. Yes? Then please tell me what you have been doing and how you are feeling now that the harvest is completed." Berta covered her agitation with conversation. She stood up and followed her guest to a pair of chairs across the room.

With an elegant bow, Wootters offered her a bouquet of autumn flowers.

"I have brought you some wildflowers, but I fear that they are too rustic to adorn such an elegant room as this," he said. "They could not add to the roses that you have arranged."

"You are very kind to say such things," Berta said. "But I am sure that these will be the last rose blossoms of the season and what you have brought will be a very nice addition to the décor."

Berta looked more closely at her guest. He wore a gray army uniform, although it seemed much newer than his usual attire, and his beard was neatly trimmed. She thought he exuded maturity and confidence, which could have been intimidating except that his eyes and smile radiated the enthusiasm of youth.

Oscar entered the room with the tea service, which he placed on the low table beside the chairs, and she asked him to place the flowers from Wootters in a suitable vase on the dining table.

"I hope you are planning to dine with us this evening, Captain Wootters," she said. "My parents and I will be very disappointed if you have other plans."

"Hannah will insist that Captain Wootters stay, as she has already set a place for him," Oscar said. Berta noted that he looked elegant in his suit; she was very pleased with Oscar's genteel presentation of the tea set.

"I will be honored to stay for dinner," Wootters said. "I can think of no greater pleasure than sharing a meal with you and your parents in your lovely home."

He noticed that Berta was wearing a white, frilly skirt, enhanced by petticoats, with a blue bodice and a white lace collar. Her red hair was adorned by a blue ribbon. She was, in his mind, the picture of beauty.

"Miss Smith, you have never looked lovelier," he said. "That blue ribbon, is it the same one I helped you select some years ago when we first met at my uncle's store?"

"Thank you for your compliments," Berta said, turning several shades of pink. " But we have obtained new ribbons in the past five years. I certainly remember our first meeting, however, as you made an encouraging remark about my piano playing. Your kind words then may have been responsible for my continuing efforts to improve my technique."

"You were very skilled then, but the level of your expertise at the graduation recital last year was truly remarkable," he said. "I have heard your parents mention the possibility of you seeking further training at prestigious institutions in the east. Does that interest you?"

Berta noticed that with that question, Wootters' eyes reflected a certain tension that she did not understand. Perhaps he did not think she was old enough to be away from home. Not wanting to encourage that impression, Berta sat up straight as she looked directly at him.

"I have thought that travel to the great cities and conservatories of the east, or even in Europe, would be a wonderful adventure and could certainly help me achieve the full use of whatever talents I may have," she said. "At the time of my graduation I was seriously considering such a plan."

"And what have you decided?" Wootters said, leaning forward.

"Over the past year, I have become aware of different opportunities I think I must consider," she said. Wootters could see the enthusiasm in her eyes and in her face as she described for him, in some detail, her efforts at teaching reading and writing skills to the local children and to others at the Cedar Branch community. Moreover, he was not aware of her mother's frail state and the satisfaction that Berta got from being there to help and comfort her.

The late afternoon passed quickly as she showed him some of the knitted and embroidered items that she and Anna Jane had made on behalf of the Dorcas Aid Society. She described for him her pleasure at the success of her rose gardening efforts, and he was amused at the pride she had in her ability to make a cobbler.

Their conversation was interrupted by Hannah, who came in to light the candles. It was then that Berta realized their visit had extended into the early evening hours, and she had not given her guest the opportunity to do much of the talking.

"I am sorry to have been so talkative," Berta said, feeling flustered. "I haven't given you a chance to tell me about your activities and plans for the future."

Wootters laughed. He enjoyed hearing about her activities; he was, in fact, more than pleased that she was finding life in Houston County to be so interesting and productive. His life, on the other hand, had been rather ordinary, but he was hoping that his efforts would have reasonable prospects. His land had enjoyed a much better harvest than expected, and the cotton brokerage company was growing, although it required more travel than he would have liked. It would take time for that venture to produce results, but the first year of work had seemed favorable thus far.

The sun had sunk below the horizon and the golden puffs of clouds reflected its departing rays. Candles illuminated the room with their flickering light. As she looked at her guest, Berta's eyes fell on the rose sitting behind him; it was on her piano in a slender vase at the end of the keyboard where candles would usually sit to illuminate her music. She felt somewhat overcome by the moment.

"I am very pleased to see you feeling so well and appearing as happy as one could ever hope for," she said. "Tell me about the plans for your future as this year's planting efforts have met with such success."

He wanted to further expand his farming acreage and cotton brokerage business. Over the next year, he and his partner would have their finances in order to begin accepting consignment of cotton crops. There were plans, he said, to build a railroad line to Crockett from Galveston through Houston, but it would still be several years before that could be completed. The track, which was supposed to extend to Palestine, would greatly improve the delivery of crops to the markets.

There was even talk of a new town where that line would cross the roadway between Augusta and the Trinity River. Wootters was anticipating these developments and had already bought land in the area, land that would be suitable for a house, as it was close enough to both my farmlands, the major roadways and eventually the railroad.

"It sounds as if you have made excellent plans," she said. "I am very happy for you, and from the enthusiasm in your smile, I can see that these activities have brought you much satisfaction. I have no doubt you will succeed."

"There is one matter that I have not been able to resolve," Wootters said casually. "That is my wish to share the future with the one person in the world that means more to me than any other. That person is you, Miss Berta Smith, whom I love with all my heart and mind."

Suddenly the world stopped. Berta felt as if she couldn't breathe; then everything around her seemed to spin. She could feel a sensation of heat spreading up her neck. Was she blushing, or was she simply overcome by joy? At last, she was able to catch her breath and speak.

"That particular Miss Smith has been prayerfully considering her own future," she said with a smile in her voice. "There is no name by which she would prefer to be known than Mrs. John Wootters. She has loved you with her heart for a number of years, and now her mind has reached the same happy conclusion. I could never, however, agree without the blessing of my dear parents."

Wootters, who had reached out to prevent her collapsing when she turned red, held her closely as she fell into his arms. The relief that he felt from having avoided a dreaded rejection of his proposal made him laugh aloud as he suppressed a brief urge to release a rebel yell. .

"Berta, I have had such a conversation with your father and received his tentative blessing depending on your willingness. He has informed me that you have a mind of your own, and he would only agree to whatever you have already decided."

"Indeed, if I have such a mind, then it is fully made up and is very pleased to say 'yes' to your proposal," she said, as they shared gentle kisses. "I really do love you, John Wootters, and you have made me a very happy person."

Soon thereafter Hannah knocked on the parlor door and announced that Major and Mrs. Smith were seated at the dining room table and would be very pleased if Berta and Captain Wootters would join them."

When the couple entered the dining room, Major Smith arose and extended his hand in greeting to Wootters, who greeted them with a lilt in his voice.

"It is a great pleasure to be here and to have you be the first to know what is, for me, the best news imaginable," Wootters said. "Berta has accepted my proposal of marriage and made me the happiest man in the state of Texas. We would ask for your blessings on this happy circumstance."

Major Smith embraced the young man and Anna Jane clasped her arms around Berta, as both women's tears of happiness began to flow.

"I am so happy for you !" Anna Jane said. "I thank the Lord that I have lived to see this day."

Major Smith, who was overcome with emotion, wiped his eyes with a handkerchief. "This is the happiest of days. Not only do I have a daughter, but I will also now have a son. The Lord took Lucius from me, but has given me John," he said, grasping the younger man's hand. "In honor of this occasion, I want you to have a certain horse. He is the son of Magnus, the horse that Lucius would be riding today if he were alive. I know he would want you to have him."

"I am honored by your gift," Wootters said, humbled by his future father-in-law's gesture. "As I ride him, I will always be reminded of Lucius' service and devotion to his country."

In anticipation of this announcement, the servants had gathered just around the corner and heard all that happened. Berta asked her mother to ring the bell so they could share the good news with them. On the first tinkle of the small bell, they burst into the dining room, faces beaming, and added their embraces to the celebration.

"Just as the Bible's Abigail found her King David, my own Abigail has her Captain Wootters!" Hannah exclaimed. "Praise the Lord!"

After an extended round of congratulations, Hannah's daughter Addie entered the room carrying a large platter of fried chicken and warned them cheerfully to not be too slow in beginning their meal as the dinner wouldn't stay warm for much longer. The four members of the soon-to-be-extended family sat at the dinner table where, after saying grace, they enjoyed an abundant and delicious meal.

Anna Jane seemed more vigorous than usual and eagerly engaged Berta in a discussion of the upcoming nuptials. It was determined that the wedding would be held at their plantation home and that Berta would have as her attendants Fannie and Martha Meriwether, her friend Betty Graves and as many of The Mystic Seven as would be able to attend. John would ask his brother, Major James Wootters, and his comrades from the Crockett Southrons, especially Captain Wall and Lieutenant Aldrich, to be with him for the ceremony. His sister and her family and James Wootters' wife and children would also be part of the celebration.

Although Captain Wootters wanted to marry in the next few weeks, it was agreed that they would wait until after Christmas. That time would also give him the opportunity to further the construction of his new home, where the couple would eventually live. They would ask the minister from Crockett, Reverend Pritchard, to perform the ceremony.

Once the meal was over and Berta had been complimented on the berry cobbler, Anna Jane excused herself and went to bed. The excitement of the evening had taken its toll on her stamina. Major Smith agreed that it had been one of the most eventful days he could remember and assisted her upstairs .

As Hannah and Addie cleared the table, Berta and Captain Wootters retired to the front veranda, where the cooling breeze welcomed them. They sat holding hands on the porch swing. Berta was reminded of the many times she had enjoyed similar peaceful moments. Things would be different from now on; peaceful still, but on a different course. She realized that her life had taken a fork in the road that would be the most important decision she had ever made.

Would she regret not pursuing musical opportunities and expanding her experiences with distant travel? What would be the future of her homeland as it faced the uncertainty of becoming a new society? She silently thanked God for having answered so many of her prayers, and she knew she had made the right decision.

Berta excused herself as she got up from the porch swing and went into the music room. Taking the rose from the vase on her piano, she returned to the veranda and after a gentle kiss she offered it to her future husband.

"Take this, John, it's for you," she said. "It is my rose of love, and it has finally bloomed."

EPILOGUE

The wedding on January 17, 1867, concluded my story. However, this event began the life journey of Berta Smith Wootters and Captain John Henry Wootters and their family. The Wootters had seven children; their first child, John Smith Wootters, was born on October 3, 1870, at Smith Landing Plantation, and was followed by two girls, both of whom died in infancy. In 1877, the family moved to Crockett, which would be their home for the rest of their lives and where their subsequent children were born. These included daughters Ethel (1877), Lucia (1879), Frances (1883) and a son, Leon Blum Wootters (1886). It has been suggested that the need for better educational opportunities for their children was a factor in their move to the county seat.

John Smith Wootters, their first born, attended the University of Texas and received his M.D. degree from Tulane University in 1891. He also studied at the Jefferson Medical College in Philadelphia and received another degree in 1892. Dr. Wootters practiced medicine in Crockett for fifty-eight years until shortly before his death on October 23, 1950 at the age of eighty.

The oldest surviving daughter, Ethel, studied piano and voice during her college education at North Texas Female College and Conservatory of Music in Sherman, Texas.[86] This institution was preeminent in fine arts and musical education, and attracted many distinguished teachers from Europe. Ethel gained recognition for her performance at the World's Fair – the Columbian Exposition in Chicago – in 1893. Two years later, she received two certificates of proficiency from the president of the college, Lucy Kidd-Key.

---

[86] Wolz, L. "Kidd-Key College," Handbook of Texas Online.

In 1909, Ethel married Willis Higginbotham and moved to Stephenville, Texas, which was his family's home. There, she taught piano at Tarleton College, now known as Tarleton State University, which has been part of the Texas A&M University System since 1917. The school continues to offer educational opportunities in piano and other musical performance. After the death of Mr. Higginbotham, she returned to Crockett where she taught music until a few years before her death in 1973 at the age of ninety-six.

The second daughter, Lucia, attended the University of Texas and married James H. Painter, an attorney who practiced law in Galveston, Crockett and Houston. The youngest daughter, Frances, attended Hollins College in Virginia and, on graduating, became the first student from west of the Mississippi River to receive the medal for piano performance. She moved to Lufkin, Texas, at the urging of her Hollins classmate, Lillian Denman, and obtained a certification to teach in Texas public schools. While teaching music in Lufkin, she met her future husband, Dr. Peyton R. Denman, her former classmate's older brother. Once married, Dr. and Mrs. Denman moved to Houston, where they lived for the remainder of their lives.

The youngest child of Berta and John Wootters, Leon Blum Wootters, graduated from Baylor University in 1909 and become a banker in Santa Fe, New Mexico, and in Houston.

Although the availability of educational opportunities for their children was certainly a factor in the family's move to Crockett, it is likely that business factors were also a consideration. In the first few years after the Civil War, due to the great demand for cotton and the fortunate relationships with the population of freedmen in the area, both Captain Wootters and Major Smith prospered in their agricultural activities, and Wootters' brokerage business seemed to have a bright future.

The agricultural economy in Texas prospered; in 1870, the price of cotton and the value of the crop were the highest that would be recorded for the next 140 years. The arrival of the Houston and Great Northern Railroad in 1872 proved to be an economic boost for Houston County. This railroad offered passenger and freight transport between Houston and Crockett via the town of New Waverly. In 1873, the line was extended through Grapeland to Palestine, Texas, which was a center for more widespread rail service. The availability of dependable transportation was a boon to cotton production in the area and contributed greatly to its prosperity.[87] The town of Grapeland, Texas, located between Crockett to Palestine where the road crossed from Augusta to the Trinity River, was developed with the arrival of the railroad in Houston County; and Wootters was an early property owner in the town. Grapeland was so named due to the profusion of wild grapevines in the area. That fruit, and the mayhaw jelly into which it was made, was a great favorite of the local residents.[88]

This economic activity and prosperity did not reach the public sector for a number of years after the Civil War, as the tax base for public services had been decimated. It would be several years before local communities recovered enough to provide both effective law enforcement and educational opportunities. Although the idea of public education had been discussed since the establishment of the Republic of Texas, such institutions didn't yet exist at the end of the war.

The economy of rural Texas, as throughout the South, was moribund, and education for the children was not at the top of the priority list. With the elimination of slavery, a major component of the tax base for both the state and counties was also eliminated. Slaves had constituted more than half of the taxable property and accounted for 36 percent of the total tax assessment. Farm values in Houston County would fall from over $1.1 million in 1860 to $57,000 in 1870.[89] Road improvements that had, in the past, been undertaken by slave labor (which the plantation owners were required to provide as an in-kind assessment) became an unaffordable luxury.

In March 1865, the Federal Congress established the Bureau of Refugees, Freedmen, and Abandoned Lands, known as the Freedmen's Bureau. It was led by a national commissioner, Union Army General Oliver Otis Howard, who appointed assistants to head the program in states that had a large population of former slaves. The Bureau in Texas was led

---

[87]   Young, N.B. "Houston and Great Northern Railroad," Handbook of Texas Online.

[88]   Bishop, E. "Houston County," Handbook of Texas Online.

[89]   Campbell, R.B. "An Empire for Slavery: the peculiar institution in Texas, 1821-1865."

initially by Edgar M. Gregory; his position was considered to be the "post of greatest peril," as the program faced considerable hostility from some of the state's white citizens.

Those who supported the program believed that long-term protection of the freedmen depended on the establishment of a free agricultural labor system and of schools to help prepare them to function in a literate society.[90] This program, which began in January 1866 with sixteen schools, ten teachers, and 1,041 students, had within six months expanded to ninety schools, forty-three teachers and 4,590 students, both children and adults.

The other major function of the Bureau was the supervision of labor contracts; that function soon evolved into a military court system handling legal issues. However, the Bureau's most widely recognized achievements were in the field of education: by the end of 1865, more than 90,000 former slaves were enrolled in schools across the southland.[91]

Although the 1870s began on a positive note for the agricultural economy in Houston County, 1873 marked the beginning of the worst economic depression to date in the U. S. and around the world, although the Great Depression of 1929 would surpass it. There were a number of factors leading to this circumstance, referred to as the "Panic of 1873" and the subsequent "Long Depression," which in some European markets persisted until 1896.[92]

This particular economic disaster can be traced to the collapse of the Vienna Stock Exchange on Black Friday, May 9, 1873. Inflationary factors related to the large war debt incurred by France for reparations resulting from the Franco-Prussian War caused a speculative boom in central European financial markets.

The Panic began in the U.S. on September 18, 1873 with the failure of Jay Cooke and Company, which had incurred large amounts of debt for the Northern Pacific Railway expansion. The overbuilding of railroad facilities in the U.S. through the use of excessive debt led to the collapse

---

[90] Harper, C. "Freedman's Bureau," Handbook of Texas Online.

[91] McPherson, J.M. "The Abolitionist Legacy: From Reconstruction to the NAACP." (1975)

[92] Moseley, F. "Depression of 1873-1879." In Glasner and Cooley, eds. Business Cycles and Depressions: An Encyclopedia.

of major national banks. The German Empire discontinued the use of silver to back its currency. Similar measures by the U.S., in an attempt to return to the gold standard after the Civil War, contributed to a depression in silver mining activities in the West. Ensuing high interest rates and a slowdown in the domestic money supply had a negative impact on agricultural interests, which depended greatly on the credit markets.

The value of cotton fell drastically, as the crop in 1880 was twice as large as in 1860 but had only 25 percent the value. In addition, the opening of the Suez Canal gave cotton production in Egypt and India greater access to European markets; British shipping interests took a thumping, and tariffs increased as a result. Between 1873 and 1875 in the U.S., a total of 18,000 businesses folded, while unemployment reached a staggering 14 percent.

One of the businesses that failed was the cotton brokerage firm of Duble and Wootters. With the downturn of his personal agricultural venture, it is likely that John Henry Wootters faced challenges as difficult as those he and his unit encountered with Hood's Texas Brigade ten years earlier. This author does not have definite evidence of the role played by Mr. Duble, but the obituary of Captain Wootters suggested that Wootters personally accepted the responsibility for the firm's debts and eventually satisfied his creditors without the assistance of his former partner.[93]

In later years, Wootters was actively involved with his brother in the mercantile business known as the J.C. Wootters firm. Their letterhead stated that they were a "Dealer in Staple and Fancy Dry Goods, Groceries, Ready Made Clothing [including] Hardware, Saddlery, Plantation Implements and Machinery at Factory Prices". Wootters was also one of the founders of the First National Bank in Crockett, and he continued his agricultural ventures with the advice and counsel of his father-in-law, Major John Smith.

Berta Smith Wootters devoted much of her efforts towards the care and nurture of her family, including her parents. Her mother, Anna Jane Pouncey Smith, died on June 9, 1874, from complications due to her progressive disability; she was buried in a family cemetery on the Smith Landing Plantation property.[94] According to his family Bible, Major John

---

[93]   Appendix I. Obituary of John H. Wootters.
[94]   Appendix I. Obituary of Anna Jane Pouncey Smith.

Smith was remarried to Mrs. Margie Dailey on July 1, 1875, and they lived in the plantation home until her death in 1883 from tuberculosis. Soon thereafter, Major Smith moved to Crockett, and lived with John and Berta Wootters and their children until his death in 1890.

His obituary stated that "Major John Smith had owned one of the finest plantations in East Texas and was regarded as one of the county's most successful planters. For several years he has done nothing other than exercise supervision over some farming interests of his son-in-law, Capt. John H. Wootters. Major Smith was a gentleman after the old school type--highly educated, intelligent, courteous, and patriotic."[95] He was buried next to Anna Jane in their family cemetery at Smith Landing Plantation.

Berta Smith Wootters was an active member of the First Baptist Church in Crockett, and provided inspiration and leadership to the Dorcas Aid Society throughout her life. She had her oversized piano moved from Smith Landing Plantation to their home in Crockett, where she continued to both teach and perform. Captain John Wootters was also an active member of the First Baptist Church, where he served as a deacon and leader of the Sunday school. He was active in the Masonic lodge and the Hood's Brigade Association, whose yearly reunions he regularly attended throughout his lifetime.

Captain Wootters died on January 21, 1892, at the age of fifty-two after a short illness that may have been congestive heart failure. Berta Smith Wootters died unexpectedly on February 5, 1915, at 67, following an apparent myocardial infarction. She was attended in her final illness by her son, Dr. John Smith Wootters.[96] Berta and John Wootters' five surviving children all had the benefit of university educations, despite their father's untimely death when the youngest child was five years old. Their Christian faith and dependence on the direction of God's will for their lives were guiding principles for their family.

Betty Williams Graves, friend and mentor of Berta Smith, was born in 1840 and continued to live and teach in Fairfield, Texas after the end of the war. In 1870, she married Theodoric G. Jones, a distinguished lawyer and judge who had completed his education in Tennessee and practiced

<hr>

[95]   Obituaries, Houston Co., TX, Ancestry.com

[96]   Appendix II. Obituaries of Captain John Wootters and Mrs. Berta Smith Wootters.

law in Mississippi before moving to Texas. They had one son and lived in Palestine, Texas, until Judge Jones died in 1898 at the age of seventy-five.[97] Betty Graves Jones subsequently moved to Dallas where she lived until her death in 1935 at the age of ninety-five.[98]

The comrades of Captain John Wootters who returned to Houston County included his close friend Captain William B. Wall, who recovered after his injury at the battle of Gaines' Mill in 1862. He married Miss Nettie Cooper on December 6, 1866, and they had long and productive lives in Crockett. Wall was elected county judge in 1878, serving for eight years, and was elected state representative for Houston County in 1896.[99] Albert Augustus (Gus) Aldrich married Miss Josephine Coleman, but they had no surviving children. Gus was the commander of Company I of the 1st Texas Regiment following the injury to Captain John Wootters. His younger brother, Colin Aldrich, was the mess sergeant for their company and later married Miss Bettie Kyle of Augusta. Bettie died after the birth of their first child and Colin married Bettie's sister Julia. They lived in Crockett and had a large family.[100]

Hannah and Oscar Pouncey lived at the Cedar Branch community their entire lives. A daughter, Addie Pouncey, continued to work in the home of Captain and Mrs. John Wootters for many years. Her grandson, also named Edgar Pouncey, was a well-educated man and served on the Board of Trustees of the Grapeland School District with which the Cedar Branch school had affiliated in earlier years.[101] Those who maintained their ownership of the land from Smith Landing Plantation likely benefited from the discovery of oil in the Navarro oil field in that area in the 1930s.[102]

To complete this story, a brief word about the piano is in order. After its move to Crockett, the piano gradually lost its ability to sustain proper tune and was replaced by more modern instruments. Because of its size, beauty and historical significance it remained at the home in Crockett until their youngest daughter, Frances Wootters Denman, brought it to

[97] Obituary, Theodoric G. Jones, Ancestry.com.
[98] Obituary, Betty Graves Jones, Ancestry.com.
[99] History of Houston County, Texas 1687-1979, p. 609.
[100] Ibid. p. 226.
[101] Ibid. p. 573.
[102] Ibid. p. 26.

Houston following her marriage to Dr. Peyton R. Denman. Despite their best efforts, the piano could never be restored to a functional musical instrument status and was left to Frances' grandson in her will when she died in 1975. He had apparently expressed appreciation for the piano as a child while living with his grandparents during World War II, and he continues to provide it a home. Thanks to the benefit of modern electronics, the piano now produces acceptable quality sounds. The author of this work enjoys hearing such works as Für Elise and Pathetique sonatas, although they are probably not rendered with the same sensitivity demonstrated by a young, red-haired girl one hundred fifty years ago.

BIBLIOGRAPHY

1st Texas Volunteer Infantry Regiment. Nineteenth Century Living History

Association, Inc. (http://texas-brigade.org/1st tex/1tex.htm)

Baker, William D. The Camden Expedition of 1864. Arkansas Historic Preservation Program. Little Rock, AR.

Barr, Alwyn. Black Texans: A History of African Americans in Texas, 1528-1995. Norman, OK: University of Oklahoma Press, 1996.

Barr, Alwyn. "Battle of Galveston," Handbook of Texas Online. (http://www.tshaonline.org/handbook/online/articles/qeg01). Uploaded June 15, 2010. Modified March 4, 2011. Published by the Texas State Historical Association.

Barr, Alwyn. "Green, Thomas." Handbook of Texas Online. (http://www.tshaonline.org/handbook/online/articles/fgr38). Uploaded June 15, 2010. Modified March 4, 2011. Published by the Texas State Historical Association.

Barr, Alwyn. "Sabine Pass, Battle of. " Handbook of Texas Online. (http://www.tshaonline.org/handbook/online/articles/qes02) Uploaded June 15, 2010. Published by the Texas State Historical Association.

Bilby, Joseph. Civil War Firearms: Their Historical Background and Tactical Use. Conshohocken, PA: Combined Publishing, 1996.

Bishop, Eliza H. "Houston County." Handbook of Texas Online. (http://www.tshaonline.org/handbook/online/articles/hch19). Uploaded June 15, 2010. Published by the Texas State Historical Association.

Bladen County N.C. Genealogy and History. (www.ncgenweb.us/bladen/).

Block, William T. The Battle of Sabine Pass – Its Causes and Effects. (http://www.wtblock.com/wtblockjr/battleof.htm).

Boles, John B. Masters & Slaves in the House of the Lord: Race and Religion in the American South, 1740-1870. Lexington, KY: The University Press of Kentucky, 1990.

Boles, John B. The South Through Time: A History of An American Region, Third Edition, Volume I and II. Hoboken, NJ: Pearson, 2004.

Braynard, O. Frank. S.S. Savannah, the Elegant Steam Ship. Athens, GA: University of Georgia Press, 2008.

Breiner, Thomas L. Pork Belly Politics or How Longstreet Brought Home the Bacon: James Longstreet and the Suffolk Campaign. Cincinnati Civil War Round Table, September 16, 1999. (http://www.cincinnaticwrt.org/data/ccwrt_history/talks_text/breiner_longstreet_suffolk.html)

"A Brief History of Public Education." Texas State Historical Association, Texas Almanac.

Briseno, E.X. "Samuel May Williams: Texas Pioneer, Businessman, and Freemason."

Browne, Philip Dale. "Graves, Henry Lee." Handbook of Texas Online. (http://www.tshaonline.org/handbook/online/articles/fgr14) Uploaded June 15, 2010. Published by the Texas State Historical Association.

Burns, Ken. The Civil War: A Film by Ken Burns. A production of Florentine Films and WETA-TV, American Documentaries, Inc, 1990.

Campbell, R.B. An Empire for Slavery: The Peculiar Institution in Texas, 1821-1865. Baton Rouge, LA: Louisiana State University Press, 1989.

Campbell, Randolph B. and Curtis Bishop. "Davis, Jefferson." The Handbook of Texas Online. Texas State Historical Association.

Carroll, H. Bailey. Texas Santa Fe Expedition. Handbook of Texas Online. (https://www.tshaonline.org/handbook/online/articles/fda42) Uploaded on June 12, 2010. Modified on January 18, 2013. Published by the Texas State Historical Association.

Cassel, Daniel Kolb. A Genealogical History of the Kolb, Kulp or Culp Family, and Its Branches in America, With Biographical Sketches of Their Descendants from the Earliest Available Records. Norristown, PA: Morgan R. Wills, 1895.

Catton, Bruce. The Coming Fury: The Centennial History of the Civil War, Volume 1. Garden City, NY: Doubleday and Company, Inc., 1961.

Catton, Bruce. Terrible Swift Sword: The Centennial History of the Civil War, Volume 2. Garden City, NY: Doubleday and Company Inc., 1963.

Catton, Bruce. Never Call Retreat: The Centennial History of the Civil War, Volume 3. Garden City, NY: Doubleday & Company, Inc., 1965.

Chance, J.E. "Second Texas Infantry." Handbook of Texas Online. (http://www.tshaonline.org/handbook/online/articles/qks04) Uploaded June 15, 2010. Published by the Texas State Historical Association.

Chilton, F.B. Unveiling and Dedication of Monument to Hood's Brigade on the Capitol Grounds at Austin, Texas. Houston, TX, 1911. From the Library of Congress Internet Archive.

Cotham, Edward T. Jr. Battle on the Bay: The Civil War Struggle for Galveston. Austin, TX: University of Texas Press, 1998.

Cozzens, Peter. This Terrible Sound: The Battle of Chickamauga. Urbana, IL: University of Illinois Press, 1992.

Cromartie, Shamella. The Cape Fear River: Road to Bladen County. (http://bladenroadwork.pbworks.com.) A Roadwork project by Bladen County Public Library and Bladen County Historical Society. North Carolina Humanities Council.

Crofts, Daniel W. Reluctant Confederates: Upper South Unionists in the Secession Crisis. Chapel Hill, NC: University of North Carolina Press, 1989.

Cutrer, Thomas W. "McLeod, Hugh." Handbook of Texas Online. (https://www.tshaonline.org/handbook/online/articles/fmc90) Uploaded June 15, 2010. Modified on April 3, 2011. Published by the Texas State Historical Association.

Cutrer, Thomas W. "Smith, Edmund Kirby." Handbook of Texas Online. (http://www.tshaonline.org/handbook/online/articles/fsm09). Uploaded June 15, 2010. Published by the Texas State Historical Association.

Cutrer, T.W. and D.P. Smith. "Twiggs, David Emanuel." Handbook of Texas Online. Uploaded June 15, 2010. Modified on March 8, 2011. Published by the Texas State Historical Association.

Dattel, Gene. Cotton and Race in the Making of America: The Human Costs of Economic Power. Lanham, MD: Ivan R. Dee, Publisher, 2009.

DeFazio, Joe. "Morse's Telegraph – A Gift Refused." From Preserving Texas History at Ancestry.com. (http://freepages.history.rootsweb.ancestry.com/~unclejoe/tx/telegraph.html)

Flachmeier, J.E. "Johnston, Albert Sidney." Handbook of Texas Online. (http://www.tshaonline.org/handbook/online/articles/fjo32) Uploaded on June 15, 2010. Modified on March 13, 2013. Published by the Texas State Historical Association.

Foote, Shelby. The Civil War: A Narrative, Volumes 1, 2 and 3. New York: Random House, 1986.

Frazier, Donald S. "Val Verde Battery." Handbook of Texas Online. (http://www.tshaonline.org/handbook/online/articles/qkv01) Uploaded on June 15, 2010. Modified on March 8, 2011. Published by the Texas State Historical Association.

Ferguson, Ernest B. "The Battle of Bull Run: The End of Illusions." Smithsonian Magazine, July- August, 2011: 57-64.

Gilmore, G.W. The New Schaff-Herzog Encyclopedia of Religious Knowledge. Vol. 1: 469-470. (http://www.ccel.org/s/schaff/encyc/encyc13/htm/TOC.htm)

Goodwin, Doris Kearns. Team of Rivals: The Political Genius of Abraham Lincoln. New York, NY: Simon & Schuster, 2005.

Gorman, M.D. Hospitals in Richmond During the Civil War, Civil War Richmond. From the Richmond Sentinel, May 17, 1864. (http://www.mdgorman.com/Hospitals/hospitals.htm).

Gorman, M.D. Information about General Hospital #9 in Richmond, VA during the Civil War, Civil War Richmond. (http://www.mdgorman.com/Hospitals/general_hospital_9.htm).

Gorman, M.D. Information about Howard's Grove Hospital in Richmond, VA during the Civil War, Civil War Richmond. (http://www.mdgorman.com/Hospitals/howards_grove_hospital.htm).

Gorman, M.D. Notice to All, Civil War Richmond. From the Richmond Examiner, May 17, 1864. (http://www.mdgorman.com/Written_Accounts/Examiner/1864/richmond_examiner_5171864.htm)

Gorman, M.D. Palmer CSR, Florida Hospital, Civil War Richmond. From the National Archives. (http://www.mdgorman.com/Written_Accounts/NARA/Palmer_CSR1.htm).

Gregg, Rev. Alexander. History of the Old Cheraws. Originally published in 1867. Austin, TX: DMK Heritage, republished in 2009.

Gunn, Jack W. "Mexican Invasions of 1842." Handbook of Texas Online. (http://www.tshaonline.org/handbook/online/articles/qem02) Uploaded on June 15, 2010. Published by the Texas State Historical Association.

Hall, Martin Hardwick. "Jordan, Powhatan." Handbook of Texas Online. (https://www.tshaonline.org/handbook/online/articles/fjo72). Uploaded on June 15, 2010. Modified on March 2, 2011. Published by the Texas State Historical Association.

Harper, Cecil, Jr. "Freedmen's Bureau." Handbook of Texas Online. (http://www.tshaonline.org/handbook/online/articles/ncf01) Uploaded on June 12, 2010. Published Texas State Historical Association.by the

Hazlewood, Claudia. "Augusta, Texas." Handbook of Texas Online. (https://www.tshaonline.org/handbook/online/articles/hna50) Uploaded on June 9, 2010. Published by the Texas State Historical Association.

Henson, Margaret Swett. "Williams, Samuel May." Handbook of Texas Online. (http://www.tshaonline.org/handbook/online/articles/fwi35) Uploaded on June 15, 2010. Published by the Texas State Historical Association.

History of Houston County, Texas 1687-1979. Compiled and edited by the Houston County

Historical Commission, Crockett, Texas. Tulsa, OK: Heritage Publishing Company, 1979.

Johnson, L. "The Welsh in the Carolinas in the Eighteenth Century." North American Journal of Welsh Studies, Vol. 4, no 1 (2004): 12-19. (http://www.flint.umich.edu/~wllis/Lloyd2.pdf)

Johnson, Lloyd. "Naval Stores." North Carolina History Project. (http://www.northcarolinahistory.org/encyclopedia/103/entry/)

Joiner, Gary Dillard. One Damn Blunder from Beginning to End: the Red River Campaign of 1864. Lanham, MD: Rowman & Littlefield Publishers, 2002.

Jordan, John Woolf. Colonial and Revolutionary Families of Pennsylvania: Genealogical and Personal Memoirs. Volume II. Originally published by Lewis Publishing Co. in 1911.

King, C. Richard. "Ballinger, William Pitt." Handbook of Texas Online. (http://www.tshaonline.org/handbook/online/articles/fba52) Uploaded on June 12, 2010. Modified on March 1, 2011. Published by the Texas State Historical Association.

Leatherwood, Art. Red River Campaign. Handbook of Texas Online. (http://www.tshaonline.org/handbook/online/articles/qdr01) Uploaded on June 15, 2010. Modified on March 8, 2011. Published by the Texas State Historical Association.

Long, Christopher. "Daly's, Texas." Handbook of Texas Online. (http://www.tshaonline.org/handbook/online/articles/hrdzm). Uploaded on June 12, 2010. Published by the Texas State Historical Association.

Long, Christopher. "Gossett, Elijah" Handbook of Texas Online. (http://www.tshaonline.org/handbook/online/articles/fgohw). Uploaded on June 15, 2010. Published by the Texas State Historical Association.

Lowe, Richard G. Walker's Texas Division. Baton Rouge, LA: Louisiana State University Press, 2004.

Maberry, Robert Jr. Texas Flags. College Station, TX: Texas A&M Press, 2001.

Mainer, Thomas N. Houston County in the Civil War. Crockett, TX: Publications Development Company, 1981.

The Family of Col. Kolb and Some of their Neighbors. Marlboro County, South Carolina Genealogy Trails. (http://genealogytrails.com/scar/marlboro/hx_col_kolb.htm)

McPherson, James M. The Abolitionist Legacy: From Reconstruction to the NAACP. Princeton, NJ: Princeton University Press, 1975.

McPherson, James M. Crossroads of Freedom: Antietam, The Battle that Changed the Course of the Civil War. New York, Oxford: Oxford University Press, 2002.

Miller, Aragorm Storm. "Wootters, James C." Handbook of Texas Online. (http://www.tshaonline.org/handbook/online/articles/fwo61). Uploaded on April 21, 2011. Modified on April 25, 2011. Published by the Texas State Historical Association.

Moseley, Fred. "Depression of 1873-1879." In Business Cycles and Depressions: An Encyclopedia, edited by D. Glasner and T. Cooley, 148-149. New York, NY: Routledge, 1997.

Nance, John Milton. "Mier Expedition." Handbook of Texas Online. (http://www.tshaonline.org/handbook/online/articles/qym02), Uploaded on June 15, 2010. Published by the Texas State Historical Association.

National Register of Historic Places, North Carolina, Bladen County, Historic Districts. (www.nationalregisterofhistoricplaces.com/nc/bladen)

NOTE: THIS ENTRY IS INCOMPLETE AND THE LINK DOES NOT WORK
Obituaries, Houston Co. Tx (www.rootsweb.ancestry.com/txhousto/obituaries page1.htm).

NOTE: THIS LINK DOES NOT WORK
Old Fairfield College. Transcribed from the Fairfield Recorder, September 21, 1923 by Modene Knight Thornton, The GenWeb. (http://www.txgenweb2.org/txfreestone/histories/fairfieldfemale.htm).

"Old San Antonio Road." Handbook of Texas Online. (http://www.tshaonline.org/handbook/online/articles/exo04). Uploaded on June 15, 2010. Published by the Texas State Historical Association

Polley. J.B. Hood's Texas Brigade: It's Marches, It's Battles, It's Achievements. New York, Washington DC: The Neale Publishing Co., 1910.

Presidential Election of 1864: A Resource Guide From the Library of Congress http://www.loc.gov/rr/program/bib/elections/election1864.html

Proctor, Victoria. The Welsh Neck Baptist Church. Part One: Brief History. Marlboro County, SC Churches. (http://sciway3.net/proctor/marlboro/church/Welsh_Neck_Baptist.html)

Proctor, Victoria. The Welsh Neck Baptist Church. Part Two: An Abstract of the Records of the Welsh Neck Baptist Church, Society Hill, S.C. Marlboro County, SC Churches. (http://sciway3.net/proctor/marlboro/church/Welsh_Neck_Baptist2.html)

Roasting Ears Battle, August 23, 1864. Civilwartalk.com. (http://www.civilwartalk.com)

Robertson, James. The Untold Civil War: Exploring the Human Side of the War. Edited by Neil Kagan. Washington, DC: National Geographic Society, 2011.

Sears, S.W. To the Gates of Richmond: The Peninsula Campaign. New York, NY: Ticknor & Fields, 1992.

Sheehan-Dean, Aaron. Struggle for a Vast Future: The American Civil War. New York, NY: Random House, 2006.

Shields, Douglas R. "Fairfield Female College." Handbook of Texas Online. (http://www.tshaonline.org/handbook/online/articles/kbf01). Uploaded on June 12, 2010. Published by the Texas State Historical Association.

Silber, Irwin. Songs of the Civil War. Dover Publications Inc., 1995.

Silverthorne, Elizabeth. "Smith, Ashbel." Handbook of Texas Online. (http://www.tshaonline.org/handbook/online/articles/fsm04). Uploaded on June 15, 2010. Published by the Texas State Historical Association.

NOTE: THIS LINK DOES NOT WORK
Sparkman, Grady. Keatchie College. The Baptist Messenger, March 14,

1957, p.6-7 as referenced in DeSoto Parish Louisiana, The US GenWeb Project, (http://www.countywebgen.com/DeSotoParishLA/Keatchie college.htm).

Stockard, Sallie W. The History of Guilford County, North Carolina. Knoxville, TN: Gaut-Ogden Company, 1902.

Taylor, John. Bloody Valverde: A Civil War Battle on the Rio Grande, February 21, 1862. Albuquerque, NM: University of New Mexico Press, 1995.

Tew, Jerome D. "The Battle of Elizabethtown." The Sampson Independent, 2012. (www.clintonnc.com).

The New York Times, February 1, 1864. "The Draft for Half a Million of Men." New York Times Complete Civil War, 1861-1865, edited by Harold Holzer and Craig L. Symonds. New York, NY: Black Dog & Levinthal Publishers, Inc, 2010.

The New York Times Complete Civil War, 1861-1865. Edited by Harold Holzer & Craig L. Symonds. New York, NY: Black Dog & Levinthal Publishers, Inc, 2010.

Walbert, David. "Naval Stores and the longleaf pine." Learn NC, a program of the UNC School of Education. (http://www.learnnc.org/lp/editions/nchist-colonial/4069)

Walter, John. The Rifle Story. Barnsley, UK: Greenhill Books, 2006.

Wilson, Anna Victoria. "Education for African Americans." Handbook of Texas Online. (http://www.tshaonline.org/handbook/online/articles/kde02). Uploaded on June 12, 2010. Published by the Texas State Historical Association.

Wolz, Larry "Kidd-Key College." Handbook of Texas Online. Texas State Historical Association. (http://www.tshaonline.org/handbook/online/articles/kbk02). Uploaded on June 15, 2010. Modified on October 24, 2011. Published by the

Wooster, Ralph A. "Murrah, Pendleton." Handbook of Texas Online. (http://www.tshaonline.org/handbook/online/articles/fmu15). Uploaded on June 15, 2010. Modified on March 3, 2011. Published by the Texas State Historical Association.

Young, N.B. "Houston and Great Northern Railroad." Handbook of Texas Online. (http://www.tshaonline.org/handbook/online/articles/eqh08). Uploaded on June 15, 2010. Published by the Texas State Historical Association.

04089914-00835746

Printed in the United States
by Baker & Taylor Publisher Services